||||| ||||| ||||| |||||

Chiat/Day: The First Twenty Years

First published in the
United States of America in 1990 by
Rizzoli International Publications, Inc.
300 Park Avenue South
New York, New York 10010

ISBN 0-8478-1163-8

Typography by Andresen Typographics

Printed and bound in Japan

Chiat/Day: The First Twenty Years

Written by Stephen Kessler   Designed by Jill Savini

RIZZOLI
NEW YORK

For my mom,
who yelled when I
took a copywriting job
for $175 a week.

And for my partners:
Ralph, Marv, Frank, Marc,
and especially for Harry.

Special thanks to Amy Miyano,
who made sure this book got finished.
And to Mel Abert, Rick Boyko,
David Butler, Robert Chandler,
Jay Chiat, Pam Cunningham, Ed Cole,
Guy Day, Bob Dion,
Steve Garey, Fred Goldberg,
Jeff Gorman, Bill Hamilton,
Steve Hayden, Elizabeth Hayes,
Hank Hinton, Penny Kapasouz,
Phil Lanier, Mike Moser,
Mel Newhoff, Jane Newman,
Dave O'Hare, Brian O'Neill,
Richard O'Neill, Steve Rabosky,
Mary Teresa Rainey, Robin Raj,
Marv Rich, Jeff Roll,
Jamie Seltzer, Chuck Silverman,
Mark Sitley, Dick Sittig,
Brent Thomas, Ross Van Dusen,
Bob Wolf and Hy Yablonka for talking.
And to Sherry Johannes, Debra Kessler
and Irene Mar for helping.
And to Lee Clow,
who always makes me do things
better than I can.

This book is about aggravation,
frustration, triumphs, heartbreak, exhilaration,
joy, tears, love and a carload of passion.
You know, a typical day at the agency.

But most of all, it's about trying.
Trying to make the advertising better.
More provocative; friendlier; more motivating;
exciting and, most important, more effective.

It takes an incredibly special group
of agency people and clients to keep trying
to do all that. And I was lucky enough
to be able to work with them.

God, has it really been 20 years?

Jay Chiat

Preface

"No army is better than its soldiers."
— General George S. Patton

It's a funny thing: nobody remembers much. It seems like it all happened so fast to so many people who came in days and nights and yelled and screamed and argued over ads that when it was all over, most people just forgot most of what, specifically, went on from day to day. For so many people I talked to, Chiat/Day was like going into a fifteen-round heavyweight championship prizefight and winning by a decision—they remembered the fight, but forgot about the beating.

To give you an idea of what I mean, here is a portion of the transcripts of a discussion I had with one of Chiat/Day's earlier creative teams.

I think we did that ad in '75.
Can't be. I wasn't here in '75. We did it in '76.
I wasn't here in '76.
Well, maybe we did it '74.
We didn't have the account in '74.
When the hell did we do it then?
Maybe I did that ad with someone else.
Y'know, I think you're right. I don't think I worked on that ad.
And so on.

Besides a birthday, what makes Chiat/Day a worthwhile subject for a book? For one thing, it's influence on individual advertising categories. Its 20-page magazine ads for Yamaha motorcycles were a first in the motorcycle industry; now, everybody does them. Apple advertising changed the way business talked to business. And before Nike, if you asked someone what category would be doing the most creative advertising on television five years in the future, they probably would have been hard pressed to say, "Sneakers."

Chiat/Day, for the first time, made it permissible for companies to seek out good advertising in cities other than New York and Chicago. In 1968, if you were an ad manager at a major corporation and you needed an ad agency, you looked to those two cities, period, the end, don't show me anyplace else. Twenty years later, the most creative agencies in the country are found in places like Minneapolis, Portland, Seattle, Virginia, North Carolina, San Francisco, and Los Angeles. If you are not in advertising and want to know just how far things have come, consider this: last year, the Wall Street Journal went to Minnesota to have its advertising done.

Chiat/Day was the first American agency to institute Account Planning, a research-based discipline that establishes a dialogue with consumers before, during, and after the creative development process, to ensure that the advertising being done is grounded in something that's really relevant to its target audience.

While many agencies have talked about the importance of doing good creative work, Chiat/Day has, for two decades, made an earnest attempt to do it. It is an agency built on Jay Chiat and Guy Day's belief that if you take the best people you can find, put them in an environment that encourages their best work, and then stick up for them when they do it, you'll get good advertising. So far, it seems to be working.

But enough of that.

Has every Chiat/Day ad been a good one? Not nearly, no. In the course of twenty years, you are bound to produce a few ideas that will not catch fire in the hearts and minds of consumers. Among them:

The ad for Novus, National Semiconductor's short-lived consumer products division, that tried to convince parents that the best thing you could do for a bad math student was buy him a pocket calculator. The copy said that this would free the child from the drudgery of working with numbers and "turn him on to the concepts of math."

The ad that tried to convince professional photographers that the best place they could take their film was Fotomat.

The campaign for Midori that tried to persuade America that just about anything tasted better with a little melon liqueur mixed in (although, in the post-disco, pre-Reagan era, this colorful premise actually worked for quite some time.)

About this book. There is a lot I have left out. I have not talked very much about the men and women in Account Management, those people who make sure that the accounts actually run from day to day. It is one thing for a creative person to have an unusual idea; it is another for an account person to have to walk into a client's office and say, "Fred, I really feel you're going to like this." They are a valued part of Chiat/Day and as responsible for its success as any other department. They are part of a proud tradition that gets too much grief and too little credit; far be it from me to break with tradition.

I have not talked enough about Account Planning and the planners who fly around the country day in and day out, telling people, "My opinion isn't important. I want to know how *you* feel about pizza." Planners have made Chiat/Day's creative work more than just creative, they have made it consistently and thoroughly effective. Chiat/Day was always recognized as having a creative edge; with the implementation of Account Planning, it is now recognized as having a marketing edge, too.

I have not talked at all about Chiat/Day's former Seattle office, which opened in 1976, and today exists on its own as Livingston and Company, although much of Chiat/Day Seattle's work is represented here.

Thanks to my own sloth, I did not interview every creative person I would have liked to. Here and there, I have left out a good story, mixed up facts, maybe even gotten a date wrong once or twice. I have used the word "just" too much. I have used too many colons. Of these and other transgressions, I can only say this:

It's hard to write a book.

The growth of Chiat/Day, in many ways, parallels the growth of Southern California. In the beginning, the accounts were mostly industrial and technical. As Guy Day put it, "There was heavy industry, Carnation, and electronics. We clearly weren't going to get Carnation." Then came the real estate boom, then the expansion of Japanese businesses like Pioneer, Mitsubishi, and Yamaha into the American market, then the growth of computers and high technology. As you look at the work, you will see it all.

The work also reflects the changing times in which it was created. The psychedelic Viviane Woodard ads, the swinging singles of the early Honda work (check out the Peggy Lipton Mod Squad hairstyles), the anti-heroin campaigns of the late sixties and early seventies, the denim-clad executive in Apple's "I'll be home for breakfast" commercial—these are only a few examples. You will find dozens more.

This book is about the building of a business, but it is also about creative work and how it gets done. Although I tell many stories about creative people, and it is mostly their voices you will read next to the work they created throughout the book, I have chosen not to use their names. This was my reasoning: If you know who these people are, you do not need their names in print to tell you; if you do not know them, the names aren't important, the stories are. Also, by leaving out everyone's name, I have left out no one, so none of my friends will be tempted to clear a room when I enter it. Every creative person has a story. If you are sitting near one, I suggest you ask about their's. It is sure to be a good time, and if they are on an expense account, you may not even have to pay for the drinks.

This book should really be called Chiat/Day: The Work, because in the end, it is the work that it is important; it is the work that people remember.

A last word about all the people who took the time to tell me their best Chiat/Day stories from the last two decades. And here, I would like to quote none other than that great song stylist and Academy Award nominated actress, Diana Ross. At the conclusion of Motown's Twenty-Fifth Anniversary Celebration, Ms. Ross said, "Although a lot of people have come and gone, Motown isn't about the people who've left. It is about the people who came back. And tonight, everyone came back."

When it came time to talk about what Chiat/Day was and what it is and what it means, everyone came back.

Even me.

—S.K., January, 1989

1968: The Year Of The Merger Faust/Day, Chiat Join Forces

Tom Faust Exits F/D, Day Wins Presidential Toss

Los Angeles—"The urge to merge" has hit the West Coast advertising industry. Last week, The Wyman Co. joined forces with Anderson-McConnell to form Wyman/Anderson-McConnell. This week Faust/Day and Jay Chiat & Associates have announced plans effective immediately to become Chiat/Day Inc., a new $8 million agency.

Ingredients for the Chiat/Day merger: Flip a coin to see who's going to be president. Get rid of $350,000 in conflicting business (See story below). Combine staffs and move two blocks up the street.

Although informal discussions have been going on for several months, the actual merger took four days to accomplish the nitty gritty details, including notification of clients and employees.

In the new organization, Day will be president — a decision literally determined by a toss of the coin. Tom Faust, who is leaving the agency business and will announce his new plans shortly, flipped the coin. "We plan to make this C/D Presidential Coin Flip a semi-annual affair and chances are Jay Chiat will be our next president," reports Day.

The key staff at the new shop includes: Tom Burr as director of client services; Hy Yablonka, executive art director; Bill Manning, general manager; Warren Halperin, director of marketing services; Lenore Plotkin, media director; Dennis Juett, director of design group; and Sid Salinger, production manager. Yablonka and Miss Plotkin currently are members of the Chiat staff.

Three of Chiat's people — including art director Tom Pfahlert, production manager Les Slifkin and Miss Plotkin — have worked for both agencies.

F/D brings to the merger about $5 million in billing including, Fairchild Semiconductor, Fairchild Instrumentation, Property Research Corp., Aerospace Corp. and Vivianne Woodard Cosmetics. The Chiat shop bills about $3.6 million, including Equitable Savings & Loan Assn., Cary Instruments, Leach Corp. and Commonwealth United Corp.

Although the merger becomes effective immediately, the physical combination of the two shops (which are located two blocks apart) will be accomplished about October 1. At that time, the Chiat staff will move in with the F/D people at 1300 W. Olympic Blvd.

New president Guy Day told *MAC* that the agency is in the process of adding several new people which will bring the total staff to about 50.

Tom Faust and Guy Day started their agency in January 1962, three months prior to the debut of the Chiat shop.

Before launching the agency six years ago, Guy Day was with Carson/Roberts. Prior to that, he was with Hixson & Jorgensen, where he met Tom Faust. Both worked at H&J on copy and contact for about five years. Chiat's background includes the Leland Oliver Co., Orange; McCann-Erickson, New York; and NBC.

"Now that I've got you all here, I want to see headlines."

This is how it happened:
Two men, two small agencies.
Guy Day calls Jay Chiat on the phone. He's never met the man, but he likes his work. He says he'd like to get together and talk. Jay says fine and invites him over. Guy is thinking this: I'm losing my partner, there's going to be negative publicity, I want to move forward, I don't want to do it alone. Jay is thinking: If there's an opportunity for the two of us together to grow faster than either one of us alone, let's do it.
The meeting takes about an hour. Guy says he thinks that if they combine, they'll be big enough to go after some decent accounts. Jay says fine again, and suggests they work out the details at a Dodger game he's gonna take his kid to tomorrow.
They go, they stuff the kids with hot dogs and popcorn, and by the sixth inning, they have a deal.
Don Drysdale pitches his fourth consecutive shutout.
The fifty some odd employees of Chiat Advertising and Faust/Day are gathered in a conference room at Faust/Day, and in what will soon become known as the new agency's laid-back management style, are informed that they now work for Chiat/Day, that it's going to be good for everyone involved, that they are pitching the South Bay Club apartment complex, and that headlines are needed. Now.
Everyone starts working.
They get the account, and within a month, they are asked to pitch their first major piece of consumer business, the Equitable Savings Bank.
For the newly formed Chiat/Day, it is an enormous opportunity. Equitable is a major television advertiser. The problem is, neither Chiat nor Day nor any of their employees have done any television commercials.

So this is what they do: they go out and rent a Concord videotape machine, and position it in the corner of the conference room, making it as conspicuously inconspicuous as possible. This way, when the Equitable people come in, they will know that this is obviously an agency that knows how to do TV commercials.
The meeting goes great, and soon, Equitable Savings Bank has a new ad agency.
The videotape machine is used to record the celebration, then promptly returned.
Chiat/Day is in business.

MUSIC: (THROUGHOUT AS EDIFICE GROWS. LYRICS ARE REPETITIVE AND RHYTHMIC): "Chick, chick, boom, pow, yeah, yeah," etc.
SFX: Construction sounds are worked in with the music.

CONSTRUCTION SOUNDS
THROUGHOUT.
ANNCR. VO: When you open an
account at Equitable for a thou-
sand dollars or more . . .
FROG CROAKS.
ANNCR VO: We'll give you a free
safe deposit box.
DOORS SLAMMING, CLANGING
SHUT.
ANNCR VO: and we do mean *safe*.

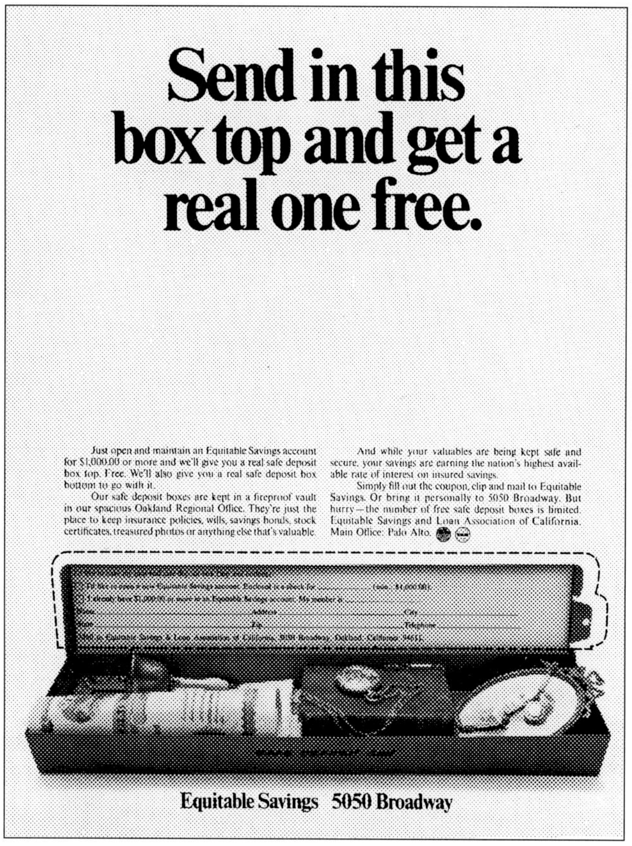

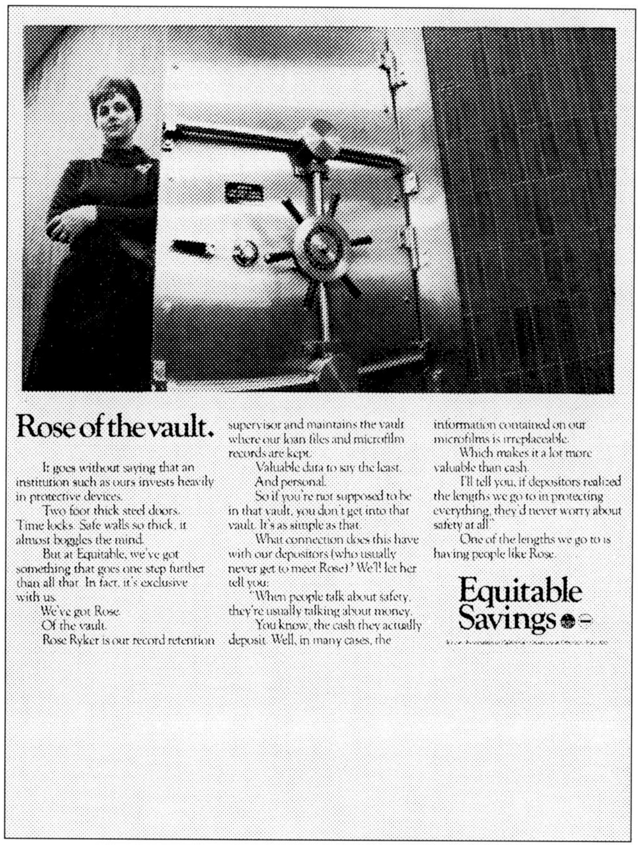

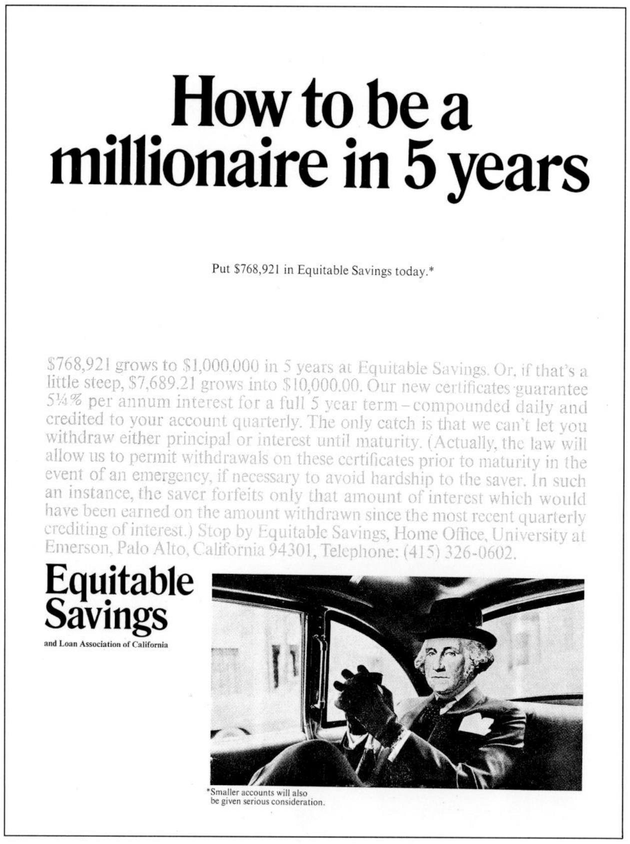

1968

Send in this box top and get a real one free.

How to be a millionaire in 5 years

Equitable Savings

One thousand and one.

One thousand and two.

One thousand and three.

One thousand and four.

One thousand and five.

One thousand and six.

One thousand and seven.

One thousand and eight.

One thousand and nine.

One thousand and ten.

One thousand and eleven.

One thousand and twelve.

One thousand and thirteen.

One thousand and fourteen.

One thousand and fifteen.

One thousand and sixteen.

One thousand and seventeen.

One thousand and eighteen.

One thousand and nineteen.

One thousand and twenty.

The end of the 20-second stall.

Twenty seconds is a long, long time for a customer to listen to nothing. And, when the twenty seconds is being used by a clerk to find product, credit or account information, a hard-earned reputation for customer service hangs in the balance.

That's why so many service-oriented companies are switching to CARD.

CARD is a low-cost data storage and retrieval system that holds 73,000 pages of information and displays any one of them in four seconds or less. All the data you use every day. Plus all the data it takes days to locate. Right at your clerk's fingertips. Only a couple of buttonpunches away.

Large multiple-product companies use CARD as a pushbutton catalog. Airlines use CARD to store a world of travel information. Department stores use CARD for instant credit checks. Insurance companies use CARD for rapid retrieval of policy holder history. Banks use CARD for signature verification and account balance retrieval. And a lot of other industries use CARD every day to save time and money in information storage and retrieval. CARD can go on-line to any digital computer now or when you go on-line, allowing a low cost direct address to your customer files with millions of bits of displayed information in less than four seconds.

Right now, over 5,000 CARD units are eliminating the 20-second stall in companies throughout the world. We'd like to tell you exactly how they do it. Call or write Image Systems, Inc., 11244 Playa Court, Culver City, California 90230, (213) 390-3378.

image systems

Find the mistakes in this picture   and save a million dollars.

We'll give you a hint: There are at least 80 mistakes in the picture. They're called keypunch operators. They cost you about a million dollars a year. In salaries. Errors. Equipment. Errors. Cards. And errors.

For about the same price, you can buy our computer input machine. It doesn't make mistakes. And it saves a lot more than it costs.

We call our machine the Electronic Retina* Computing Reader. It reads information from original documents.

Ordinary type faces from almost any typewriter or office machine in the world. Complete alphabets. Upper and lower case letters. Typed or handprinted numbers. Symbols. Punctuation. The works. Then it records the data on magnetic tape in computer language. And feeds the information directly into the computer. No human effort. No human errors.

Our machine is cutting data processing costs from Los Angeles to Liverpool. At banks, airlines, oil companies, credit card companies, the Library of Congress, the U.S. Army, and dozens of other organizations. There's no other machine quite like it. Which is one reason Recognition Equipment is the largest manufacturer of optical reading systems in the world. (Every week, our systems process over 100 million documents—more than all the other optical readers in use combined.)

If this is beginning to sound like another promise-them-everything computer ad, do us a favor. And yourself, too. Go talk to your data processing manager. Ask him about input bottlenecks. And overtime. And sick leave. And trainees. And turnover. And all the ways a mistake can get into your computer. Then ask him to ask us about our reading machine.

Recognition Equipment Incorporated
1500 West Mockingbird Lane
Dallas, Texas 75235 (214) 637-2210

Offices in principal cities throughout the United States
Subsidiaries in Frankfurt, London, Paris, Rome, Stockholm, Tokyo and Toronto.
*Electronic Retina is a Trademark of Recognition Equipment Incorporated.

"I think I'd rather work for these guys."

Chiat/Day is looking for new accounts, and Sid the Production Manager loves the trotters. So when the agency offers money to any employee who comes up with a new business idea that turns into a new client, Sid finally sees a way to get back some of the money he's spent over the years as an aficionado of Western Harness Racing. He may not know a bad horse, but he knows a bad ad. He shows some of the Western Harness advertising to Guy, who in turn writes a letter to the President of Western Harness.

It says: I'm going to disqualify myself from soliciting your account because of this letter. Your advertising is embarrassing. You're a major event in Southern California, and if you don't care about your advertising, you ought to find somebody who will.

Ten days later, Guy's phone rings. The President of Western Harness wants to talk. Jay and Guy go over, take along some of the agency work, have a friendly meeting, and in less than two hours find themselves back in the parking lot without an account.

Getting into the car, it occurs to them that any man who makes his living operating a race track might be interested in a bet.

So they get out of the car, go back to the president's office, and Jay says this: "I think I have an offer that may interest you. We'll bet you every dime we'd make on your account that we can increase your attendance by 15%. And if we deliver, every person over 15%, we want a dollar a head. Every person below 15%, we'll give you a dollar a head."

They go back to the parking lot. Western Harness is now an account.

Within one year, the client will request the agreement be changed to a standard commission contract.

Sid the Production Manager is happy.

Somewhere down the hall in the creative department, one of the copywriters is getting a call. It's from Doyle Dane Bernbach, agency of agencies, and they would like to meet him very much. When you get a call from Doyle Dane, it's like God wants you to come. The copywriter puts together his portfolio and goes.

He interviews, he gets offered the job, he comes back to the office, and that evening, as he sits at his crummy desk in his crummy little room, listening to an argument that is always going on between the creative team next door, he thinks about where he is, who he's with, and the work Chiat/Day has done and is doing and will do.

He says to himself, "Screw it. I think I'd rather work for these guys."

A night at the harness races can be a very rewarding experience:

Sept. 22	Happy Hal to Tooth Pick	$ 127.00
Sept. 23	Rich Dan to Nu Lu	$ 183.40
	Parkers Choice to Carnival Star	$ 351.00
	Down Town Lobell to El Mayordomo	$3,143.00
Sept. 24	Hanley Bill to Skys Pal	$ 275.50
	Trotwood Jim to Harly Abbe	$ 817.00
Sept. 25	Rico Bay to Careless Joe	$ 250.50
Sept. 26	Nu Lu to Silver Jac	$ 228.20
	Poco Caballo to Rex G.	$ 341.50
Sept. 29	Tally Ho to Happy Hal	$ 859.00
Sept. 30	Wisenheimer to Cindilla	$ 861.20
Oct. 1	Abbe Chance to Spanish Chief	$ 525.00
Oct. 2	Poco Caballo to Sampson Frisco	$ 343.50
Oct. 3	Sister Dares to Bullys Shoe	$ 350.00
	Wee Judy D. to El Denny Pegasus	$ 533.50
	Blackie Grattan to Brass Key	$ 561.50
Oct. 6	Fleur D Amour to Odette Adios	$ 636.00
Oct. 7	El Denny Pegasus to Dick's Dilemma	$ 435.00
	Final Count to Boy Trust	$1,294.50
Oct. 8	Jill's Choice to Dandy Boy Tass	$ 413.40
	C. K. Adios to Big Time	$ 338.50
Oct. 9	Roswell to Americo Tass	$ 129.50
	Abbe Chance to El Mayordomo	$ 168.00
Oct. 10	Tartar to Cousin Ann	$ 520.00
	Saint Estephe A. to Brass Key	$ 203.00
Oct. 13	Flamingo's Pride to The Fooler	$ 505.00
Oct. 14	Dellvale Fancy to Miss Meadow D.	$ 121.00
Oct. 15	Dugger Wave to Upland Queen	$ 159.50
	Gypsy Goose to Brightest	$ 201.50
Oct. 16	Silver Jac to Cisco Wilson	$ 204.00
Oct. 17	Hirams Bay to Sis Byrd	$ 264.00
	The Grumbler to Bout Due	$ 130.50
Oct. 20	Diamonte Song to Sierra Billy	$ 146.80
	Easy Faith to Peter Perkins	$ 162.50
Oct. 21	Egyptian Song to Duke Liner	$ 106.50
Oct. 22	Carelens First to Silver Dawn Truax	$ 926.80
	Speedy Patch to El Patron	$ 576.00
	Polly Jinks to Happy Otto	$ 138.00
Oct. 23	Chief Sun to Caledonia Lobell	$ 78.50
Oct. 24	Copper Duke to Dazzilum	$ 242.20
Oct. 27	Bo Bo Ranger to Diamonte Phil	$3,941.00
	Free Heather to Shawn Hill	$ 145.00
Oct. 28	Flash on Pick to Happy Hal	$ 217.00
Oct. 29	Rod V. Adios to Dusty's Colt	$ 416.40
	Lumber Dazzle to Silver Jac	$ 245.50
Oct. 30	Stoney Burke N. to Eyre Fire	$2,799.00
Oct. 31	El Denny Pegasus to Wee Can D.	$ 252.60
	Judge to Starfire Hanover	$ 495.50
	Bout Due to Majestic Lee G.	$ 113.50
Nov. 3	Game Pick to Queens Key	$ 135.40
	Chancey Guy to Latin Em Pres	$ 259.50
	Action Boy to Santa Dee	$ 359.00
Nov. 4	Peter Perkins to Tripoli Hanover	$ 126.40
Nov. 5	Daddy Gene to Kelly's Mail	$ 67.40
Nov. 6	L. R. Adios to Princess Savford	$ 218.50
	Direct Takeoff to Ruths Choice	$1,238.00
Nov. 7	Sandra Kay A to Joe Blades	$ 468.50
Nov. 10	Ensign Cleo to Brightest	$ 323.50
Nov. 11	Colvins Lad to Thorpe Aid	$ 268.40
	Topall Adios to Look Me Over	$ 221.50
Nov. 12	Beloved Lady to Rory Ranger	$ 591.40
	Silver Creek Pal to Christines Fillie	$ 671.00
Nov. 13	Lumber Dazzle to Bo Bo Ranger	$ 193.50
Nov. 14	Napoleons Dream to Jet Attack	$ 338.80
	Springtime Cheer to Swatara	$1,038.50
Nov. 17	Easter Lucky to Clever Rod	$ 314.00
	Rhode Island Red to Mister Hot Shot	$ 217.00
Nov. 18	Skipper Hal to Princess Savford	$ 142.40
	Francis Quarry to Silver Sing	$ 302.00
Nov. 19	Blazing to Dell Haven	$ 744.50
Nov. 20	Royal Cavalier to King Trick	$ 702.00
	Lumber Dazzle to Wee Herb	$ 117.50
Nov. 21	Good Move to Clear Brook	$ 355.00
	Danas Roybill to Down Town Lobell	$ 275.00
Nov. 24	Free Heather to Dream Buster	$ 218.00
Nov. 25	Rico Bay to Diamonte Queen	$ 172.80
	Saint Estephe A. to Rieds Shadow	$ 569.00
Nov. 26	Sun Shadow to Land Freight	$ 105.00
Nov. 27	Nardins Dream to Pleasant Lad N.	$ 186.00
Nov. 28	Gomer Hanover to G. G. Parker	$ 175.20
	Miss Comet Time to Meadow Cobb	$ 539.00
Nov. 30	Game Pick to Poplar Nibble	$ 102.40
	Balmacraig to Shawn Hill	$ 359.50
	Our Juanita to All Keyed Up	$ 352.50
Dec. 1	Silent Tona to Edgewood Jet	$ 139.80
	Keystone Iris to Track Master	$ 354.00
Dec. 2	Shesadoll to Russets Boy	$ 146.00
	Varsity Knight to Mary's Dawn	$ 189.00
Dec. 3	Wee Can D to Amigos Heir	$ 425.00
	Silver Creek Pal to Armbro Louann	$ 129.50
Dec. 4	Gary Paul Hoffman to Gallant Trip	$ 404.50
	Circle Thorpe to King Trick	$ 169.00
Dec. 5	Vals Playboy to Adios Dominion	$ 47.00
	Miss Comet Time to Press Agent	$ 637.00
Dec. 5	El Denny Pegasus to Balmacraig	$ 625.00
Dec. 7	Russets Boy to Silver Dawn Truax	$ 701.50
	Sis Byrd to Happy Hal	$ 189.50
Dec. 8	Mocking Dream to Whanga Earl	$ 146.40
	Ingenue to Christines Fillie	$ 144.50
	Freight Manifest to Cardinal Hanover N.	$ 798.00
Dec. 9	Edgewood Jet to Wee Judy D.	$ 453.50
	Miss Comet Time to Bout Due	$ 374.00
Dec. 10	Justice Slo to Scorcher Wave	$ 674.00
	Ruths Super to Adios Alta	$ 113.50
Dec. 11	Flashy Sky to Shawn Hill	$ 130.00
	Pleasant Lad N. to East Faith	$ 368.50
Dec. 12	Fast Craig to Gon's Mary F.	$ 143.60
	Land Freight to Bright Bridget	$ 292.00
Dec. 12	Scotty's Colt to A. Dares	$ 116.00
	Francis P. Adios to Bewitching Goldie	$ 132.50
Dec. 14	Clever Rod to Clear Brook	$ 82.00
	Armbro Guy to Ruths Super	$ 111.50
Dec. 15	Nu Lu to Texas Freight	$ 247.00
	Scorcher Wave to Tricky Dares	$ 360.50
Dec. 16	Wee Johnny D. to Colvins Suzie	$ 109.60
Dec. 17	Althea Tass to Master Redwood	$ 376.00
Dec. 18	Gomer Hanover to Peter Perkins	$1,445.00
	Ski Slope to A. Dares	$ 115.50
Dec. 19	Nevada Jack to Carnival Star	$ 136.20
Dec. 21	Chachuma Chief to Our Juanita	$ 116.50

EXACTA PAYOFFS for $2 and $5 wagers during 1970.

Harness racing starts tonight at Hollywood Park. First post, 7:45 pm.

How to tell the difference between a pacer and a trotter.

A pacer.

A trotter.

Night Racing at Hollywood Park starts Sept. 23rd.

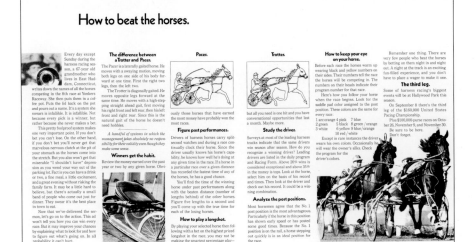

How to beat the horses.

Night Racing at Hollywood Park. Season Opens September 6.

How to feel classy at the harness races.

Night Racing Sept. 9th at Hollywood Park.

"Jay and Guy were great in presentations together. Because Guy was a leader, and he's kind of one of those guys who steps back, but he's still in charge. And Jay would be right up front."

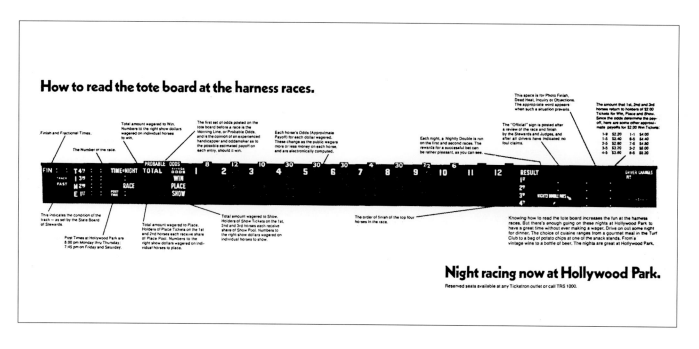

How to read the tote board at the harness races.

Night racing now at Hollywood Park.

Reserved seats available at any Ticketron outlet or call TRS 1000.

11 things you can do at the harness races that you can't do here:

1. See trotters trot and pacers pace.

2. Buy booze.

3. Make a wager openly (not out of the side of your mouth).

4. Sit in the shade (all races are at night).

5. Save 50¢ parking.

6. Get a gourmet meal or a hot dog without having to stand in line.

7. Buy a Hollywood Park pennant for your kid.

8. Win the Daily Double (optional).

9. Have a race named after you (call Ann Roberts, 678-1181).

10. Sit peacefully wherever you want (there are no rival teams—and no fanatical rival team rooters—to worry about).

11. Miss having to sit through a halftime show.

78 nights of racing at Hollywood Park Sept. 23 thru Dec. 22

We've waited 25 years for next Tuesday night.

You only have to wait 2 days.

Harness racing's 25th season starts September 22nd at Hollywood Park.

ANNCR VO: Harness Racing
WOMAN: Whinnies like a horse.
MAN #1: Whinnies like a horse.
Man #2: Whinnies like a horse.
OLD WOMAN: Blubbers like a horse.
GIRL: Giggles.
ANNCR VO: Night Harness Racing, every Tuesday through Saturday at Hollywood Park.
MAN #3: Wiggles his ears.
SPOKESMAN: Returning by popular demand…Night Harness Racing…Now at Hollywood Park.

ANNCR: Returning by popular demand, Night Harness Racing.
GIRL BEATING HERSELF WITH COCONUTS.
ANNCR: Now at Hollywood Park.
GIRL BEATING COCONUTS.

"The advertising was not widely liked in the horse circles. I mean, the insiders—the breeders, the trainers, the jockeys, they're into tradition, My Old Kentucky Home, that kind of stuff. So the president of Western Harness had a business card made up, and you turned it over like a Japanese business card, and it said something like, 'Yes, I did approve that advertising. Yes. I do think it works. Sorry you don't like it.' It was printed right on his business card."

GREAT MOMENTS IN COST ACCOUNTING: PART III

Manny Kent cures the curse of Wall Street.

NEW YORK, September 7, 1970 — Manny Kent, mild-mannered reporter for the Wall-To-Wall Journal, today found a logical solution for the market-choking Paper Plague. While covering a meeting of the Brokers' League to Eradicate Excess Paper (BLEEP), he earned the acclaim of the entire financial world by asking, "Why don't you call Dallas, Texas?" A ticker-tape parade will be given in Manny's honor on Friday.

Manny Kent was finishing a story on September Pork Bellies when the call came in from BLEEP. There was to be a meeting on Thursday morning to discuss standard sizes for stock certificates, the paper jam and related market problems. Manny was assigned to cover the meeting.

He had two days to prepare. He dug into the files on paper problems and banknote companies and security certificates and buy and sell orders. Then he got into reports on keypunching and optical reading and key-to-tape systems and error factors. Then he got into the elevator and went to lunch.

Thursday's BLEEP meeting started promptly at 10 a.m. Brian Bull, the Chairman, was the first to speak. "We've got to reduce the size of security certificates so they can be handled automatically by optical scanning or reading or something."

"Small certificates are too easy to counterfeit," Stanley Bear protested.

"And, besides, there isn't an optical machine on the market that can handle the large volumes many securities dealers have."

"What's wrong with keypunching?" someone asked.

"Too slow. Too many mistakes," Bull said. "Look at the problem we're having with buy and sell orders. Brokers write like doctors. Someone has to re-write every order by hand so keypunch operators can understand them. Even so, there are still too many errors."

The conversation continued in circles around the rectangular table. Suddenly, Manny Kent asked his now-famous question. "Why don't you call Dallas, Texas?"

A hush came over the room. It was so quiet you could hear a stock split. Finally, Bull broke the silence.

This is the third episode in a five-part attempt to convince you to cut your data processing costs in half. Reprints of the entire series are available free from Recognition Equipment Incorporated, 1500 West Mockingbird Lane, Dallas, Texas 75222.

"Dallas, Manny? Big D? Home of Neiman-Marcus and Don Meredith . . . ? Why Dallas, Manny?"

"Recognition Equipment."

"Why Recognition Equipment?"

Bull persisted. "They make that large optical reading system for oil companies and airlines, don't they?"

"Yes. The Electronic Retina* Computing Reader. Costs upwards of three-quarters of a million. It's being used by banks, credit card companies, the U.S. Army . . ."

"What's that got to do with the stock market?"

"They have a new machine. The INPUT 2 Reader," Manny exclaimed.

"Costs about half-a-million dollars. Leases for about $14,000 a month. It could read miniaturized stock certificates, handprinted buy and sell orders, dividend cash receipt forms and probably a lot of other things you're still keypunching. It reads documents just the way they come in. Typed, imprinted or handprinted. Then it records the data on magnetic tape in computer language and feeds the information directly into the computer."

"How do you know so much about Recognition Equipment?"

"They advertise in my paper."

So Wall Street got an INPUT 2 Reader, solved one of the biggest paper jams in history and saved a lot of money in the bargain. Manny got a bonus from his paper, a ticker-tape parade and an assignment on September Cotton for Monday's edition.

Recognition Equipment Incorporated
Watch for the next thrilling adventure:
"Please Fasten Your Seat Belt, We're Going To Audit Your Income."

*Electronic Retina is a trademark of Recognition Equipment Incorporated.

1969

GREAT MOMENTS IN COST ACCOUNTING: PART V

Let's all sing the gas company bill.

A cost-cutting breakthrough almost turned into a public relations problem the day the utility companies stopped punching holes in computer cards.

Willard Bach loved to receive utility bills. He collected the stubs and taped them together in long rolls. But nobody knew why, until the day he unveiled an amazing machine. A player piano that worked from keypunch cards.

"Utility bills make the best music," he would say. "Don't know why. Must be some kind of mathematical explanation."

Soon Willard Bach was famous. He even put words to his music and got a group together to record "The Sound of Water," "Kilowatt Rock," and "Love is a Natural Gas." All three songs made the top ten on rock radio stations.

Suddenly, one day, the music stopped. Instead of the familiar hole-punched cards, utility bills began arriving on plain printed paper. Phone calls poured into the utility companies.

"What about Willard Bach's music?" people asked. "What about the wonderful player piano?"

"We're sorry," utility company personnel said. "But, we've found a simpler, faster, much less expensive way to process billing information and statements."

"What could be simpler than holes?" Willard demanded.

"No holes. You see, utility billing involves two primary functions: meter reading and the processing of statements and cash receipts.

"Meter reading used to be done one of two ways. The meter reader either wrote the information manually on a simple form or marked the dial reading on a specially prepared *mark sense* form. The manual operation required keypunch operators who translated the written information into punched cards. Mark sense forms were processed by optical readers that punched the holes automatically. Either way, we had to go through an extra step and still ended up with punched cards which we used to update our billing records in the computer.

"Then, as now, the computer information was used to produce statements on a line printer. But, before statements were mailed, account numbers had to be keypunched into them.

"As you know, customers have to return a portion of the statement with their payments. Our clerks have to open every envelope that comes in to see if the payment equals the amount due. When we were still doing things the old way, any partial payment amount had to be keypunched into the card before it went to the computer for processing."

This is the final episode in a five-part attempt to convince you to cut your data processing costs in half. Reprints of the entire series are available free from Recognition Equipment Incorporated, 1500 West Mockingbird Lane, Dallas, Texas 75222.

"That makes sense to me," Willard said. "What made you stop keypunching?"

"INPUT 2. A totally new kind of optical reader that handles meter reading and statement processing without keypunching," the utility people said.

"INPUT 2 was developed by Recognition Equipment. It reads machine printing and handprinting. Records the data on magnetic tape in computer language so it can be fed directly into the computer. It costs only $550,000. Leases for $14,000 a month."

"What are you doing with it?"

"Information handprinted by meter readers is read by INPUT 2 and fed directly into the computer. Statements are sent out without keypunch holes because the new machine reads information printed by the line printer. And since there's no need for keypunching, statements are prepared on regular paper instead of card stock.

"When statement stubs come in, information about full or partial payments is handprinted by clerks and sent directly to INPUT 2 for processing. Again, no keypunching. In fact, many of the utility companies have eliminated keypunching entirely. We use INPUT 2 to process service work orders, daily time cards, cashier stubs, customer service invoices, and other forms. The new system cuts millions from our data processing costs."

"Just because the utility companies wanted to save a couple of million bucks, I have to go without music," Willard said.

"Not necessarily. We'll be glad to give you one of our obsolete keypunch machines. Then you can make all the music you want."

So Willard Bach got a utility company keypunch machine of his very own and went on to fame, fortune and his own TV show. The utility companies avoided a public relations problem, continued to find new applications for INPUT 2 and saved themselves a couple of million bucks.

Recognition Equipment Incorporated

GREAT MOMENTS IN COST ACCOUNTING: PART II

The price of success is compounded quarterly.

Rapid growth threatened to inundate Eastern National Bank in its own paper work until Hernando Sawbuck saved the day, the bank and a lot of money by writing a check for $550,000.

Eastern National Bank was getting ready to open its fifth branch in as many years. The new building was ready. The new manager was ready. The new tellers were ready. But, Hernando Sawbuck wasn't ready.

"¡Caramba!" he would say daily. "How are we going to handle the paper work from five branches when we can hardly keep up with just the debit and credit memos from four offices?"

"You'll find a way," bank president Norton von Debit would answer. "That's your job. Assistant Vice President In-Charge of the Customer-generated and Internal MICR-encoded and Non-specific Forms, Slips and Subsequent Memos Department. You'll find a way," he repeated.

"Automate something."

Automate what? Hernando mumbled to himself. The only thing that's even partially automatic is checking. But even with MICR, we still have to enter amounts on checks with proof encoders before we can update our computer files and return cancelled checks with statements.

And, that's only one of my headaches. We've got MICR account numbers on checking account deposit slips, savings account deposit and withdrawal forms, even installment loan payments. They all have to go through MICR proof encoders to have amounts put on before we can process them for our computer. I can't even distribute the workload because it's too expensive to put encoding machines at every teller window, where most of the documents come in.

Then there's the biggest headache of all. The new OmniCard credit plan. It's going to bring in a ton of charge tickets, statements and problems for the keypunch department. And they really can't stand the extra burden. Even MICR won't help them because it's impossible to preprint account numbers on charge tickets.

Hernando began a systematic investigation of each headache. Starting with the biggest one first. Being a logical person, he went first to the source of all contemporary wisdom. The Yellow Pages. There, under *Credit Cards*, he selected the name of one of the world's largest independent credit organizations. He called and asked for the data processing manager. And he found that they used to have the same kind of problem he had now. Too much to process.

"How did you fix it?" Hernando asked.

This is the second episode in a five-part attempt to convince you to cut your data processing costs in half. Reprints of the entire series are available free from Recognition Equipment Incorporated, 1500 West Mockingbird Lane, Dallas, Texas 75222.

"Optical reading with high-speed paper handling," the data processing manager said. "Eliminated keypunching and knocked several days off the billing process."

"Where can I get an optical reader?"

"Only one company makes a good one. Recognition Equipment. Dallas, Texas."

Hernando called Recognition Equipment and asked about the machine he'd heard about. He found out it's also used by most of the major oil companies, the large airlines and dozens of other companies. He also discovered that his problem wasn't as big as he thought it was. The machine cost upwards of three-quarters-of-a-million dollars and he didn't process a big enough volume to justify the price.

"What you need is our INPUT 2 Reader," the people at Recognition Equipment said. "It's brand new. Costs $550,000. Leases for about $14,000 a month. Reads machine-printing and handprinting, too. Typed. Printed. Imprinted. Even reads MICR better than MICR readers do. Then it records the data on magnetic tape in computer language.

"The INPUT 2 Reader will read the account numbers put on your credit card charge tickets with imprinters. And amounts imprinted in the field or added later. Statements printed on a line printer. You can even handprint cash receipt data on returned statements. You can do every bit of your credit card processing without keypunching."

"¡Caramba! The INPUT 2 not only solves my OmniCard problem, it solves all the others, too. I can automate all my debit and credit memo processing. I can even handprint amounts on all those deposit and withdrawal slips right at the teller's window."

So Hernando ordered an INPUT 2 Reader for Eastern National Bank, solved an impossible paper problem and told the president to go ahead and open the fifth branch. He was ready.

Recognition Equipment Incorporated
Watch for the next thrilling adventure:
"Manny Kent Cures The Curse Of Wall Street."

GREAT MOMENTS IN COST ACCOUNTING: PART IV

Please fasten your seat belt, we're going to audit your income.

A new job, a tough problem and a torn shoe all added up to instant success the day Wally Bean stepped off the third floor elevator at Mid Air Lines.

Wally Bean never thought he'd leave the oil business. But the job offer from Mid Air Lines was much too good to pass up. So, on August 3, 1970, Wally became special assistant to the president of the largest regional airline in the United States.

At 10:15 a.m. on the very first day, he was summoned to the office of Clarence Upp, president of Mid Air Lines. Mr. Upp's office was up on the third floor behind a jungle of potted plants and biplane replicas.

Wally rushed to the elevator which stopped just short of floor level. He tripped into the elevator and tore the heel off his shoe, which spun him around causing him to push the third-floor button with his nose. When the doors slid open again, he hopped out of the elevator and leaned against a statue of Otto Von Zeppelin. While he pounded the heel into place, Wally overheard a conversation between two men who were waiting for the down elevator to come up.

"I'm sorry, Bert. It's impossible. We can't possibly keep tabs on earned revenue."

"But, you heard Clarence. The auditors are going to want an accurate statement every month."

"Ridiculous. We're lucky to sample ten percent of the tickets that come in for processing. If we had to count every one, we'd need two hundred more keypunch operators and a hundred more verifiers. It's just not feasible..."

The elevator arrived and took the men out of earshot. But, Wally had heard enough. If he could come up with an instant solution to the earned revenue problem, he'd make a pretty good first impression on Upp. He went back to his office, called Mr. Upp's secretary asking for a few minutes, and then called the data processing manager at his old job.

A few minutes later, he was in the president's office.

"Wally," Clarence Upp said. "You know what our biggest problem is today?"

"Keeping tabs on earned revenue?"

"Why, that's absolutely right. How did you know?"

"Just a lucky guess."

"Well, that's our problem. The auditors want us to find a way to keep track of every dollar we earn. You see, until an airline ticket is used, the money paid for it is considered unearned revenue. We can't call the money ours until the passenger actually takes the flight. Tickets are collected on the plane and sent here for processing. Our EDP center gets thousands of tickets a day. So you can imagine how difficult it is to process every one."

"Well, sir, if I might suggest...your problem is keypunching."

This is the fourth episode in a five-part attempt to convince you to cut your data processing costs in half. Reprints of the entire series are available free from Recognition Equipment Incorporated, 1500 West Mockingbird Lane, Dallas, Texas 75222.

"Yes, I know. Not enough girls."

"No, sir, too many," Wally said.

"You shouldn't be keypunching at all. Optical reading is what you need."

"We looked into that. The reader we need is too expensive. The one we can afford isn't good enough."

"Who makes the one you need?"

"Recognition Equipment. Dallas. Great machine, but too expensive. Price starts at three quarters of a million. Almost all the big airlines are using it. United, American, TWA..."

"I know something about it. The Electronic Retina* Computing Reader. Just about every large oil company uses it to process credit card charge tickets... as I recall, it knocks about five days off the billing process... anyway, the oil company I worked for wanted one but they had the same problem you do. Not enough volume to justify the price."

"Too bad they don't make a less expensive machine."

"But they do. That's what I was getting at. Recognition Equipment has a new reading machine that's just perfect for regional airlines and smaller credit card companies.

It's called the INPUT 2 Reader.

Reads just as well as the bigger machine, but costs only $550,000. Leases for $14,000 a month. They just left off a lot of the extras that companies with smaller volumes and more uniform documents don't need. The INPUT 2 Reader reads documents just the way they come in. Typed, imprinted or handprinted. Then it records the data on magnetic tape in computer language and feeds it directly into the computer."

Wally was put in charge of solving the earned revenue problem. He had an INPUT 2 reading system installed at Mid Air Lines and soon there was no problem.

Today, Mid Air reads and processes every airline ticket that comes in. The auditors are happy because they always know how much money the airline is making. Mr. Upp is happy because the INPUT 2 Reader system is saving more than it cost. And Wally is happy because he got a new third-floor office right next to the jungle of potted plants and biplane replicas.

Recognition Equipment Incorporated
Watch for the next thrilling adventure:
"Let's All Sing The Gas Company Bill."

*Electronic Retina is a trademark of Recognition Equipment Incorporated

"I wrote these ads during my short story period."

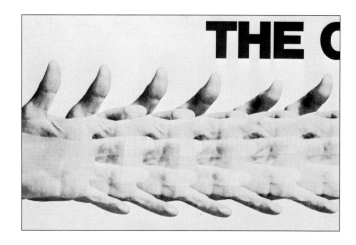

*"We got more requests for
reprints of the ad than they
sold machines."*

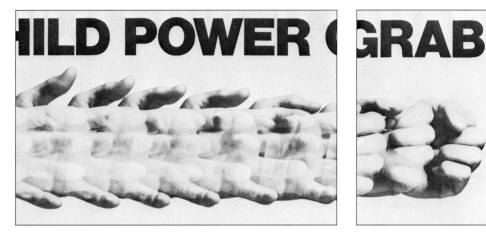

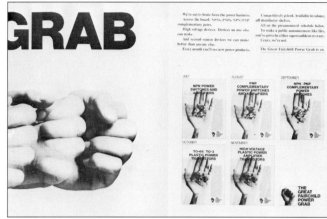

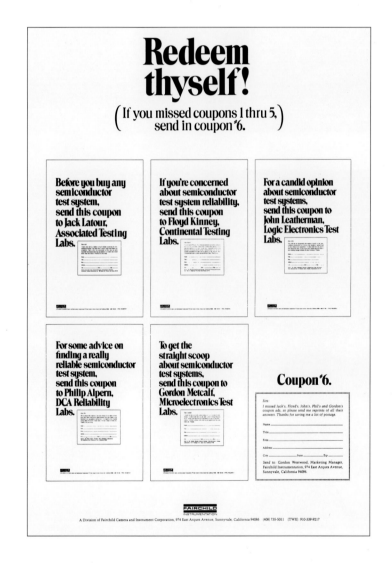

the first of the flying tankers

The day was balmy. The visibility unlimited. Over Signal Hill, California, two planes lapped wings, barely six feet apart. The lower one, a reddish Lincoln Standard. The other, a brighter red, a JN-4, Jenny.

From the Jenny's left skid, his body a pendulum, Wes May swung back and forth trying to work up onto the lower wing. Moments before he'd been on the wing of the Standard.

On his back, instead of a chute, hung a chunky fifty pound can. It pulled his body back, and for a dizzying minute, Wes hung, head down, the blackish oil derricks a splotchy lacing some 3,500 feet below.

Finally his foot hooked the skid. Slowly Wes worked his way forward, caught the outside strut and pulled himself hand over hand until he stood on the leading edge. With a wave at the pilot, Wes made his way toward the fuselage.

His back half turned to the prop, he unstrapped the can and uncapped it. With one hand clutching the plane, Wes tipped the can at the gas tank. Some fuel splashed into the tank. Most poured into the slip-stream, soaking May.

A nearby plane took photographs, because the incident was, for November 12, 1921, newsworthy. But, to the newspapers and most observers, it was still another barnstorming exhibition by misplaced youngsters who couldn't forget the War.

To May, though, it was an accomplishment. He'd bet his skill against his life, and won.

To the Jenny's pilot, Earl Daugherty, it was a great step into the future. The beginning of the fulfillment of a dream; something to do with men flying cross country in less than a day; of going around the world non-stop. It was a step. Crude. Sloppy. Sensational. The world's first air-to-air refueling.

Earl Stanley Daugherty was a problem. And a hero. He'd learned to fly in 1911 and was recognized, by those who paid any attention, as one of America's top aviators. He offered his talent to the Air Service, was appointed a 2nd Lieutenant during the War. And was almost as promptly grounded for teaching students, of all things, aerobatics.

A court martial hung over his future. And he escaped it by resigning from the service days ahead of the Armistice.

To Daugherty, aerobatics was an expression, a disciplined course in learning. Aerobatics taught a oneness between man and machine. It sharpened skills; provided limitations. It prepared one for emergencies. Properly applied it was schooling for the man, not amusement for the fool.

Back home, like others, Earl became a Barnstormer, and gained top billing at every flying circus across the land. He operated from Daugherty's Flying School at the edge of Long Beach, California, the center of Southland aviation in the twenties.

He developed double wing-walkers and men who hung from plane bellies their teeth. He molded flyers who carried off the spectacular outside loops and made screaming passes under bridges with as little as 4' clearance. Some flyers barnstormed only for the thrill. Others for a purpose as well. Like Daugherty, who claimed the use of planes only for joy riding was becoming a thing of the past; that "travel by air will become commonplace and people will be using airplanes someday as they now use trains, steamboats and automobiles." And he forecast businessmen flying from Los Angeles to New York overnight, attending to business and returning the next afternoon, adding that one day, airports would even be built on top of buildings.

Daugherty's stunts kept the crowds coming. The circuses were profitable. But, more than that, airplanes and their accomplishments and the daring of the pilots, stayed in the public eye.

Flying groups vied with flying groups for new "death defying feats." And they were always looking for firsts. Like turning off the engine, climbing out and starting it again with a hand crank. Or the mid-air transfer of gasoline, carefully planned by Daugherty, May and Frank Hawks.

Wes, the "Flying Tanker" proved gasoline could be transferred air-to-air. More than a stunt, it was the beginning of a new engineering concept to keep planes aloft longer for far-reaching missions. Just a little over a year later, an auxiliary jettisonable belly tank fitted to the bomb rack, was successfully tested at Selfridge Field, Michigan.

In June, 1923 the first pipeline refueling between two airplanes was completed in San Diego by Lts. Lowell H. Smith and John Richter. Army Air Service. January 1929 saw Major Carl Spaatz and Capt. Ira C. Eaker set a world record of 150 hours in a Fokker C2-3 Wright 200. In March 1949, the B-50 Lucky Lady made a non-stop round-the-world flight in 94 hours. The first non-stop jet was completed by B-52's in 45 hours 19 minutes in 1957.

Daugherty and May never lived to see the refinement of their art. Wes died shortly after in a freak parachute jump — and Earl when his newly purchased Laird disintegrated over Long Beach in 1928.

But today, there is an aerial hook-up made on the average of one every minute every twenty-four hours, and refueling is one of the most vital support missions in today's defense systems.

Many of these operations are monitored by recorders. Rugged ones. Sensitive ones. Reliable ones. Like the ones Leach builds. Very critically. With very high packing densities.

We once thought 2,500 bits per inch was something. Now, we're delivering recorders using saturation recording techniques to obtain 10 to 20K bits/inch/track with less than 1 error in 10^9.

Very small in size. But very big in broadband analog performance and capacity. Very custom. Very sought after. From a few ounces to hundreds of pounds — multiple track, multiple speed. Wherever permanent or temporary storage of analog and digital data is required. Military or industrial, we've done it. Leach Corporation, 405 Huntington Drive, San Marino, California 91108. Telephone (213) 682-3506. Export: Leach International S.A. **LEACH**

the day the marines made air history

The skies were leaden and damp as First Lieutenant Christian F. Schilt banked his Vought Corsair and headed straight for the tiny settlement of Quilali. Below, in the wetness of the Nicaraguan jungle, a 260-man Marine patrol struggled to hold off a guerrilla band of more than 400 led by the rebel-bandit, Augusto Sandino.

Schilt's mission called for nerves of steel. Quilali was surrounded on three sides by thick jungle. On the fourth side, a sharp cliff dropped off for several hundred feet. Even for a veteran pilot like Schilt, landing on such terrain would be hazardous — if not impossible. He would have to fly in over the top of the cliff, land and stop within 300 feet or smash into the jungle wall. Then he would take off with a wounded man (two would dangerously overload the Vought Corsair). There would be many trips, many men to get out. Success would mean the first air-evacuation in history. Failure would be forgotten.

JUNGLE AMBUSH

The drama of this day had begun several days earlier, on January 2, 1928. A 200-man patrol of the Second Marine Brigade had been sent out to attack Sandino's main camp, a fort in the mountains. A smaller patrol would meet them near Quilali. Suddenly, there was an ambush and the leaders of both patrols were seriously wounded along with several enlisted men.

THE PLAN

According to a prearranged system, an "emergency" message was air-hooked by an observation plane and flown to Marine Headquarters at Managua. A thirteen-year veteran pilot, Schilt was chosen to make the evacuation flights. The wounded men would be ferried one by one from Quilali to Ocotal, just 30 miles away. From there, they would be taken in a larger plane to Managua.

On paper, the plan for the first air-evacuation was simple. And, typically Marine. Observation planes would drop axes, shovels and supplies to the men on the ground who would hack out an airstrip under fire. Then, Schilt would fly in and out as many times as necessary to air-lift the seriously wounded men. His only advantage was that his Vought Corsair was light, powerful and easily maneuverable. But it had never been used for a mission like this before. Nor had any other plane.

For the next three days, the mood at Managua remained tense as reports of the work at Quilali filtered in. The men of the trapped patrols were being plagued by constant downpours and never-ending volleys of gunfire from the rebels in the jungle.

TAKE-OFF AND MORE TROUBLE

At 6:40 on the morning of January 6, 1928, Schilt made a last-minute check of his aircraft and took off for Quilali with Captain Roger Peard who would, take over as patrol commander and direct the march out of the jungle once the wounded men had been evacuated.

The tires of the Vought were now those of a DeHavilland because larger tires would be safer in a muddy landing. All excess weight had been removed, including Schilt's parachute (a fact known only to the young pilot himself).

By 8:00, Schilt was over Quilali and could see that he would have to come in as low as possible over the clifftop. Signaling to Peard, Schilt dove for the cliff. A fierce downdraft caught the ship. The nose dipped crazily as Schilt fought for control. Past the top of the cliff, the Vought bounced onto the muddy ground and headed straight for the jungle wall. Then, the mucky terrain took hold and brought the craft to a rocking halt just a few feet from the end of the airstrip.

Schilt taxied back toward the cliff for the return trip take-off and one of the critically wounded patrol leaders was carried under heavy guard and gently lowered into the rear cockpit. "Get a medical corpsman in here," said a weary Marine. Schilt nodded, knowing that only a corpsman could set up the priority of those to be evacuated. Then, Schilt revved his 450 h.p. engine to full pitch and the Vought Corsair lurched forward. Gaining more speed, the craft lifted itself from the muddy turf, climbed quickly and soared over the treetops. The first air-evacuation was now underway. Just how many more times he could land and take-off from this precarious jungle perch, Schilt did not know. Two hours later, he was back for another wounded man.

TWO AT A TIME

The next day, during the fifth flight, it was decided to evacuate two men at a time. Although this would increase the danger of overweight, it was felt necessary to save as many lives as possible.

Three days and two planes later, Schilt had made a total of ten flights and had evacuated 18 seriously wounded Marines. The air-lift completed, the patrol proceeded to smash its way out of the jungle.

For his actions, Christian F. Schilt was awarded the Navy Medal of Honor — the only such citation issued in 1928.

OUR NEWEST, TOUGHEST RELAY

Our new Series G, 150-grid relays were designed to satisfy the requirement for smaller, lighter, more reliable airborne components and equipment. They can handle loads from dry circuit to 2 amps and qualify to MIL-R-5757/37 (airborne). And even though they're half the size and half the weight of ½-crystal can relays, they make higher packing density possible. For details, write Leach Corporation, Corporate Offices, 1499 Huntington Drive, South Pasadena, California 91030. **LEACH**

"Even though they might have had small accounts, Chiat/Day always managed to run, like, a spread, four-color, it may have happened once a year for that account, but people would know about the account because they would see that one ad. That's I think what attracted me to Chiat/Day. I used to see big ads from them all the time. And I could never figure out how they did it without any big clients."

"A lot of people started hearing about us for the first time through our public service work. If you do public service right, it transcends 'is it better for us or is it better for them?' It should be better for both of you."

MY IDOL, THE PIMP.

When you're born in a ghetto, odds are ten to one you'll never get out.

What's worse is, you know it. You know it from the first day you step into society and fail. That first day of school.

So what do you do?

Well, you look down the street at the corner. And you see a guy with a chick on each arm, a $200 custom tailored suit, and you say:

"Man, I'm gonna be just like him. He was born here. He lives here. And he's beaten it. He lives here and he ain't part of the garbage. I'm gonna be just like him."

Not like O. J. Simpson. Not like Willie Mays. Not like Mike Garrett or Bill Russell. Because nobody's *really* like them. At least, nobody you know.

So right then and there you decide. 11 years old and you decide to place a value on your future.

You're going to be a pimp.

Because when you're born in a ghetto, that's what you do.

But you weren't born in a ghetto, were you? And it really isn't your problem.

Right. It's ours.

Direction Sports.

We help kids.
Bright underprivileged kids.
Not by recognizing the symptoms, but by attacking the causes.

We're interested in building self esteem. We're interested in giving these kids an identity. And attitudes. And a reason for being.

How do we do all this?

As our name implies, with sports. But as our name also implies, with direction.

Quite simply, we took the universal magnetism of everyday sports and turned it into a tool for teaching and motivating.

It works.

Because no matter who you are, no matter where you come from, when you're 11 or 12 years old, a baseball or a football is magic. Once you're hooked, you're hooked.

Then you become part of a team. And you're not alone.

If you miss a basket the first time, you learn how to make it the second time. Or the third.

If you never could understand math, you suddenly become a pro at batting averages.

And instead of being a boy from the ghetto, you're Tommy Brown. Football player. Number 16.

You're somebody.

Here's where you can help.

We need money. $10. $20. $50.

We need it for helmets, for sneakers, for footballs.

And for whatever else it takes to make these kids feel like pros.

We want you to use the coupon.

In return for your contribution, which is tax deductible, we'll send you an autographed picture of one of our teams and a schedule of the games for this season.

If the plight of these underprivileged kids isn't enough to move you, if the little reward

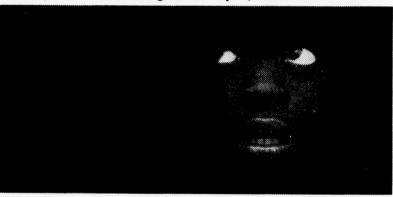

we can offer isn't enough reason, maybe this is:

No matter what your profession is, no matter where you grew up, or who your father was, no matter if you couldn't afford a movie *every* Saturday, no matter what course your life may have taken, or how many failures you've experienced, when you were eleven years old, you never dreamed of being a pimp.

"A chick on each arm and a $200 suit."

At the last minute, the copywriter is pulled into the meeting. There's Jay, there's Guy, there's his art director, and there's this guy he's never seen, telling them all a story. The guy is from a non-profit group called Direction Sports; the story is about O.J. Simpson.

The guy says that where Simpson grew up, there weren't many role models. You looked up to the men in the neighborhood who had the money, and those men were all hustlers and pimps and crooks. Simpson got out, but most kids didn't. The guy says that the goal of Direction Sports is to get kids involved in a real athletic program while they're young, give them teams and uniforms and something positive to identify with, give them an alternative to hanging out and getting into trouble.

Is there a way Chiat/Day could tell this story?

Now, it's lunch. The copywriter sits in the meeting room alone with an art director, who is constantly drawing. The art director says, whattaya think? The writer says, how about "My Idol, The Pimp"? Great, the art director says. "Are you sure?" the copywriter asks. Pretty strong word, pimp, it's not the kind of word you see in an ad, maybe it has too much edge to it, maybe it's offensive, and before his maybes are finished, the art director's hand is floating over the page and he flips the pad over and there's the layout. No picture yet, but the headline and the logo in the middle, and the open coupon.

Now it's a week later, the Direction Sports guy likes the ad and Chiat/Day's production department is pasting it up, when a kid from Art Center comes in, hoping to show someone some of the photographs he's taken while at school. One of them is a picture of a young boy.

Can we buy that picture from you? We need it for an ad. Now.

The kid from Art Center says he'll rent it, and the ad is finished.

Guy and Jay have a meeting with the media and everyone agrees to run the ad for free, except for one major television publication that finds "pimp" offensive, but will later run the ad as "My Idol, The Thief," a decision which will bother the copywriter all that day and for many years after that.

Otherwise, the ad gets produced as is. Nothing is changed—not a word, not the layout, not the crazy looking coupon. And then suddenly, it's running. And it's bringing in money.

Now it's a couple of months later, and the copywriter is asked if he'd like to take a ride down to the Venice Pavilion with a few people from the agency and the guy from Direction Sports.

When they get there, this is what he sees: tables filled with brand new t-shirts and helmets and numbers and uniforms, all lined up, gleaming in the sun. And shortly after that, there are buses pulling up and kids getting off and faces beaming and uniforms being pulled on over street clothes and there is smiling and shouting and laughing everywhere, and it is glorious, glorious.

Twenty years later, he will remember it like it was yesterday.

This little piggy went to market,
This little piggy took dope,
This little piggy had withdrawal,
This little piggy...died.

UNITED STUDENTS AGAINST DRUG ABUSE

PO NT OF NO RETURN

UNITED STUDENTS AGAINST DRUG ABUSE

"In those days, 'My Idol, The Pimp,' all those ads were very adventuresome. Today they're extremely mild by comparison."

Les Fleurs Enchantées

The mysterious essence of woman
is captured in a new fragrance . . .
Les Fleurs Enchantées, created by
Viviane Woodard.   An enchanted garden
of delicate scents blended into a flowery mist
of fragrance . . . Les Fleurs Enchantées emerges as a
complete collection of beautiful fragrance forms.

Your Viviane Woodard consultant brings you
total beauty with Les Fleurs Enchantées and a superb
collection of facial care and make-up products.

In your home . . . by appointment only

Viviane Woodard® Cosmetics . . . as near as your telephone

"That psychedelic stuff? I know I did it, but I can't think of anything to say about it."

Lesson One.

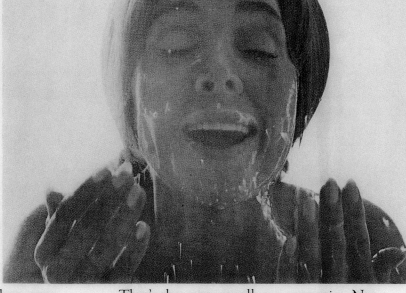

It begins with moisture. With basic skin care.

Because that's where every pretty face begins. With pretty skin. And then it goes on to make up. How to choose it. And how to apply it.

When does it start?

When you call a Viviane Woodard Cosmetic Consultant. She'll come to your home and give you a complimentary lesson in skin care and make up, Lesson One.

First she'll show you how to clean your skin. So it's really clean. So clean it glows.

Then how to refresh and stimulate your skin so it feels cool and tingly. How to protect it against the wind and weather. And how to keep it soft and smooth.

Then she'll show you how to select just the right shades and colors of make up. And how to apply them. You learn how to conceal any little blemishes or wrinkles that bother you. How to high light your best features. And soften others.

How to make your eyes look bigger. Or your chin look smaller. How to apply rouge in the most flattering fashion.

And how to wear powder so it doesn't look like you're wearing powder.

That's the way we sell our cosmetics. Not by the bottle. But by the person. Individually. And not in a store. Only in your own home. Where you can try on different things 'til you find what's really you.

And where you can get directions from a trained beauty advisor instead of from the back of a bottle.

At Viviane Woodard we know how to make excellent cosmetics. And we know something else, too. That even the best cosmetics in the world won't make you look good if you don't know how to use them. That's why we show you how to use ours. Starting with Lesson One.

Viviane Woodard would like to give you a complimentary skin care and make-up lesson. There's no obligation of course. Just mail in this coupon and a Viviane Woodard consultant will make an appointment to show you how to apply the latest make-up techniques.

Send to: Viviane Woodard Corporation, 14621 Titus Street, Panorama City, California 91412. A Subsidiary of General Foods.

NAME_____

ADDRESS_____

CITY_____

STATE_____ ZIP_____

PHONE_____

Viviane Woodard® Cosmetics
LOS ANGELES · TORONTO · LONDON

"What they want to be, not what they are."

Honda, the well-known motorcycle company, has built a car. They ask Chiat/Day to pitch the account. To the advertising agencies competing against Chiat/Day, it is a chance for a nice, small piece of business—Honda expects to spend about $500,000 a year. To Chiat/Day, it is a chance to work for a national advertiser, to expose the agency's work to a whole new audience, to do ads for a new car, just like Volkswagen was a new car when Doyle Dane Bernbach got ahold of it.

The pitch begins. They need a strategy. Automotive experience tells you that for $500,000, you introduce a new car by running lots of black and white newspaper ads. Fortunately, no one at Chiat/Day has any automotive experience.

Jay, Guy, and about six other people sit down, and figure things like this: Forget the budget. It's temporary. It'll grow. We should be pitching what they want to be, not what they are. That means television, magazine spreads, color, music.

It bears repeating, because it is a strategy Chiat/Day will use again and again for its clients over the years: Just because you are small doesn't mean you advertise small.

The pitch is getting closer. People are working 48 hours straight, no sleep, and in typical Chiat/Day fashion, nobody is satisfied with any of the work. They realize that it's not enough to show television storyboards, they're going to have to make a commercial. So on a Friday, they find a camera, they find a Honda, they find a location, and they get ready for what is arguably the most important film shoot in Chiat/Day's short history.

Saturday morning, it rains.

They film anyway. They've already paid for the camera. They produce original music, and not only do they put it in the commercial, they pipe it into the building's elevators so the Honda people will be listening to it on the way up and on the way down.

The day of the pitch, the Honda executives arrive at Chiat/Day, having already sat through three days of black and white newspaper ads.

Most of them speak very little English. They are asked to look at a television in the corner, and when the lights go down, they see this: their little Honda driving in circles in the rain, around and around to the elevator music.

They have never seen their car in an American context on film before. They are mesmerized.

Jay and Guy speak no Japanese, so they just keep saying, "Would you like to see the commercial again?" They show it about thirty times.

And Honda becomes a Chiat/Day account.

When it comes time to actually do the first ads introducing the car, they write hundreds of headlines, until one copywriter comes up with the line that says it all.

"Introducing The Honda Car."

"After all," he argues, "What would you say if Volkswagen came out with a motorcycle?"

With that unerring logic, Chiat/Day makes its first foray into the big time.

THE HONDA CAR.

That's right.

Car.

It's called the 600 Sedan and has a base price that looks more like a down payment.

For a lot of you, that's probably all the reason you need to at least go look at it.

Our name. And our price.

But before you get a few surprises driving it on the road, get a few surprises reading about it on this page.

First, you should know what our price includes.

Without leaving anything out, here's what you get without having to pay extra for it:

Self-adjusting front power disc brakes.

Four-speed transmission.

Flow-through ventilation (believe it or not, you don't get that on all small cars).

Bucket seats with headrests (the latter is mandatory, of course, but the former isn't).

Hinged rear side windows.

And front bumper overrides to protect the grille, lights and front end.

There's only one thing you don't get. A large gas tank. It isn't even medium sized. It's tiny. It holds 6.9 gallons of regular gas and costs somewhere around $2 to fill.

Here's the incredible part: with that 6.9 gallons, you'll be able to drive over 270 miles! Figure it out. That's almost 40 miles to a gallon.

The engine?

It's an overhead cam, four-stroke design that's air-cooled. And it's mounted sideways over the front wheels for better traction.

If we stopped right here, more than likely you'd come to the following conclusion:

The Honda 600 Sedan is an incredibly low-priced car that offers more value and performance per dollar than anything you've seen so far. It has a list of options that aren't options. And a fuel consumption that shouldn't even be called consumption.

But, there's more to the story.

Before we designed our body, we took a look at yours.

We built our inside before we built our outside. But, if you think we're going to tell you it has a lot of room, wrong.

It has just enough. (Ever drive in a car where the dash seems ten feet away? That's too much room.)

But just enough for what? Driving? All cars have that, big or small. When you drive a car, you do more than drive. You twist your head left and right to look in other lanes. You flip ashes into an ashtray. Look for a tissue in the glove compartment.

You do lots of things.

In the Honda 600, you do all of them comfortably. Simply because we designed it from the inside out.

Visibility is superb.

When you look out the right rear window to switch lanes (you do do that, don't you?) you'll see a hunk of road instead of a hunk of metal.

Or a hunk of metal if there happens to be another car there. Whatever, you'll see it. And at 75 miles an hour (yes, the Honda does 75) that's important.

WE KNOW. YOU'RE SKEPTICAL ABOUT SAFETY IN SMALL CARS.

Before you judge the new Honda at face value, consider this: There are two things you don't build overnight. A car. And a reputation. We've got the best of both.

The Honda name is known all over the world. Honda cars are known almost all over the world. We've been building good, sensible small cars since 1964. If you've traveled abroad, you've probably seen them. In Europe, Australia, or Asia.

Now we're introducing the 600. Our first entry into the U.S. auto market.

So, if you're concerned about safety, how do you think we feel?

Right. When we say the Honda 600 meets or exceeds all applicable U.S. Federal Motor Vehicle Safety Standards, it's not just a line the government gave us to use. It's a commitment.

Again, if we stopped right here, you'd probably draw even more conclusions than before, and be even more anxious to test drive it.

We're stopping right here.

$1395.*

"The first year, they were selling cars out of motorcycle shops."

"It suddenly strikes me. I said, 'This is ridiculous. How can you say Honda and not allude to motorcycles? Let's just say the Honda car.' And my partner says, 'Gee, that's very dull.' I said, 'Oh yeah?' And I wrote 'The Volkswagen Motorcycle' on a piece of paper. And I said, 'If this ran in the paper tomorrow, would you read it?' He said, 'Yeah. Present it to Jay just like that.'"

HONDA: THE CAR EVERYBODY'S BEEN TRYING TO BUILD.

The auto industry is on a mini kick. They've finally discovered what people want most from the cars they buy. Transportation. Reliable, convenient, economical transportation.

We've known it for years. Honda started building good, sensible small cars in 1964. If you've traveled abroad, you've probably seen them. In Europe, Australia, or Asia.

Now we have a model specially designed for the United States. The Honda 600 Sedan. A good basic car with good basic features. Like up to 40 miles per gallon on regular gas. An air-cooled, four-stroke overhead cam engine. Front-wheel drive. A top speed of 75 miles an hour.

The only thing it doesn't have is options. (Those extras you'd normally expect to pay extra for.) All the really important things are already included: Self-adjusting front disc brakes. A four-speed transmission. Flow-through ventilation. Bucket seats with headrests. Hinged rear side windows.

It's a very complete little car.

See for yourself. Honda built the car everybody's been trying to build.

And we did it for a price nobody's been able to beat.

THE HONDA CAR. $1395. Suggested retail. Does not include dealer new car preparation, local transportation, tax and license. Prices and specifications subject to change without notice. Copyright 1970 American Honda Motor Co., Inc. Meets or exceeds all applicable U.S. Federal Motor Vehicle Safety Standards.

In one year many new cars depreciate as much as our new car costs.

The Kelley Blue Book of used car prices is a book of horror stories.

For most new car buyers, it's "read 'em and weep".

The January/February '72 Blue Book shows the following depreciation for various one-year-old 1971 cars ("F.O.B" new car price, less current Blue Book wholesale price):

Pontiac Bonneville Sedans depreciated $2040. Chrysler New Yorker 4-door Hardtops, $2034. Buick Riviera Sport Coupes, $1984.

Down the drain.

That's more than the Honda Sedan costs in the first place.

Including standard equipment that sounds more like optional extras: responsive rack and pinion steering,

smooth 4-speed synchromesh transmission, power-assisted front disc brakes and front bucket seats. And gas mileage that sounds more like wishful thinking: up to 40 miles to the gallon.

It's up to you.

You can spend between $1500 and $2000 for depreciation on a big expensive new car, and in a year have nothing to show for it.

Or you can spend between $1500 and $2000 for a Honda Sedan, and in a year have a car to show for it.

The Honda Sedan. Under $1600.
It makes a lot of sense.

*SUGGESTED RETAIL P.O.E. DEALER PREPARATION, TRANSPORTATION, TAX AND LICENSE EXTRA. ©1972 AMERICAN HONDA MOTOR CO., INC.

The less you spend on a car, the more you can spend on other things.

This car gets up to 40 miles to the gallon.

Up to 75 miles an hour.

Overhead cam engine, rack and pinion steering, 4-speed synchromesh transmission, power-assisted front disc brakes, front bucket seats, radial tires, tachometer, racing mirror. All standard equipment.

Oh, it doesn't have automatic

transmission, air conditioning, and a 400-horsepower engine.

But which would you rather have? Automatic transmission, air conditioning, and a 400-horse-power engine?

Or Michelle and Tammy and Alison?

The Honda Coupe. Under $1700.
It makes a lot of sense.

*SUGGESTED RETAIL P.O.E. DEALER PREPARATION, TRANSPORTATION, TAX AND LICENSE EXTRA. ©1972 AMERICAN HONDA MOTOR CO., INC.

Should your first car be a used car?

Most young people buying a car for the first time automatically think of a used car.

It's understandable. The way new cars cost these days.

But it's too bad. Because most first-timers don't know too much about it. And if ever a person needed to know the ins and outs of cars it's when he buys a used one. Or, he could end up buying somebody else's headache.

The answer is a new car that you can afford.

A Honda Sedan.

It costs less than a lot of used cars, gets up to 40 miles to the gallon, and is covered by a one year/12,000-mile warranty.

So, instead of a used car, maybe your first car should be an unused car. A new Honda.

The Honda Sedan. $0000. New.
It makes a lot of sense.

(Dealer Name)

9 reasons why you should buy a Honda Sedan.

1. The babies who cost so much to raise these days.
2. The lovely lady who costs so much to take out these days.
3. The butcher who charges so much for meat these days.
4. The banker who charges so much for big auto loans these days.
5. The girl who charges so much for popcorn at the movies these days.
6. The auto mechanic who charges so much for repairs these days.
7. The landlord who charges so much for rent these days.
8. The ski instructor who charges so much for skiing lessons these days.
9. The gas station attendant who charges so much for gas these days.

The Honda Sedan. $1595.
It makes a lot of sense.

PHONE 800 243-6000 TOLL-FREE FOR THE NAME OF YOUR NEAREST HONDA AUTOMOBILE DEALER. *SUGGESTED RETAIL, WEST COAST P.O.E. ($40 HIGHER OTHER PORTS) DEALER PREPARATION, TRANSPORTATION, TAX AND LICENSE EXTRA. PRICES SUBJECT TO CHANGE WITHOUT NOTICE. ©1972 AMERICAN HONDA MOTOR CO., INC.

"It was the first big account that, you know, both agencies had, that we had to be concerned about. Here was this big automotive account. We didn't know what the hell we were doing."

Standing Room Only

By next year this Los Angeles cemetery will be closed.

They've run out of room.

If we're even running out of space for the *dead,* the question is: how much space will there be in Southern California for the *living* by the end of this century?

So begins a half-hour KNBC television documentary called "Isn't It A Small World," narrated by Jack Cassidy.

A program dealing with Southern California's explosive population growth, and how it will affect the quality of life in the coming years.

You live here.

You ought to know what you're in for.

Isn't It A Small World
Tonight at 10:30

KNBC4!

*" 'He died for our sins.' We got a lot of
letters from Pasadena on that one."*

Southern California needs a wildlife refuge. For humans.

Remember Southern California? The place people used to go to get away from it all. Now, it all is here:

Traffic.

Factories.

Ghettos.

Ticky-tacky housing.

Unbreathable air.

Unpalatable water.

All the wonderful by-products of progress.

The rush West didn't give Southern California a chance to get organized. It grew up too fast. Bulldozed hill by bulldozed hill. One stucco-lined street after another.

Whatever happened to the San Fernando Valley?

Enough of history. What about today? After three decades of heaping civilization upon the land, perhaps we're wising up. Thinking things through. Planning for tomorrow. Before it's too late.

Unfortunately, compared to what we once had, there's precious little good land left. Livable land that's never been black-topped or super-developed or defoliated. The kind of land young men used to go West for. The kind of rich California ranchland Walter Vail bought in 1904 to establish a giant cattle empire.

But, this is 1971. Nostalgia is about as useful as hindsight. Isn't it a little late to close the barn door?

No.

Thirty-five miles due east of Laguna Beach, about halfway between Los Angeles and San Diego is the very land Walter Vail kept from the clutches of progress. One hundred and forty square miles of it. For sixty years, while Southern California boomed and suburbanized, no one but the Vails, their ranch hands and their friends set foot on the property. Until 1964, all those miles of gently rolling grasslands, oak-studded hills and mountain plateaus were the exclusive domain of Black Angus cattle and their brethren.

Rancho California

For the past six years, this 95,000-acre chunk of yesterday has been Rancho California; a very carefully planned refuge for people who want to take another crack at living. This time, with a very real sense of knowing what *not* to do. And a plan for tomorrow that says *no* to a lot of things that ruined a large part of Orange and Los Angeles Counties.

How big is 95,080 acres? You could get three and a half San Franciscos in it. You could spend all day at Rancho California and only see a quarter of it. You could stand on its northeastern border and be fifty miles from Palm Springs, or climb a hill on its western edge and see the Pacific Ocean only twelve miles away.

What's happened to the Vail Ranch since it became Rancho California? We know what you're thinking and you're wrong. It hasn't been mindlessly bulldozed, blacktopped or stuccoed. It hasn't been turned into a crazy-quilt of instant suburbs (go ahead, try to spot a neon sign). Oh, there's been development. Six years and over $100 million worth. But it doesn't stick out like a sore thumb. That's the whole idea.

Rancho California is a place where you can buy land. If you've got extra dollars and a good tax counselor, you know why that's a good idea. Rancho's also a place where you can buy refuge from environmental abuse. If you've got eyes, ears, and a nose, you know why *that's* a good idea.

Pick a day to get away from the way you live. Come to Rancho. You'll like what you see. You'll like what you hear. Its sounds are the sounds of a new life being born: tractors in grape vineyards and citrus farms. Families building new homes out of old dreams. Thoroughbred hoofs on the training center track. Men's boots on wooden walks in the Plaza. Spinning reels on Vail Lake. Children singing in a brand new school. Interstate trucks pulling up to low, modern industrial plants (no pollution-belchers). A constant ocean breeze rustling through oak trees and across vast open fields.

The funny smell is clean air.

If you've ever had the urge to go back in time without giving up a lot of modern conveniences, come down to Rancho California.

See what it was like to own a piece of the West when the West was worth owning.

Rancho California: A Project of Kaiser Aetna

Yesterday is over the hill.

Just over the Santa Ana mountains, about
halfway between Los Angeles and San Diego,
the Twentieth Century is just getting started.

The air smells like breakfast. The tallest
building is a barn. Time walks.

The sign on the highway says Rancho California.

You pull in at the Plaza, and for the next
ninety-five thousand acres, it's 1904. Yesterday.
Pure, unspoiled rolling hills. Oak-studded
mountain plateaus. A wildlife refuge for humans.

If you like what you see and feel and breathe,
you can take some home with you.
A piece of paper that says you own a piece of
Rancho California. For getting even
with your tax bracket, for planting new roots,
for today, for tomorrow.

Pick a day and get away from it all.

Come to Rancho California and
spend yesterday with us.

Photo taken within DeLuz Rancho area at Rancho California.

Rancho California
(714) 676-5295

Buy a little time.

We know a place where nobody's pushed
around by the second hand. A place
about 90 miles south of Los Angeles
where you can climb a hill, sink a
putt, jump a creek, chew a weed, land a
bass, buy a drink, eat a steak, shop for
clothes, watch a cow, play a set, ride a
pony, sail a boat, take a hike, ride a bike,
kick a clump, crack a bat, catch a frog,
take a dip, train a horse, go to school,
own a home, buy some time, live a life.

The kind of place a few people remember
but nobody expects to find anymore. Big
country, where there's room to breathe.

Rancho California; one-hundred and
forty square miles of active tranquility.

Take a little time. Come to Rancho
and poke around. See California the way
it was before it tried to beat the clock.

Photograph taken at Vail Lake in Rancho California.

Rancho California
(714) 676-5295

Welcome back.

Teddy Roosevelt just became President.
Kittyhawk was last year.
Babe Ruth is playing sandlot ball.
Ernest Hemingway is five.
The wild West is still a little wild.
The air still smells like air.

Welcome to 1904.

Welcome to Rancho California. A big slice of
yesterday smack in the middle of 1971.

Rancho California isn't Southern California's
latest amusement park. It's a place people go to
get away from what's become of civilization.

You can buy land there.
For living. For recreation.
For getting even with your tax bracket.

Rancho California is 140-square miles
of rolling grasslands, oak-studded hills and
mountain plateaus. Enough *yesterday*
for a thousand tomorrows. A wildlife refuge
for humans.

Pick a day and go back.

Come down to Rancho California.
See what it was like to own a piece of the West
when the West was worth owning.

Photo taken at original Vail family summer home in Rancho California.

Rancho California
(714) 676-5295

SUPER: Comparison Test #263
The Honda vs. the Chair.
ANNCR: This is the new economical Honda Civic.
This is a chair.
The Honda has front wheel drive, rack and pinion steering.
The chair doesn't.
The Honda has room for four adults.
The chair doesn't.
The Honda comes in both the sedan and hatchback models.
The chair doesn't.

SUPER: Comparison Test #262
The Honda vs. the Apple.
ANNCR: This is the economical new Honda Civic.
This is an Apple.
The Honda has front wheel drive, rack and pinion steering and gets up to 30 miles to a gallon of gas.
The apple doesn't.
The Honda has room for four adults.
The apple...two maybe, three worms tops.
The Honda comes in both sedan and hatchback models.
The apple...no chance.

"I recently did a spot for a client that's a lot like 'Honda and the Apple.' And when I presented it to the client, the guy said, 'Hey, that's Honda versus the Apple.' I said, 'You son of a bitch, that spot's 20 years old, how the hell do you remember it?' He said, 'I remember it.' And I said, 'Well, it's never beneath me to keep a good idea going year after year.'"

ANNCR VO: How to prepare your town for the new Honda Sedan. First drive down to Main Street. Since the Honda needs very little parking space, you can make more spaces for parking there... and the Honda gets up to 40 miles a gallon... so economy size gas pumps are another good idea...change your two-laned streets into three, 'cause Hondas don't need much space on the road...a couple of more basic adjustments and you'll have a perfect town for Honda. Honda, the new car that's already perfect for your town.

ANNCR VO: Introducing the Honda Coupe, the perfect companion to the Honda Sedan.
BOY: Hello.
GIRL: Oh. Hi.
BOY: Yeah, I have a Honda, too.
GIRL: Yeah?
BOY: How many miles do you get?
GIRL: Up to 40 to the gallon.
BOY: You really got a really unique body design.
GIRL: This particular model is an arrow dynamic.
BOY: Radial tires!!!!
GIRL: 4 radial tires and one in the trunk.
MAN: Would you mind if I took a look around the back?
GIRL: Okay...but be careful...
BOY: Hey, the back flips up.
GIRL: Yeah.
BOY: Look at the room in this...would you mind if I came inside and sat down next to you?

GIRL: Well yeah you can come in...ummm... would you leave the door open though?
BOY: Oh yeah...
GIRL: Thank you.
BOY: Can I put my leg in?
GIRL: Yeah okay?
BOY: Look at that dash, that tac...Ooooo... the four-speed synchromesh.
GIRL: No, it's a gear shift.
BOY: Ooooh...I don't suppose you're doing anything tonight.
GIRL: No...I mean, yes I'm not.
BOY: Would you like to go with me to a Lithuanian film festival?
GIRL: Your car or mine?

NATIONAL ANTHEM

ALL THE NEWS THAT FITS

A Review of New Products and Literature from National Semiconductor

Bi-FET™ Sample/Hold:

Fast Acquisition, Ultra-High Accuracy, Low Droop Rate

The headline tells the story. National's BI-FET™ technology, which combines FET and bipolar devices on the same chip, first yielded fantastic new op amps (*National Anthem* No. 1, January 1976). Now BI-FET technology yields new sample-and-hold circuits: dc gain accuracy of 0.002% (typ.) in a unity-gain follower configuration; acquisition times as low as 6 μs to 0.01% with a 1000-pF hold capacitor; droop rates as low as 5 mV/minute with a 1-μF hold capacitor!

We're talking about our LF198/298/398, which eliminate input/output feedthrough in the hold mode even for signals equal to the supply voltages—±5 V all the way to ±18 V. In addition, these parts feature a single-pin input offset adjustment that does not degrade input offset drift; an input impedance of 10^{10} ohms, which means that high source impedances will not degrade accuracy; a bandwidth sufficient to allow stable insertion of these circuits within the feedback loop of 1-MHz op amps; and a TTL/PMOS/CMOS-compatible logic input . . . all contained in a little, 8-pin, TO-5 metal can.

Universal Timer Circuit

The MM5865 is a new timing circuit ideal for use in stop watches, kitchen and oven timers, event timers/counters, rally and navigation timers, etc. Its single chip contains all the logic required to control the timer's two 4-digit counters, to compare them, to blank leading zeros, and to cascade another MM5865.

Input-pin functions start, stop, reset, and set the counters, and determine which of the timer's seven functions is to be performed, the display resolution (0.01, 0.1, 1.0 sec., or external clock), and the divide modulo.

The MM5865's seven functions are start/stop with total elapsed time, start/stop with accumulative event time, split, sequential with total elapsed time, rally with total elapsed time, program up-count, and program down-count. The circuit uses either a 32.8-kHz crystal or an external clock, and is packaged in a 40-pin molded DIP.

4K, 8K, and 16K Static ROMs

Fabricated using N-channel enhancement- and depletion-mode silicon gate technology, our three-member family of static ROMS is ideally suited to a wide range of uses such as table look-up, microprogramming, random logic synthesis, control logic, etc.

The MM5238 (512 x 8), MM5242 (1024 x 8), and MM5246 (2048 x 8) are TTL/DTL-compatible and operate from a single +5 V supply. They feature a 500-ns (max.) access time, full decoding, and true static operation.

In addition, the MM5238/5242/5246 have programmable Chip Select inputs that control their Tri-State® outputs, which means that bus interfacing and memory expansion are simple indeed.

SC/MP: a Simple to use Cost-effective/MicroProcessor

National's single-chip SC/MP marks the birth of a new generation of microprocessors. As the first, *low-cost* true microprocessor, SC/MP needs only one memory chip (any standard ROM, PROM, or RAM) to form a complete, fully programmable, general-purpose microprocessor system.

And this system, because of its low cost, is ideally suited to replace "sheet metal" logic in toys and games, traffic controls, home appliances, vending machines, home and building security and environment controls, on-board automotive computers, and so on.

SC/MP's features make it all happen: 8-bit data handling is combined with 16-bit addressing; an on-chip clock simplifies system design; a serial I/O port makes for easy interfacing; built-in flags and jump conditions simplify control tasks; an interrupt structure that gives fast response to asynchronous events; a delay instruction to simplify timer systems. And all of these are supported by a set of 46 control-oriented instructions.

Getting started with SC/MP is super simple. Aside from the CPU chip itself, we offer two kits. The basic kit includes all ICS, firmware, discretes, and mechanical hardware to let you explore SC/MP's capabilities. The SC/MP LCDS (Low-Cost Development System) goes further, and includes a keyboard, a display, more memory, etc.—it's a complete microcomputer, in fact, which lets you rapidly develop and debug programs, and experiment with interrupts and interface structures.

Three New 4K Static RAMs In Two Organizations, Two Lead Counts

We've got a family of ion-implanted N-channel, silicon gate, non-refresh RAMS that'll satisfy a great number of you 4K read/write users out there.

While all three family members share the same operating specs, the organizations, package pin-outs, and lead functions differ. The MM5255, for example, is organized 1024 x 4, has four common I/O ports, and is housed in an 18-pin DIP. The MM5256, also 1024 x 4, has four input pins, four output pins, and is in a 22-pin DIP. The MM5257, with its 4096 x 1 organization, has, of course, one input pin and one output pin, and is packaged in an 18-pin DIP.

All the parts are TTL compatible and operate from a single +5 V supply. These RAMS feature fast access (250 ns), a standby mode controlled by the Chip Enable (standby power is less than 200 mW typ.), low operating power (less than 400 mW typ.), and on-chip address and data registers.

You can sample the MM5255/5256/5257 next month (June), and have production quantities in the third calendar quarter of this year.

8-bit ADCs Combine Low Cost, High Performance

A new, National-proprietary ladder design is the key to the low, low price/performance ratio of our MM4357/MM5357. There simply is nothing comparable on the market at anything near the prices we've put on these monolithic ADCS—less than $8.00 each in 100-piece lots!

The MM4357, for example, is fully spec'd over the military temperature range—and there are many, far more costly ADCS around that cannot make such a claim. While the MM5357 is for commercial (0°–70°C) temperature range uses, both ADCS feature ±5 V or 0–10 V input ranges, no missing codes, high input impedance (100 MΩ, min.), ratiometric conversion, TTL compatibility, built-in output latches, and Tri-State® outputs.

Key specifications include 8-bit resolution, ±½-LSB linearity (a "B" version loosens this spec slightly), 40-μs (max.) conversion speed, and clocking rates from 5 kHz to 2 MHz. Supply voltages required are +5 V and −12 V. The MM4357/MM5357 are available in both cavity and molded 18-pin DIPS.

INTERFACE CIRCUITS IN HIGH-DISSIPATION MOLDED DIPS

National's new, high-dissipation DIPS use a copper lead frame, rather than the common Kovar lead frames. And this means increased power dissipation capabilities *with* improved reliability and increased part life.

If this sounds a bit too much like eating your cake and having it still, consider this: a circuit that in a Kovar lead frame is limited to a 625-mW dissipation in a 75°C ambient can, with a copper lead frame, dissipate 938 mW in the same ambient. Put another way, at a dissipation of 625 mW, a device in a Kovar lead frame will have a junction temperature of 150°C, while in a copper lead frame the junction temperature will drop to 125°C.

At last count, we've switched 45 interface parts to this wondrous package—dual peripheral drivers (including CMOS-compatible types), RAM interfaces, relay drivers, clock drivers, core memory drivers, etc. (See our Interface Data Book for specific thermal ratings.)

And by the way . . . If you think you can get similar high-dissipation parts from the competition, better forget it. Because there *isn't* any.

High Voltage, High Slew Rate Op Amps

Unique characteristics of our LM144/344 op amps include operation from ±4 V to ±36 V, a 30-V output swing capability, a slew rate of 30 V/μs (typ.) and an externally compensated power bandwidth of 120 kHz (both at $A_V \geq 10$), a low input-bias current of 8 nA (typ.), an input offset current of only 1 nA (typ.), and a gain of 100k (min.).

With specs such as these, the LM144/344 increase both accuracy and useful frequency range in many existing applications. The LM144, for example, is a direct replacement for the LM101A, and can replace others as well.

The LM144 operates between −55° and +125°C; the LM344, intended for less severe supply voltage and temperature environments, is spec'd from 0° to +70°C.

LARGEST-DISPLAY CLOCK MODULES NOW AVAILABLE

The outstanding feature of our new MA1010 electronic clock module is its stand-out display: a 0.84-inch, 4-digit, LED display with mitred corners, which shows hours and minutes; a blinking colon indicates seconds. There's nothing else as large, as readable, or as attractive on the market. We repeat: *nothing*. You've just got to see this one to believe it.

The module is complete on a single, 1.75 x 3.75-inch PC board, and all connections are at the bottom of the card. You add only a power transformer and switches to complete a pre-tested digital clock ideal for clock radios, desk and wall clocks, alarm clocks, TV/stereo clocks, instrument panel clocks, etc.

Timekeeping may be from 50 or 60 Hz, and you may choose a 12-hour or 24-hour format. Features include alarm ON, PM, and power failure indicators, an alarm output that drives an 8-Ω speaker, sleep and snooze timers, fast and slow set controls, and a display brightness-control output (you determine the method of control appropriate to your design). Direct (non-mux'd) LED drive eliminates RFI. Use of the module allows a low-cost, extremely compact clock design.

PROCESSOR IS CALCULATOR-ORIENTED

Looking for a versatile, low-cost, dedicated or custom-programmable calculator or control system? We've got it! Our MM5799 contains all system timing functions, all arithmetic and logic functions, all RAM functions (384 bits), and all control ROM functions (1536 microinstructions 8-bits wide, 10-μs/microcycle) that you'll need to implement a variety of small control and microprocessor systems.

A single MOS/LSI chip, the MM5799 can scan 56 keyboard switches, or you can enter BCD data words. Its eight outputs present information in either a BCD or a seven-segment-plus-decimal-point format, and four additional latched outputs give you encoded digit-timing information. Further, a serial-in port and a serial-out port let you expand the basic RAM store and interface to peripherals.

And speaking of peripherals and extra storage, our MM5788 printer interface, DS8664 Series oscillator and decoder/drivers, MM5785 RAM interface, and MM2102 and MM74C930 1-K static RAMS are a perfect match to an MM5799-based system.

SC/MP HANDBOOK TELLS ALL!

Amply illustrated, the 65-page *SC/MP Technical Description* matches SC/MP's applications-oriented design in that the text stresses applications and how-to-use information.

Opening with a discussion of SC/MP's general features and support components, the *SC/MP Technical Description* proceeds to a detailed description of the CPU chip, and from there to SC/MP's application cards. SC/MP's Development Systems are also described. Based on SC/MP's CPU, the Development Systems are powerful tools for the prototyping and use of SC/MP-based control systems.

To order a copy of the *SC/MP Technical Description*, send a check for $3.00 (California residents add 6% sales tax) payable to National Semiconductor. Direct your order to Marketing Services/520.

EET75

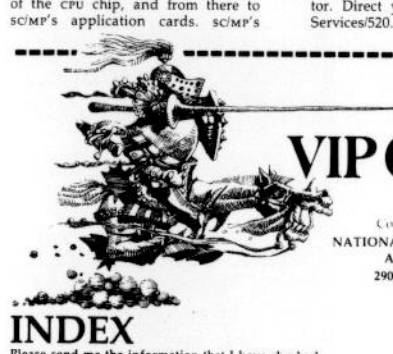

VIP CARD

Complete card and mail to
NATIONAL SEMICONDUCTOR
Attn: Marketing Services
2900 Semiconductor Drive,
Santa Clara, CA 95051

INDEX

Please send me the information that I have checked:

- ☐ **SC/MP,** Page A, Col. 3
- ☐ **SC/MP Kit,** Page A, Col. 4
- ☐ **SC/MP LCDS,** Page A, Col. 4
- ☐ **MM4357/5357 ADCs,** Page A, Col. 4
- ☐ **MM5255/56/57 RAMs,** Page A, Col. 2
- ☐ **MM5238/42/46 ROMs,** Page A, Col. 2
- ☐ **Hi-Diss. Interface Ccts,** Page A, Col. 2
- ☐ **LF198 Sample-and-Hold,** Page A, Col. 1
- ☐ **LM144/344 Op Amps,** Page A, Col. 4
- ☐ **MM5865 Timer,** Page A, Col. 1
- ☐ **MM5799 Processor,** Page B, Col. 2
- ☐ **NPD5564/8301 JFETs,** Page B, Col. 3
- ☐ **Durawatt 92-Plus Parts,** Page B, Col. 3
- ☐ **MA1010 Clock Module,** Page B, Col. 1

Please send me the literature that I have checked:

- ☐ **AN-135** IMP-16L DMA—What It Is and How To Use It
- ☐ **AN-154** 1.3-V IC Flasher, Oscillator, Trigger or Alarm
- ☐ **AN-155** Digital Voltmeters and the MM5330
- ☐ **AN-156** Specifying A/D and D/A Converters
- ☐ **μSpec 10** IMP-16P/004A RAM Memory Card
- ☐ **μSpec 11** IMP-16P/008P ROM/PROM Memory Card

Your End Product or Application: ____________

Have Salesman Call ☐ YES ☐ NO

Please print clearly; this information will be used for our mailing list.

NAME ____________ TITLE ____________

COMPANY ____________

ADDRESS ____________

CITY ____________ STATE ____________ ZIP ____________

APPLICATIONS CORNER

How to symmetrically limit the output of an op amp

A common way to symmetrically limit the output of an op amp is to use back-to-back Zeners across the feedback resistor. One of our readers, realizing that this is not the best way to do things, has asked us for a better way, and also wants to know what to expect from an op amp when symmetrical limiting is attempted by tying back-to-back Zeners from the output to ground, making use of the amp's current-limiting characteristics. Since we suspect that a great many of you are perplexed by the same problem, here are our answers.

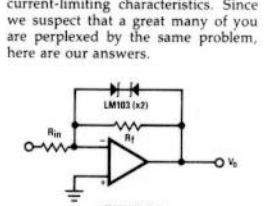

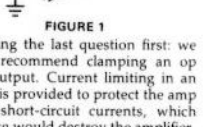

FIGURE 1

Answering the last question first: we do not recommend clamping an op amp's output. Current limiting in an op amp is provided to protect the amp against short-circuit currents, which otherwise would destroy the amplifier. But short-circuit currents are not well defined, nor is the recovery time of the amplifier from such conditions. Further, positive and negative current-limiting may not be symmetrical. Thus, using the current-limiting characteristics to limit an output signal really is an attempt to make ill-defined internal parameters yield a well-defined external result. Not a good idea.

In the current-limited mode the op amp's feedback loop opens, which forces the internal biases away from their nominal values. Some amps may take several milliseconds to recover, in addition to the recovery time of the external feedback component itself. If the amp is connected as an integrator, for example, the recovery time may be several minutes.

If you're still not dissuaded from clamping the amp's output, consider the radical increase in power dissipation in such a situation. This increases chip temperature, which degrades the op amp's dc parameters.

Now let's get back to back-to-back limiting. Figure 1 shows a typical circuit. It suffers from a lowered high-frequency corner (thanks to the Zener's capacitance), Zener leakage across R_f at low and medium voltages, asymmetrical limiting, and possibly even soft limiting if the Zeners have poor knees. At low voltages, use of our LM103 active Zener improves things, but only to a certain extent.

Figure 2, however, improves limiting, and in fact performs quite well. Here, the diodes do not add much capacitance across the feedback resistor. And all diode leakages are absorbed by the 1-kΩ resistor. *D7* will be, typically, a 9.1-V Zener for an 11.8-V limit. At V_0 = 10 V, leakage will be less than a nanoamp; but at ±11.8 V the limiting circuitry will conduct more than 2 mA. As the same Zener conducts for both polarities of the input, output symmetry is very good.

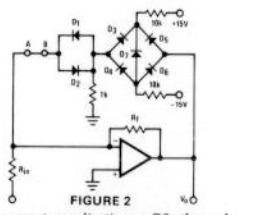

FIGURE 2

For most applications, *D3* through *D6* can be low-capacitance, fast-recovery 1N914s. But operation at elevated temperatures may require the use of low-leakage types, such as 1N457s or FD300s. (*D7* isn't critical; it never turns off, so its capacitance and knee characteristics are unimportant.)

For super-critical low-leakage applications, add an extra stage of resistor-diode network between points *A* and *B*. For non-critical work, you can delete *D1* and *D2*.

And now...A full line of Durawatt 92-Plus™ Power Transistors

Durawatt 92-Plus™ . . . National's unique power transistor package concept that actually improves performance *and* reliability while letting you retain a cost-effective design. As described in *National Anthem* No. 1, January 1976, Durawatt 92-Plus packaging eliminates the no-man's land of power transistor usage, that limbo between 800 mW and 2 W dissipation.

Our new, standard line of 92-Plus transistors operates at a solid 1.2 W, and features a 6-W maximum dissipation rating! The series comprises six generic families of general purpose complementary power types and Darlingtons (rated at 2 A/45-100 V), and high-voltage line drivers (100-500 mA/250-300 V)—21 92PXXX types, and only National has them.

Not yet using NSC's dual JFETs? Get your head examined!

Tactless? Perhaps. But if the headline caught your attention you're already ahead of the game. After all, National *invented* the monolithic dual JFET. And we still supply the best quality parts in the marketplace, and supply them to the tightest specs. Period.

Take our new NPD5564 Series, for example. Low noise (spot NF = 1 db max. at 10 Hz, R_g = 1 MΩ) . . . high speed, wide bandwidth (C_{iss} = 12 pF max.) . . . low offset and offset drift (5–20 mV max., and 10–50 μV/°C max., depending on the type) . . . an easily guarded gate pin for low leakage operation . . . and an 8-lead molded MiniDIP package that's ideal for auto-insertion (also a 6-pin, TO-71 can). Top these features with low cost, and you're guaranteed the lowest price/performance ratio JFETS that money can buy.

Samples of the NPD5564 Series—or of any of our JFETS—are available through your local National rep, or by a letterhead request to Mike Turner, JFET marketing manager here in Santa Clara. And while you're at it, check out our new NPD8301 Series—three MiniDIP duals that replace 39 different metal can and plastic duals!

"My partner and I would have meetings with Jay at 8:30 in the morning—we'd have our group therapy so we could work together for the day. We would talk for a half hour, and by 5 o'clock we would be yelling at each other again."

"We always tried to invest in people. And then work their asses off."

Before, you always felt like there were still two agencies—Chiat's and Day's. You had probably come from one or the other, or worked mostly with the people who had come from one or the other. But now, things are different.

Now, there is Honda.

Chiat/Day finally feels like one agency. It has to. There is no time to feel any other way.

Some examples:

It is the first big Honda presentation. A ton of work. The clients are using a dictionary to translate headlines, one word at a time. Upon the conclusion of the presentation, they suggest that the copywriter and art director go away and wash their minds. The art director goes home, and the next morning informs his partner that last night he washed his mind, and now he can't do a thing with it.

It is the first rough cut of a television commercial that Chiat/Day has done for Honda, and the agency is so excited that they bring the rough cut to one of Honda's top executives to see it. He watches the commercial, and then spits at the screen.

The creative people are not disheartened. They have been exposed to other kinds of rejection, but never spitting. Spitting, the creative director decides, is an interesting visual.

KNBC, a local television station, is introducing a new anchorman to Los Angeles by the name of Tom Snyder. The creative team who had been asked to wash their minds comes up with a big print campaign around lines like "Tom Who?" and "Tom Snyder never heard of you, either." They hear from KNBC that Tom Snyder hates it, thinks they're the worst ads he's ever seen.

Two months later, he is seen driving around town with a "Tom Who?" license plate.

In the midst of a vicious presidential cam-

paign, Jay and Guy decide to do a house ad entitled "Chiat/Day versus Politics," pledging never to do political advertising.

One creative team spends its weekends at the Ontario Motor Speedway. A copywriter is sent to live at Rancho California for a couple of weeks so he can really understand it.

And an art director is delighted when he is told that he will be traveling to New Jersey for a week to photograph large quantities of potatoes frying in a machine called the Hunt-Wesson Frymax.

"Great," he thinks. "At last, a vacation."

THE CALIFORNIA 500
SUNDAY SEPT. 3 1972
ONTARIO

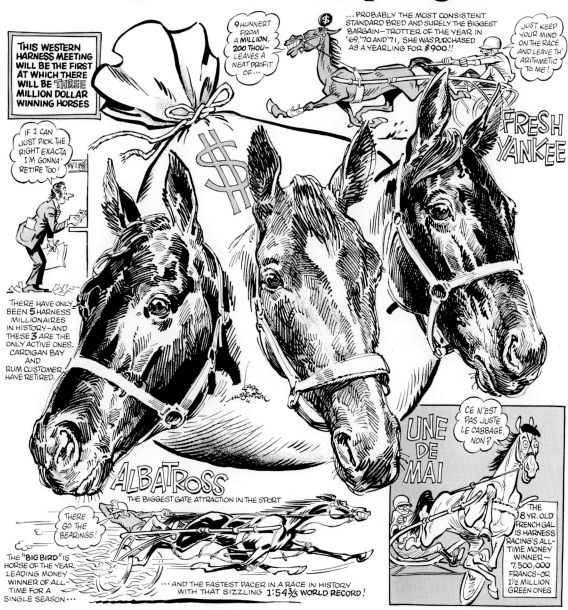

Chiat/Day vs. Politics

Since things are now quiet in political advertising, it's a good time to slip in a public announcement of what has been a private policy: Chiat/Day won't work on political advertising accounts.

It's been our observation that on the polar extremes, political advertising can either tell the truth and lose or lie and win. And there's not much satisfaction to be gleaned anywhere in between.

In line with our viewpoint, we've sent a letter to the Federal Trade Commission suggesting that they keep careful record of all advertised political campaign promises for comparison against performance in office.

It seems to us that if the FTC is really intent on punishing false and misleading advertisers, they ought to go after the worst offenders first.

For our money, a liar in elective office is one hell of a lot more dangerous to the public than Wonder Bread's nutritional claims.

Welcome back.

Yesterday is over the hill.

You know what they say about real estate accounts...
We used to say the same things.
Then along came Rancho California.
Super guys. Super land. And an honest desire to do it right:
Two pages, four colors, no lies.

CHIAT/DAY ADVERTISING

"We were doing some pretty neat work that nobody saw, running in places like Aviation Week and the American Gas Journal. And the only way we could get visibility was to run our own ads with our work in them. And largely, I think that was good advertising because people started to say, 'Well, I've never heard of the company, but at least they do good work.' And I think it was a way of saying to the audience, 'We have a lot of pride in what we do.' Rather than the typical agency baloney."

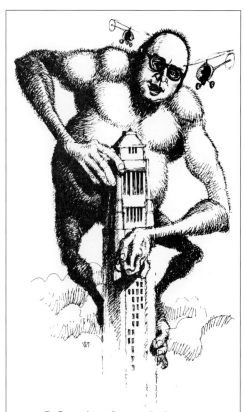

Is Los Angeles ready for Jerry Della Femina?

Jerry's in town, open for business, and he's got a Savings & Loan account. Right there you know he's crazy.

Easterners don't make it from scratch in L.A. They've got to buy their way in. Even then they don't make it. Well, hardly ever.

Then there's the S&L. As an advertising category, they've got to be the local joke. It's not only hard to do a good S&L ad. It's illegal.

Consensus is that Jerry will blow it. But what do they know?

Before you write Della Femina off, better take another look at his work. And his people. And his track record.

What's in it for L.A.?

Another good agency doing good advertising. Another voice saying, "This is right and that's not."

Another marketing success or two based on bright, responsive advertising.

It certainly can't hurt. In fact, it just might help any of us who are really serious about the selling power of good advertising.

L.A. may not be ready for Jerry. But neither was New York five years ago.

CHIAT/DAY INC. ADV.

Dear Sirs,

It was with great enthusiasm that our family looked forward to seeing one of our favorite movies on T.V... "Ben Hur."... popcorn and all. In spite of the commercials, We all enjoyed it. Just in case anyone is interested, the following are responsible for an evening's entertainment:

1. VO-5 Hairdressing
2. Lifesavers
3. Chun King
4. Magnavox
5. Great American Soup
6. Vicks
7. Betty Crocker
8. Schlitz Beer
9. Pacific Telephone
10. Mrs. Paul's Fish Sticks
11. Contac
12. Air Wick
13. Pepto-Bismol
14. Cheer
15. Audi
16. Desinex
17. Fleischmann's Margarine
18. Hertz Cars
19. Sta-puf
20. Chun King
21. Wishbone Dressing
22. Lipton Soup
23. Pan Am
24. Ovaltine
25. Dodge
26. Safeguard
27. Flair
28. Techmatic Razor
29. Anacin
30. Dristan
31. F.D.S.
32. Dodge
33. Cantrece
34. Dreyfus Fund
35. Great American Soup
36. Wonder Bread
37. Dodge
38. Green Giant
39. Sinarest
40. Chevy Van
41. Oppenheimer Fund
42. Right Time
43. Air Wick
44. Motorola
45. Mrs. Paul's Onion Rings
46. Cheerios
47. Gold Medal Flour
48. Lipton Tea
49. Wishbone Dressing
50. U.C.B.
51. Oldsmobile
52. Nyquil
53. Miller
54. Midas Mufflers
55. Playtex Bra
56. Playtex Nipple Nurser
57. Oldsmobile
58. Miller Beer
59. Hills Brothers Coffee
60. American Airlines

A Star Is Born.

Variety put it this way: "Another Jingle Jangled Into Pop Platter." But, there's a simpler explanation.

Last January, Chiat/Day produced a radio spot for Channel 4 TV promoting Tom Brokaw and the KNBC Newservice. It featured an original song—"The World Had Quite a Day Today"—by singer/composer James Stein. After hearing the commercial, Bell Records signed Stein to a recording contract and released the song as a single. It's already on the air.

If you'd like to hear the KNBC spot and a few other fantastic radio offerings from Chiat/Day, just pick up your phone and dial…

384-9193

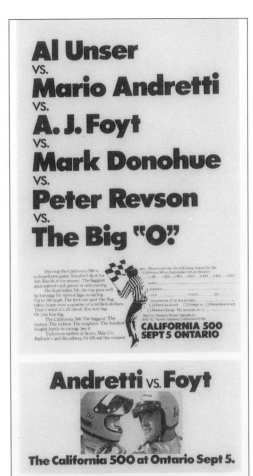

What's the appeal of auto racing? Some say it's the thrill. Others say it's the risk. We say it's the attendance. And on September 5, we're betting over 160,000 fans will show up for the California 500. Check your daily paper on September 6. Find out how many really did.

CHIAT/DAY, INC.

"I remember one thing we worked on a lot was the ads that Chiat/Day ran in AdWeek every week on the front page column. And you moved that assignment around 'cause it was the toughest assignment in the shop, 'cause Jay would have to approve it and it had to be the right tone and all that stuff. So everybody got a shot at it. And frankly we had time to work on that thing. 'Cause there wasn't that much business."

HHT

"God, these are a bunch of nuts."

She has come for a job in the art department, where the ads are physically, painstakingly laid out. She will be interviewed by a man who talked to her over the phone about perfection, about Chiat/Day's seriousness and dedication to quality.

As she looks around the office, she cannot believe what she sees.

When she is led to the interview room, she hears screaming. It is her introduction to Jay Chiat and Guy Day, who are using the room next door to have a discussion.

As her interview ensues, a copywriter bursts into the room and says "Hire her, hire her!" and runs out. He is a total stranger.

"What kind of people are these?" she thinks to herself.

She doesn't know the half of it. She has not yet seen:

The man who is interviewing her, when he is raving mad and swearing that he will hunt down and kill anyone who leaves art materials sitting out in the production department.

The copywriter who spends his free time making announcements over the P.A. system like "Wayne Newton, white courtesy telephone." Although he himself looks more like a biker, he often dresses up his five-year-old child in a suit, gives him a huge briefcase, takes him to work, and refers to him as Mr. Durkee when introducing him to strangers.

The art director who brings a baby goat to work, which leaves an odor that will stay in the halls

of Chiat/Day long after the art director has left.

The creative team that brings stray dogs and cats to work and lets them roam the halls, hoping someone will adopt them.

The copywriter who complains he is entitled to two art directors. The more they refuse to hire him a second partner, the testier he gets. He argues that he can get more done with two art directors. He says that if he doesn't get a second art director, he'll find one himself. For months, when art directors see him coming, they hide.

The art director whose disdain for conversation is so widely known that he comes to be referred to as "The Smiling Wall."

The copywriter who tries to convince Jay to invest in the first All-Robot musical.

The one particularly hirsute young art director, who in order to get hired, spends months bombarding the agency with a "Hire the Hairy" campaign, the highlight of which is a jack-in-the-box that looks just like him. Eventually, he gets the job, which over the years will be the cause of considerable hair loss.

Or the copywriter who spends his lunch hours dressing up as a construction worker and going to condemned building sites in order to "remove" materials that he can use to build himself a new home.

In time, she will see them all. Against her better judgement, she accepts the job.

In years to come, she will take the place of the man who interviewed her. And eventually, she too will hunt down and kill anyone who makes a mess in her department.

HAS THE WHOLE IDEA OF MOTELS GOTTEN OUT OF HAND?

Whatever happened to the original idea behind motels?

Motels were invented as an alternative to the bother and expense of a hotel. Someplace simple where you could drive right up to your door and have a nice functional little room for the night without taking out a bank loan to do it.

But today many motels are just a little simpler and slightly plainer than Buckingham Palace.

What happened?

Runaway luxury.

That's what happened.

Somebody started building a motel that was a little fancier than the next guy's. And the next guy got fancier right back to meet the competition.

Just about the time one motel got to thinking they offered the most services, somebody else figured they had to top them.

Don't be too surprised some day soon if room service arrives with a maitre d' supervising things.

The television explosion.

Or take the case of television.

First, no motels had it. Then a few got it, and it helped their business.

But pretty soon most motels had it, so it didn't particularly help anybody's business. Then to get something that *would* help business, some motels put in *color* TV sets.

The whole domino theory again. Where will it all end? Well, here's a start.

We're what motels started out to be.

At Motel 6 our idea of a motel room is more like the original idea.

A nice functional, inexpensive little place to put up for the night.

And to get it inexpensive we naturally had to sacrifice some of the luxuries and frills that twenty dollar motels have.

Like room service and bellhops and chandeliers and posh wallpaper and scrollwork mirrors and valets and manicurists.

And gymnasiums and saunas and ballrooms and doors on closets and a lot of paintings and sculpture that are almost always ugly anyway.

With all that stuff out of the way we could set some rather attractive rates...

All rooms $6.60 to $9.90.

We have only two kinds of rooms.

Rooms with one double bed, and rooms with two double beds.

One bed, one person, is $6.60 a night. One bed, two persons, $7.70 a night.

Two beds, two persons, $8.80 a night. And two beds, three or four persons, $9.90.

That's the price. Every day of the year. At every one of our 120 motels.

Controlled luxury.

At Motel 6, we build simple motels. But we didn't get carried away with the whole thing.

We have swimming pools and first-class mattresses and high quality thick shag carpeting and black-and-white coin-operated TV.

And, except for a few motels in cool climates that don't need it, air conditioning.

What you get at Motel 6 is what you need.

A decent place for spending the night.

Without spending the bankroll.

Sirs: Please rush me a copy of your latest Motel 6 Directory and a packet of Advance Reservation Forms so I can mail ahead for my accommodations.

Name _____

Address _____

City _____ State _____ Zip _____

Telephone (use Area Code) _____

Mail to: MOTEL 6, P.O. Box 3550, 51 Hitchcock Way, Santa Barbara, California 93105.

MOTEL 6

A City Investing company

Our rooms aren't fancy. Our prices aren't fancy.

"*The agency was chaos then, and chaos was good. This was before people like Tom Peters wrote books about casual environment and creative management and management by walking around and...of course, we didn't know it was gonna become in vogue to be crazy.*"

MOTEL 6 GIVES YOU FEWER UGLY PAINTINGS THAN OTHER MOTEL ROOMS.

What's uglier than the paintings on the walls of hotel and motel rooms?

Almost nothing.

Remember?

Well, Motel 6 has done something about this problem.

No, not by putting up a lot of paintings that aren't ugly. Our paintings are probably as ugly as anybody else's. But we put up fewer of them.

There is only one painting on the wall of every Motel 6 room.

Actually, we didn't do this to save you ugliness. We did it to save you money.

Pictures cost money. Money that has to come from charging a little more for the motel room.

That's one of the reasons Motel 6 rooms cost so little.

What we don't give you.

There are many such things we don't give you in our rooms.

No water glasses (plastic cups instead), no bathtub (just a shower), no chandeliers and fancy fixtures.

Add it all up, and it saves you quite a bit.

All rooms $6.60 to $9.90.

We have only two kinds of rooms. Rooms with one double bed, and rooms with two double beds.

One bed, one person, is $6.60 a night. One bed, two persons, $7.70 a night. Two beds, two persons, $8.80. And two beds, three or four persons, $9.90.

That's the price. Every day of the year. At every one of our 120 motels. (If you'd like a free booklet showing where all those Motel 6's are, write: Motel 6, P. O. Box 3550, Santa Barbara, Calif. 93105.)

What we do give you.

So now you know what you don't get from us. What do you get?

A clean room (we're very, very fussy about that). A good bed. A swimming pool. A black-and-white coin-operated TV. Thick carpeting. And except for a few motels in cool climates that don't need it, air conditioning.

But no frills.

We figure that pictures of horses and sunsets on the wall are nice, but pictures of Abraham Lincoln and Alexander Hamilton in your wallet are even nicer.

Our rooms aren't fancy. Our prices aren't fancy.

HOW TO SPEND THE NIGHT IN SEATTLE/TACOMA FOR $6.60.

That's all it takes at a new motel in town called Motel 6. The newest in our national chain of 100 motels.

Our rate for one person is $6.60 a night. Which is something to keep in mind if your Aunt Emma comes to town for a visit.

(If Aunt Emma has a husband she's bringing along, it's $7.70 a night for a room with one double bed, or $8.80 a night with two double beds. If they bring the kids, the rate for up to four people is $9.90 a night.)

We give you a lot for so little.

A swimming pool. Air conditioning. Nice thick carpeting. A comfortable bed with a first-class mattress. A telephone in the room. And everything spotlessly clean. Aunt Emma will love it.

A City Investing company

**18900 47th Avenue
206-246-5520**

HOW TO TAKE A BATH AT MOTEL 6.

For some people there are slight inconveniences involved in staying at our motels.

People who won't take anything but a sit-down bath have something of a problem. Because our rooms don't have bathtubs in them, just showers.

Afterwards, if you want to bask under a sunlamp, you'll have to bring your own. We don't have them.

And you'll have to go out and get your own food, too. We don't have room service.

Why we're so stingy.

Things like bathtubs and sunlamps and room service cost a lot of money.

And the result is that the average motel room in the eleven major chains in this country today also costs a lot of money. $16.65.

But, you see, we don't have a lot of fancy frills. So our motel rooms aren't $16.65.

All rooms $6.60 to $9.90.

We have only two kinds of rooms. Rooms with one double bed and rooms with two double beds.

our 120 motels. (If you'd like a free booklet showing where all those Motel 6's are, write: Motel 6, P. O. Box 3550, Santa Barbara, California 93105.)

Things we're not stingy about.

Of course, one has to draw the line somewhere on this saving money thing.

So at every Motel 6 you'll find a swimming pool, a first-class mattress, high quality thick shag carpeting, and (except for a few motels in cool climates that don't need it) air conditioning.

Most of all, you'll find a spotlessly clean room.

But we don't splurge on very many things.

Because if we did, we wouldn't have prices like we do.

Think of it this way.

We don't give you a bathtub.

But we don't soak you $20 a night for a room, either.

One bed, one person, we charge $6.60 a night. One bed, two persons, $7.70 a night. Two beds, two persons, $8.80. And two beds, three or four persons, $9.90.

That's the price. Every day of the year. At every one of

A City Investing company

Our rooms aren't fancy. Our prices aren't fancy.

IN THE DARK OUR MOTEL ROOMS LOOK AS GOOD AS ANYBODY'S.

Turn off the lights and close your eyes and we defy you to tell our under-$10 rooms apart from those fancy $20-a-night rooms.

And isn't that the way you spend most of your time in a motel room, sleeping?

We figure the average person spends a mere two waking hours in a motel room.

That's a pretty expensive two hours.

A $20 motel room costs $10 more than a $10 room. That's five dollars an hour extra for the two hours in the room that you're awake. Five dollars an hour for the privilege of looking at a spiffy room.

When the lights go on again.

Our motel rooms may be as nice as anybody's in the dark, but turn on the lights and you'll see that they're, well, sort of plain looking, and lacking certain luxury features.

We do have a swimming pool and air conditioning, but no bathtub (just a shower). No color TV (just a black-and-white coin-operated set). No chandeliers or statues or lush wallpaper.

No frills.

That saves a lot of money. And we pass the savings on to you.

Cleanliness is next to you-know-what.

One thing we don't try to save money on is keeping our rooms clean.

Our rooms are inspected by a head housekeeper to be sure they're spic and span. Also by an executive housekeeper and our motel managers.

If a dusty table slips through a system like that, it's practically a miracle.

All rooms $6.60 to $9.90.

We have only two kinds of rooms. Rooms with one double

bed, and rooms with two double beds.

One bed, one person, is $6.60 a night. One bed, two persons, $7.70 a night. Two beds, two persons, $8.80. And two beds, three or four persons, $9.90.

That's the price. Every day of the year. At every one of our 120 motels.

If you'd like a booklet showing where all those Motel 6's are, write: Motel 6, P.O. Box 3550, Santa Barbara, Calif. 93105.

A City Investing company

Our rooms aren't fancy. Our prices aren't fancy.

"I've sweated, fought bedbugs, slept on the floor, eaten out of a can, and pushed a canoe halfway up a river in Borneo, so your clients won't have to."
Ron Harris, President, Travelworld.

At Travelworld the guy who evaluates new places for our tours is the guy who runs the place.

And he doesn't do it behind a big desk. He does it on the spot in the four corners of the world.

Our President, Ron Harris, travels almost a quarter of a million miles a year checking out possible new tour attractions. Four months out of every year, this is what he does.

So when we send your clients to a new place, we know what they're getting into.

An awful spot in Borneo.

For example, we heard about a terrific, unspoiled native Long House in a remote part of the interior of North Borneo that sounded promising.

Off Ron Harris went.

And here's what he found.

A shower out in front...and the natives were selling postcards!

And the luxurious accommodations turned out to be 30 mattresses on the floor of a 60-foot-long room.

Mr. Harris and friends.

The roses among the thorns.

Of course, not all of the places and excursions Ron Harris checks out turn out badly.

This year he found a new lodge in Africa that was, in his words, "the most luxurious game lodge in Africa." We'll be going there in '75.

And a helicopter flight over the Himalayan mountains that he calls "the most fantastic excursion I've ever been on." We're going there in '74.

The end result.

The end result of all this is some sensational tour packages.

To places where your clients aren't apt to find disasters of one kind or another.

To places and things that are unique in the tour business, such as our Himalayan flight.

We tour the South Pacific. The Orient. Africa. South America. Around the World. And the Middle East.

Our full-color catalogs have all the details. Departures, itineraries, pictures, the works. Write for your free supply (enough to give out to your interested clients).

And remember. Even though we're a big international company backed by General Mills, we haven't lost the personal touch that's so important in the travel business. Everyplace we go has been checked out by our President.

In his words: "I won't send anybody anyplace I haven't been myself."

Every tour has scenic wonders. Only Travelworld has Sid Maddocks.

Sid Maddocks is one of our Tour Escorts.

He is living proof of our belief that Tour Escorts can make or break any tour, and that we've got the best Tour Escorts in the business.

Let us tell you just a few highlights off the top of Sid's head about some of his recent experiences escorting our tours.

On Yanuca Island in the Fiji Islands a hurricane hit, washing out bridges and isolating our tour group.

A disaster? A ruined trip? Not with Sid around.

He rounded up some candles, food and liquor, and organized a Hurricane Party. And everybody had a ball.

Or another time, a lady on one of Sid's tours had a handbag full of Travelers Checks stolen. Incredibly, Sid tracked down the thief and apprehended him himself. And the lady got all her Travelers Checks back.

Another time Sid drove one of the safari vehicles in Africa when the driver didn't show up.

Another time on a hot night in Timbuctoo, Africa he gave up his room (which had a ceiling fan) to

two of his tour members so they could get some sleep.

And another time a tour member had an earache in Bangkok. Guess who knew the name of an ear specialist in Bangkok who speaks English?

All of those mishaps were things that could have made for some mighty unhappy clients. Unhappy with us...and therefore unhappy with you. But escorts like Sid Maddocks help see that this doesn't happen.

But a good Tour Escort can also help people have a better trip even when something *doesn't* go wrong.

Sid can tell your clients where to find a good German beer garden in Tokyo. Or fettuccini and hamburgers in Bali.

He can get Sumo wrestling tickets for them in Tokyo.

Or arrange for a fishing junket in New Zealand if somebody has a big thing for fishing.

He can tell your clients how to avoid having a Masai tribesman in East Africa throw a spear at them as they take pictures. (Pay him first).

Or where to find just about the best lobster in the world in Cape Town, South Africa. (A little rundown, out-of-the-way place called the Harbor Cafe.)

It's no surprise that we get clients coming back for a second tour with us who ask if they can go with Sid Maddocks again. Sid brings *us* repeat business. And you, too.

Sid Maddocks is not unique.

But good as Sid is, he's just one of dozens of top Tour Escorts we have.

We could tell you about Elfreda Reynolds, who—because one of her tour members had a thing for apple pie—got the chef at the Hilton in Hong Kong to bake one for him.

Or Dave Edwards who actually talked a hijacker out of hijacking the plane we were scheduled to take.

Or...well, you get the idea.

And it's something to keep in mind next time you book a tour to any of our destinations.

Where in the world do we go?

We offer 45 different all-expense deluxe tours, from 15 to 66 days.

We tour the South Pacific. The Orient. Africa. South America. Around the World. And the Middle East.

Our full-color catalogs have all the details. Departures, itineraries, maps, pictures, the works. Write for your free supply (enough to give out to your interested clients).

Why sell us?

Well, we could talk about our higher commissions. 12½% (from the first booking) to 15%.

Or the fact that we have more offices around the world to serve you and your clients (13).

Or the financial stability of our being a part of the General Mills family of companies.

Or the fact that we've been in business for 29 years and have offered more tours to more places exclusively through travel agents than any other company.

Or our reputation in the business, which is second to none.

But the best reason we can think of for your selling Travelworld tours in 1974 is Sid Maddocks.

Sportscoach vs. 32¢ a gal.

When we designed the Sportscoach, gasoline cost about 32¢ a gallon. So nobody was particularly worried about saving gas.

But our engineers kept talking about the efficiency of the Sportscoach. And when an engineer says efficiency, he means savings.

For example:

Instead of a flat, stub nose, ours is shaped more like a jet plane. It cuts through the wind, rather than hitting it flat on. We can't tell you exactly how much that increases fuel economy, but our drivers report getting as much as 30% better mileage than drivers of other makes.

Because most of the materials we use were born in the aerospace industry, our rig is strong without being heavy. More efficiency. Check our GVW (Gross Vehicle Weight) against anybody's.

We put the engine up front and the drive wheels in the rear for the most efficient use of power. Or, to put it another way, the most efficient use of gas.

Finally, every Sportscoach comes equipped with cruise control. Before the gasoline shortage, most people thought cruise control was just a luxury device that lets your foot take a rest on long trips. Our engineers knew better.

Maintaining a constant speed and accelerating at a steady ratio on hills is great for mileage. Efficiency again.

So if you find that you're buying less gas than the drivers of conventional motor homes, you can thank the Sportscoach engineers who thought about the problem. Before it was a problem.

Sportscoach
9601 Canoga Ave., Chatsworth, Calif. 91311.

WHY WE PUSH INSTEAD OF PULL.

Zion National Park, Utah

If the world were flat, it wouldn't much matter whether a motor home had rear wheel drive or front wheel drive. Either way, you'd probably reach your destination.

But if you've ever traveled in the Rockies, the Blue Ridge Mountains, the Berkshires, San Francisco or even the rolling hills near your home, you can appreciate why we designed the Sportscoach the way we did.

You have a choice.

There are two basic ways to propel a motor home.

Front wheel drive puts the power to two front wheels.

Rear wheel drive puts the power to four rear wheels.

When it comes to chassis design, nobody knows more than Detroit's big three, Chevrolet, Ford and Dodge.

And they build a motor home chassis only one way: With rear wheel drive.

These are the experts who build the chassis for Sportscoach.

Although we give you a lot of fresh thinking in our rig, we never use a fundamental engineering principle that hasn't proved itself in actual motor home usage.

So much for policy. Now we'd like to tell you why our engineers like rear wheel drive.

A motor home is not a car.

Maybe you're wondering what's wrong with front wheel drive. Some automobile manufacturers have been very successful with it on their cars. There is a reason.

The engine of a car is usually its heaviest part, so the engine provides excellent traction up front.

Motor homes are different. They weigh more, to begin with. And the bulk of this weight happens to be in the rear.

In fact, more than 60% of the weight on most large rigs is supported by the rear wheels.

This is fine if you have rear wheel drive. Not so good if you have front wheel drive.

How you run into trouble.

With front wheel drive you're operating at a disadvantage, even on level ground. About 40% of the weight is on top of your drive wheels. And weight is needed for traction.

When you go up an incline, the problem gets worse. Your weight shifts toward the rear of the coach, away from the front drive wheels. Here's an example. On a 15% grade, 10% of the weight on your front wheels shifts to the rear wheels.

This means a rig with front wheel drive begins to lose some of its ability to grip the road as soon as it starts up a hill.

Sportscoach doesn't have that problem on an incline. The steeper the grade, the greater the weight on our four rear driving wheels. And the better our traction becomes.

A rainy day comparison.

Just to show you what we mean, we have charted Sportscoach performance on a wet surface* and compared it with the performance of similar size motor homes with front wheel drive.

The Sportscoach can climb a 30% grade before there is any problem. The two tires on a rig with

front wheel drive will begin to slip at about 15%.

Of course, you'll never have to worry about a 15% incline on any major thoroughfares. But you'll

sometimes find them on secondary roads, in the mountains, or in a few cities like San Francisco or even Los Angeles.

If you happen to be on an unpaved road, you can run into the same sort of situation. Sportscoach can climb a grade of about 15% on loose dirt.* The other rigs can't do much better than 10%.

Maybe this doesn't matter to you. It won't matter if you plan to stay on the flat world of highways, freeways and blacktop campgrounds. But if you're interested in traveling out beyond the mainstream of traffic, out where camping is beautiful, we think rear wheel drive makes sense.

Oh yes, the engine.

Since we have rear wheel drive, you may wonder why our engine isn't in the rear too. It's a matter of having enough room to enjoy your rig. An engine in the front takes up no valuable living space. An engine in the rear takes up lots of it.

Now you know our plan.

We give you rear wheel drive for the most efficient use of power.

We put the engine up front to give you more space for comfortable living.

These same demanding standards are applied to everything else we do. Construction. Weight distribution. Interior design. We'd like to send you more information to prove it. Write Sportscoach Corp. of America, 9601 Canoga Ave., Chatsworth, Calif. 91311.

Sportscoach

*Although percentages may vary depending on slipperiness, Sportscoach will out-perform front wheel drive in any equivalent situation.

The 8:40 a.m. Grand Prix.

This is one automobile event just about everybody participates in.

The course runs several tortuous miles from home to work. It's an obstacle course. Filled with practically everybody else in town also scrambling to get to work by 9.

But just as Monaco has its Formula I car, there is also a specially built car for your 8:40 a.m. Grand Prix.

The Honda Civic.™

The Honda has everything you need to fight the freeways. Front wheel drive, rack-and-pinion steering, front disc brakes, four wheel independent suspension, and a peppy overhead cam engine that gets up to 30 miles to a gallon of regular.

April Road Test Magazine said it all: "Now…there is a new commuter car on the mar-

ket; one which is large enough to be fairly comfortable, small enough to maneuver through rush hour traffic, gutsy enough to cruise at freeway speeds, and economical enough to operate all week on one tank of gas. This amazing little vehicle is the Honda Civic."

"Clearly the automobile has it all; it provides the most immediately viable solution to our traffic problems and does this with comfort, performance, economy, and low price. For center city commuters, Honda Civic is the car of the future. And it's here now."

Well, it's 5 pm, and we're off and running again.

Gentlemen, start your engines.

The New Honda Civic
It will get you where you're going.

Introducing the Honda Civic.
The cost of loving just went down.

We're here to propose a meaningful relationship; with a car to fit your heart as well as your head.

For the headstrong there are measurable dollar and cents appeals. Like a $2125* price tag. And up to 30 miles to the gallon. But that's only logic.

The heart of the matter is another story. The Civic™ is a car of remarkable personality and spunk (who says an economy car has to be dull?). It's for people with enough sensory perception to want more out of driving than just working the pedals and steering.

It's got front wheel drive,

rack and pinion steering, independent four-wheel suspension, power front disc brakes, and four-speed synchromesh transmission. Plus a totally new transversely mounted, overhead cam engine that delivers a disarming amount of scoot. It can add up to a very personal involvement. Test drive it. Sedan or hatchback. You'll see.

Move in on a Honda. Two may not be able to live as cheaply as one, but now there's a way to narrow the gap.

The New Honda Civic.
It will get you where you're going.

The Hatchback of Notre Dame.

There's a new face on campus this year. The Honda Civic.™ From UCLA to NYU, more and more Hondas have been squeezing into parking places.

Why? Well for openers, the Civic Hatchback costs only $2250* and gets up to 30 miles to a gallon.

Pretty nice economics.

But economy is only half the story. The Civic's performance is even more remarkable.

In comparing the Civic against other economy cars, April Road Test magazine found that its 0-60 mph acceleration was bested only by the Mazda RX-3 (which lists at about a thousand dollars more).

And March Car and Driver magazine reported: "Its acceleration is not only better than that of VW's and other small displacement competitors like the Toyota Corolla 1200, but it also exceeds that of the standard engine Pinto as well. And with a top speed of 88 mph, the Civic is no sitting duck on the freeway either."

Road Test summed it up pretty well when they said: "Clearly, the automobile has it all; it provides the most immediately viable solution to our traffic problems and does this with comfort, performance, economy and a low price. For center city commuters, the Honda Civic is the car of the future. And it's here now."

Test drive it yourself.

And find out why we believe that new face on campus will soon become a very familiar sight.

The New Honda Civic
It will get you where you're going.

His partner isn't talking to him. They are in the middle of doing a huge campaign, and the art director's partner will not speak to him, will not look at him, will literally stare right past him as if he is not there.

He notes to himself that the relationship has always been a little rocky, but this is definitely a turn for the worse.

The campaign they are doing is for a bank called U.S. Life, and it is built around this idea: if you can very graphically show people what happens to those who don't save for the future, you can make a very strong case for saving money. He and his partner are in the midst of finding older people who will talk openly about the financial problems they face. They are also creating a print campaign that will show people how to save for retirement.

They are also, if he reads the note correctly that his partner has left in his in-box, not speaking to each other anymore. His partner feels he lacks the intensity necessary to create great advertising. He, on the other hand, always found his partner to be fairly intense, but thought he was keeping up with him.

He wonders how they will get their work done. It becomes clear a few days later, when he goes to his mail box and finds a note from his partner, with several ideas for headlines. The note is very civil. And the headlines aren't bad, either.

This goes on for several weeks. He will get a few headlines and crude drawings in his mail box, and he will either send them back and reject them, or draw them up.

He is going crazy. He decides to talk to somebody about the problem. He goes to see Guy.

"My partner is so mad at me he won't even talk to me."

Guy thinks this is the funniest thing. He starts laughing in the hall. Jay walks by, and asks Guy what's so funny. Guy tells him how these two guys aren't talking to each other, and they're doing all this great work, and now Jay laughs. And the two of them are standing in the hall having the biggest laugh of all time, and the art director is trying to smile about his problem, and as the three of them stand there, something awful happens.

His partner walks by.

Now his partner thinks he's trying to get him fired. Now his partner is really furious.

Sometime afterward, they shoot the commercial. It is with a 75-year-old retired gentleman, who simply says he is not an actor, he is now in some financial difficulty although he was once quite well-off, and that he suggests people start to save money now at a place like U.S. Life. He closes by saying, "I'm glad I had a chance to do this commercial. I needed the money."

The art director stops working with his partner after the commercial is completed, and not long after that, decides to take a sabbatical. He is a sculptor, and to calm himself, he goes away to pound on wood for about ten months.

For Chiat/Day, the commercial is a landmark. It is the first television work the company has done that will win Southern California's biggest advertising award, the Belding Bowl Sweepstakes.

When he goes to the Beldings, the art director sees his partner.

"Hi," the partner says, as if nothing's ever happened. "Where've you been?"

MAN: I'm not an actor. I'm a 74-year-old man in some financial difficulty.

I retired 10 years ago with what I thought was plenty to see me through my retirement in comfort.

But it just wasn't enough. I've got one piece of advice for young people.

The time to start saving for retirement is when you first start working.

And the company that asked me to do this commerical, US Life Savings, is a good place to do it.

I'm glad I had the chance to do this commercial for US Life Savings.

I needed the money.

MAN: I'm an actor. I've made a lot of money, but I've spent a lot of money.

You know, cars, boats, a lovely house, entertaining, the usual things.

Out there one lives in a make believe world. The thing an actor tries not to think about is getting old.

So when it happens we're even less prepared than most. If I had to do it all over again, I hope I wouldn't do the same thing.

This time I'd put more of my money in a safe place, like the place that asked me to do this commercial. U.S. Life Savings.

Yes, I'm an actor.

But at this moment I'm not acting.

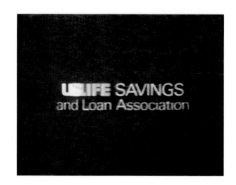

"Cars like the Honda Civic don't just happen. They are designed, engineered. Then somebody goes out and lives with the prototype and then brings it back and screams for eight solid hours and sends the designers and engineers back to their little drawing boards until they get it right. And they've gotten it right with the Civic."
Motor Trend (9/73)

"The factory has spent its money on engineering, on making the car nimble and useful."
Road & Track ('74 Buyer's Guide)

"This brilliantly conceived and executed sedan is *the* answer to basic personal transportation needs for the immediate and foreseeable future."
Road Test (1/74)

"The amazing Honda Civic combines driver comfort, quality, sporty appeal and pure economy in the best match seen in the United States."
Motor Trend (1/74)

"Naturally, the question most often asked about the Civic concerns its gas mileage. And the EPA was not wrong in awarding Honda good marks. It's overall average in the CAR & DRIVER driving cycle...was 30.1 mpg, dropping to 27.6 mpg in the city... reaching a high of 39.7 mpg at a constant 60 mph. You will find that you have to drive very hard indeed to fall below 27 mpg on the road..."
Car & Driver (9/74)

"It did 0-60 in just over 14 sec and had a top speed of over 90 mph, all the while doing an even 30 miles per gallon of fuel."
Road & Track ('74 Fuel Savers Issue)

"Happiness is 32 miles per gallon."
Hot Rod (4/74)

"The ratios in the standard 4-speed manual transmission are well matched to the engine characteristics, and shifting is crisp and positive due to an uncomplicated linkage."
Road Test (1/74)

"Its compact dimensions allow you to squeeze through the smallest cracks in traffic and park in spaces rejected by Volkswagens. The Civic's maneuverability is exceeded only by that of a bicycle."
Car & Driver (9/74)

"What we have in the Honda Civic is a car that will perform the necessities as well as any car made and provide a larger portion of luxury and fun than just about anything else you can buy for close to the Honda's base..."
Hot Rod (4/74)

"Due to the relatively short wheelbase, the turning circle is small and steering response is quick. Just about all driving can be done without the need to reposition the hands on the steering wheel, including 90-degree turns at street corners."
Road Test (1/74)

"The shift linkage is somewhat reminiscent of early Porsche Speedsters in that you're continually amazed that it's in the right gear—because it's so easy and because there is so little sensory awareness of the process."
Motor Trend (9/73)

"The space utilization is marvelous: Civic drivers can compare feats of loading capacity the way racers talk lap times."
Road & Track ('74 Buyer's Guide)

"Service and serviceability on the Civic promises to be right in line with its economy image. Access to just about everything on the car that needs periodic service or could conceivably require repair can be had by simply opening the hood."
Road Test (1/74)

"...the Honda Civic goes way beyond analytical reportage. The thing's an almost mystical experience..."
Motor Trend (9/73)

"...the Civic is the perfect antidote to the gasoline shortage and runaway prices, the two most pressing problems

with which we have to deal in 1974 and the years ahead..."
Road Test (1/74)

"As an 'only car' we would judge the Civic to be every bit as satisfactory as a Volkswagen...and better for pure urban driving."
Car & Driver (9/74)

"...once in each generation of new cars, an automobile appears that is so right for its time and application that it's a wonder all cars that follow aren't carved... in its image. The Honda Civic–how shall I put it?–is a *revolution on wheels*, and, *boy*, does it work!"
Motor Trend (9/73)

The Honda Civic. Enough said.

Why a man buys a Honda Civic:

1. handles like a sports car
2. gets super mileage
3. when you step on the gas, adios
4. maneuvers into impossible parking spots
5. quiet
6. roomy
7. and comfortable
8. classy lines
9. sensible sticker price
10. gangbusters on the freeway
11. panorama visibility
12. solid grip on the road
13. fun to drive
14. ditto
15. ditto

Why a woman buys a Honda Civic:

1. handles like a sports car
2. gets super mileage
3. when you step on the gas, adios
4. maneuvers into impossible parking spots
5. quiet
6. roomy
7. and comfortable
8. classy lines
9. sensible sticker price
10. gangbusters on the freeway
11. panorama visibility
12. solid grip on the road
13. fun to drive
14. ditto
15. ditto

"Women don't understand rack-and-pinion steering."

You may be wondering why we didn't save our rack-and-pinion ad for Playboy.

What do you care about a precise steering mechanism?

Well, we get stacks of letters from women who own Hondas and not one of them has ever gushed over the shade of blue or the texture of the fabric.

But they love the way our Honda Civic handles on curves.

(Like a sports car.)

The way it maneuvers into impossible parking spaces.

The feeling of control: When you drive a Honda, you're boss—not just tagging along.

The truth is, women buy cars for pretty much the same reasons men do.

And if other car manufacturers don't know it yet, we hope they don't see this ad.

Honda Civic.
We don't make "a woman's car."

"Women only drive automatic transmissions."

Some car manufacturers actually believe women buy cars for different reasons than men do.

So they build "a woman's car." Oversized, hopelessly automatic and dull.

At Honda we designed just one thing. A lean, spunky economy car with so much pizzazz it handles like a sports car.

If you're bored with cars designed only to get you from point A to point B, without responding to you the driver, maybe you ought to take the Honda Civic for a spin.

We've got a stick shift with an astonishing amount of zip. Enough to surprise you. We promise.

Or, if you prefer, Hondamatic." It's a semi-automatic transmission that gives you convenience, but doesn't rob you of involvement.

Neither one is a woman's car.

Honda Civic.
We don't make "a woman's car."

CLOSE SHOT OF YELLOW PAGES. SOUND OF DRUM ROLLS AND CYMBAL CRASH. PUFF OF SMOKE FILLS THE SCREEN AND TWO GLOVED HANDS OPEN THE COVER AND PULL OUT A RABBIT. ANOTHER DRUM ROLL AND CYMBAL CRASH.

ANNCR VO: If you're looking for a magic shop...

GLOVED HANDS REACH INSIDE AGAIN AND PULL OUT TWO MORE RABBITS AND EVEN MORE RABBITS BEGIN TO EMERGE.

ANNCR VO: ...it's in the Yellow Pages.

MUSIC: YELLOW PAGES THEME.

NIGHTCLUB MUSIC THROUGHOUT. CLOSE-UP OF YELLOW PAGES. LID LIFTS AND GLAMOUROUS SHOWGIRL APPEARS, BATHED IN LAS VEGAS MAGENTA LIGHTING, COVERED WITH SPARKLES.

ANNCR VO: If you're looking for a glittering night on the town...

CLOSE UP OF HER FACE. ONE OF THE FEATHERS IN HER HEADDRESS SLIPS DOWN AND SHE BLOWS IT OUT OF THE WAY. THE HEADDRESS TIPS PRECARIOUSLY BUT SHE RECOVERS HER BALANCE AND IT STAYS IN PLACE.

ANNCR VO: ...it's in the Yellow Pages.

"This campaign was preceded by a campaign with Henny Youngman, which another team did. And I don't know what happened, but at the ninth hour we lost the Henny Youngman campaign. Whether Henny Youngman wouldn't do it or the client decided he didn't like it or what have you, and with like three days to go, they threw my partner and I into a room, and we came out with this."

1. The Memory Systems Division of National Semiconductor Corporation will be exhibiting products in Booth 3220 at the National Computer Conference.
2. The Memory Systems Division of National Semiconductor Corporation will be exhibiting products in Booth 3220 at the National Computer Conference.
3. The Memory Systems Division of National Semiconductor Corporation will be exhibiting products in Booth 3220 at the National Computer Conference.
4. The Memory Systems Division of National Semiconductor Corporation will be exhibiting products in Booth 3220 at the National Computer Conference.
5. The Memory Systems Division of National Semiconductor Corporation will be exhibiting products in Booth 3220 at the National Computer Conference.
6. The Memory Systems Division of National Semiconductor Corporation will be exhibiting products in Booth 3220 at the National Computer Conference.
7. The Memory Systems Division of National Semiconductor Corporation will be exhibiting products in Booth 3220 at the National Computer Conference.
8. The Memory Systems Division of National Semiconductor Corporation will be exhibiting products in Booth 3220 at the National Computer Conference.
9. The Memory Systems Division of National Semiconductor Corporation will be exhibiting products in Booth 3220 at the National Computer Conference.
10. The Memory Systems Division of National Semiconductor Corporation will be exhibiting products in Booth 3220 at the National Computer Conference.
11. The Memory Systems Division of National Semiconductor Corporation will be exhibiting products in Booth 3220 at the National Computer Conference.
12. The Memory Systems Division of National Semiconductor Corporation will be exhibiting products in Booth 3220 at the National Computer Conference.
13. The Memory Systems Division of National Semiconductor Corporation will be exhibiting products in Booth 3220 at the National Computer Conference.
14. The Memory Systems Division of National Semiconductor Corporation will be exhibiting products in Booth 3220 at the National Computer Conference.
15. The Memory Systems Division of National Semiconductor Corporation will be exhibiting products in Booth 3220 at the National Computer Conference.
16. The Memory Systems Division of National Semiconductor Corporation will be exhibiting products in Booth 3220 at the National Computer Conference.

And don't you forget it.

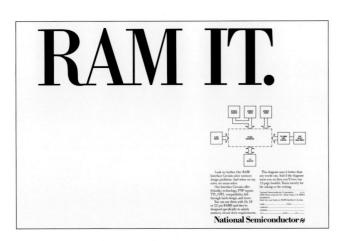

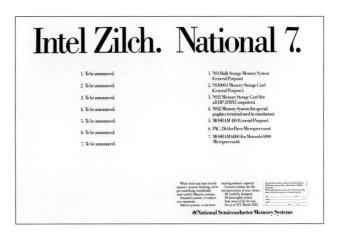

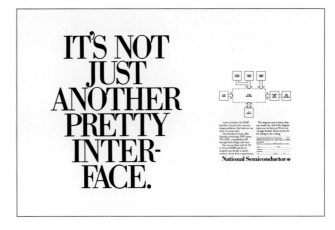

HOW CHIAT/DAY LOST THE HONDA ACCOUNT.

On November fifth and sixth, Honda's car people saw several of the finest speculative pitches money can buy.

In a period of twelve hours, over $300,000 worth of out-of-pocket dogs and ponies went on display.

Two days later, Honda had a new agency.

Chiat/Day lost a $4-million account. Needham, Harper & Steers won an $8-million plum.

As MAC reported it: "NHS met the requirements…that of a national, full-service agency."

What's it like to lose?

The classy thing for an agency to do after losing 25% of its business is to play it cool. Act like it's all a momentary inconvenience.

That's a crock.

We're not sophisticated enough to put on a fake smile and walk away from what we've done with Honda over the past five years.

Truth is, we got beat. What's worse, we got beat playing somebody else's game. We took a shamefaced shot at show-biz pitch artistry. And somewhere between the third and fifth act, some of the finest advertising ideas you'll never see got swamped in a four-hour sea of Madison Avenue buzz-words.

That's painful as hell.

"Show me a good loser and I'll show you a loser."

We're not sure where to credit that quote. But it's dead center true.

We want to go on the record as bad losers. We want you to know that we're mad as hell.

Not at Honda. They are very real gentlemen doing business in our country according to our peculiar customs.

Not at Needham. They did what they had to do and did it well (after paying those dues at Continental Airlines, maybe they had one coming).

We're mad at a system. We're mad at the way big budgets get relocated. We're mad about all the instances we see and hear about where advertising becomes a battle of logistics instead of a battle of ideas.

Most of all, we're mad at ourselves for voluntarily participating in an advertising gang-bang.

If this reads like sour grapes, you read it wrong. We don't think we could have changed the outcome. But the scarey thing is that we could have changed *us*.

The high cost of learning.

We spent a lot of money on the Honda presentation. We matched the other players dollar for dollar.

Fortunately, we had a lot of money to spend. Still do. The real pain is emotional, not fiscal.

We lost some billings. But we've never worried much about billings. They happen. If the product's good, the market's there. And, Honda aside, we added $4-million in 1974. We figure to do as well in '75.

We've still got the best account list in town. Quality.

We've still got the best concentration of talent in town (headhunters, spare your dime).

We've got money in the bank. We've got plenty to do. We're back to our real business.

Not Show Business. Advertising Business.

Chiat/Day

"How we lost the Honda account."

It doesn't seem like it was that long ago when they all sat around, trying to figure out how to introduce the Honda car in America. The account was about half a million dollars then.

Now, a little more than three years later, there are over 50,000 Hondas on the road. The account is on the verge of billing over eight million dollars a year.

And Chiat/Day is about to lose it.

Honda's automotive division has been growing at an explosive rate, and their ad agency, they feel, has not been growing along with them. They feel that Chiat/Day is understaffed creatively.

Which is true.

They feel that Chiat/Day does not have the most experienced account executives in the world.

Which is also true.

They feel, in short, that Chiat/Day is not professional enough.

The account is put into review, which is the equivalent of having to pitch it all over again. There is no question over whether or not to try and keep the business; Honda has become a major part of Chiat/Day's success.

The creative department works for six weeks on the pitch, producing tons of work tied to the theme "Our philosophy is simple."

The night before the pitch, Jay and Guy decide to send the creative team that has done most of the work on vacation. They are pretty sure this is a losing battle, and they want to get the copywriter and art director out of town before the bad news comes—they don't see any benefit in having everyone totally depressed. They decide this: if you're going to get bad news, it's always better to get it in Tahiti.

The bad news comes twelve days later: Honda is moving its car advertising to another agency. Emotionally, it's bad. Financially, it's a disaster:

Honda accounts for half of Chiat/Day's billings. Honda accounts for three-quarters of Chiat/Day's income.

Everyone in the industry, in the trade press, in the agency, is wondering the same thing: what will happen to Chiat/Day?

And that is when Guy sits down to write an ad about how Chiat/Day lost the Honda account. Rather than downplay the loss, he and Jay feel now is the time to be aggressive; they feel that nobody likes a casualty. An agency's worst times are also its most visible times, and this is the time to get people talking about Chiat/Day, to remind them what Chiat/Day is about, to let everybody know that Chiat/Day is going to be okay.

No one is laid off. The creative director goes from office to office telling people that they might have to take pay cuts for a while; the cuts never come. There are other accounts to keep the place going, and one advantage to being severely understaffed, as it turns out, is that you don't have to fire anyone when you get fired for being severely understaffed.

Two months later, Jay and Guy hire the executive vice president of Doyle Dane Bernbach's L.A. office to build a strong account management department at Chiat/Day. A few months after that, Guy decides that since he never saw himself staying in the ad business past forty, this might be a good time to get out.

"Good luck," his partner tells him. "Call if you get bored."

SUBJECTIVE CAMERA "WALKING"
ACROSS DARK STREET TO LIGHTED
PHONE BOOTH. WOMAN'S FOOTSTEPS.
BREATHING. AS IF IN DISTRESS.
ANNCR FEMALE VO: The Rape
Relief 24-Hour Crisis Line.
WOMAN: Hello? I need help.
ANNCR FEMALE VO: If you ever need
us, we're here.

WHAT'S A LITTLE RAPE BETWEEN FRIENDS?

A rapist isn't always some maniac hiding behind a garbage can. All too often, he's good old Harry.

Pruner of roses. Father of three. Friend of the family. And a great kidder at parties.

Until the day he shows up in your living room and demands the use of your body.

In one 1973 rape survey, nearly 7 out of 10 victims said they'd known their attackers before the crime.

This ugly thing is getting to be an epidemic in Seattle and nobody is immune.

And maybe the worst part is what happens afterwards.

The fears. The doubts. The feeling that you have to fight this thing all by yourself and nobody else gives a damn.

Well, we do. We have a 24-Hour Crisis Line at 632-RAPE.

And on the other end of that line, there's a sympathetic and enlightened ear. Someone who can help. Someone who's willing to stand by your side through the whole, humiliating aftermath.

632-RAPE. Write it down. And pray that some creep like Harry doesn't force you to use it.

632-RAPE
Don't keep it to yourself.

24-Hour Crisis Line. Rape Reduction Project, City of Seattle.

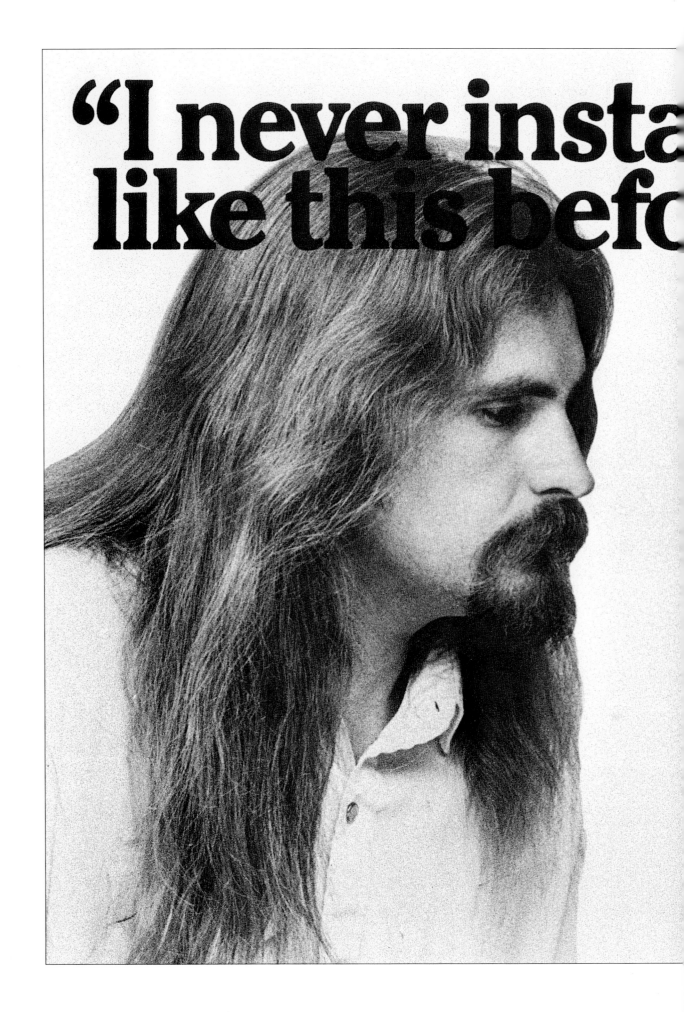

"I never insta
like this befo

led anything re."

—*Steve Tillack, installation expert.*

"Just when I think I've seen it all, the Pioneer marketing guys show up with a new quad unit. Or a cassette player with AM, FM stereo and Dolby.*

Usually, I just grab it right out of their hands and put it right in my car.

This time, it was different. I just stared.

I didn't even touch it.

'What do you think, Steve?' they asked me.

'Car stereo that looks like my receiver at home', I muttered, still staring. I think it was all they needed to hear.

How does it sound? Well, the fact that it's made by Pioneer probably tells you more about the sound than the specs. Besides, how it *sounds* in your car is going to depend a lot on how it's *put* in your car.

If you want to do it yourself (most do), I can help. After all, when it comes to installation, I wrote the book.

It's called 'How I Install Car Stereo'. And it's how you should install car stereo. No matter what kind of system you're installing. 8-track. Cassette. Under dash. In dash. Even if it isn't a Pioneer, this book will help make sure you get it right the first time.

If you want, you can also jot down a question or two about specific problems you may be having.

Enclose a stamped, self-addressed envelope, and I'll send back some answers.

Just write Pioneer Electronics, Carson, California 90746. Especially if you've never installed anything like this before."

*The word "Dolby" is the trademark of the Dolby Laboratories.

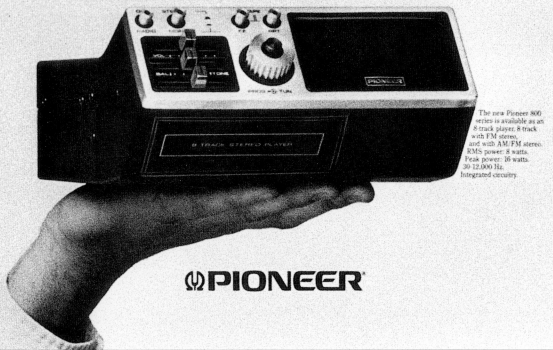

The new Pioneer 800 series is available as an 8-track player, 8-track with FM stereo, and with AM/FM stereo. RMS power: 8 watts. Peak power: 16 watts. 30-12,000 Hz. Integrated circuitry.

⚘ PIONEER

"*Pioneer went to Chiat/Day in their earliest stages of being a marketer on any sophisticated level. They had very little money. We're meeting with the president, and as I recall it, we're asking our usual questions, 'Okay, what's superior about Pioneer? What's unique? What's this, what's that?' He kept saying, 'Nothing, nothing. It's the same as everybody else's. No big deal.' 'Are your amps more powerful?' 'No, no.' 'Your faceplates are different?' 'No, nothing is unique.' That's our whole first meeting. Some time goes by and we have another meeting, kind of a work session. And it was during this meeting that we arrived at nothing again. And Pioneer's president is saying, 'Well, keep on going. I'll see you in a couple of weeks.' Then, as he's leaving the room, he does kind of like a Peter Falk, 'Oh, by the way—.' You know how Peter Falk as Columbo would turn around as he was leaving? 'By the way, I think you ought to go visit our installation set-up.' I said, 'What installation set-up is that?' 'Oh, didn't I tell you? We're the only importer of car stereos that has it's own installation facility. We have a manager, his name is Steve Tillick. Why don't you go visit him?' And the rest is just kinda ad history."*

"Can you type?"

She gets off the elevator and thinks: This is the place for me.

Two months ago, she decided to be a copywriter, so she put together a book of writing samples and went around to a lot of small agencies. One guy said to her, "You should go to Chiat/Day, they would love you there." She has stopped by to try and wangle an interview with a man named Jay Chiat, not knowing what to expect. Now, as she looks at the girl working in overalls and the guy walking down the hall, screaming, she says to herself, "This is where I want to write."

Jay isn't there, so she is sent to the creative director who sends her to the associate creative director, a guy with a beard and Jesus sandals who looks like he just crawled out of a sleeping bag. He tells her he likes her writing but hates her ads, and then spends an hour showing her how to improve her layouts and talking about the crazy way he had gotten into Chiat/Day. He tells her this: To work in this place, you've got to prove you've got the stuff. Not only the ability to write, but the dedication and the desire to hang in there.

Unable to get a job in Los Angeles, she moves to Hawaii and gets her first job in advertising, writing used car commercials. All she can think about is being a copywriter at Chiat/Day. She wonders, what would this man Jay Chiat respond to?

Her answer is to write an ad about herself. She is just about broke, but feels this is her one shot, so she spends the last $400 she has having the photo taken and the type set. She sends it special delivery, along with her return address and phone number, which happens to be the Honolulu YWCA ($200 a month, including two meals a day.)

The next night, she comes home to a message that says someone named Jay Chiat phoned. Her heart is pounding. She checks around to make sure no one at the Y is playing a trick on her, and then calls him back.

She gets through to him pretty easily. Hi, it's Jay, he says, I think you're a pretty good copywriter, but I can't hire someone with so little experience.

How about if you come and be a creative secretary? She asks what's involved. He asks, can she type? She lies and says yes. He tells her to get on a plane. She asks if she can think about it, but the minute she gets off the phone, she realizes there is nothing to think about, and calls him right back.

She shows up with a pineapple and a lei, and they stick her at a desk in the corner of a hallway. She cannot type. She cannot work the phones. And because of the way she was hired, she is hated by the other secretaries. As the weeks go by, she is given the worst secretarial jobs. She keeps asking when she is going to get a chance to write something; they keep telling her to be patient, and by the way, would you mind filing this, please?

Five months pass. One day, the head of personnel calls the girl into her office. She says, "I don't know if you know this, but we're on the verge of firing you. You're not a great secretary." The girl says, "I never said I was a great secretary, I said I was a good writer, and if somebody will just give me a chance around here, I'll prove it." The woman tells her, "if you don't learn to be a better secretary, you'll never be a writer."

She goes back to her hole in the corner, fuming. Although she doesn't know it, one day she will win awards for her work as a writer on Yamaha and Porsche and Apple. One day, she will be interviewed by the New York Times about how she wrote the landmark twenty-four page Macintosh magazine insert.

But not today. Today, she will learn how to type.

If the ads don't work, we'll give you your money back.

What advertising agency in its right mind would make an offer like that?

We would.

We're Chiat/Day.

The newest advertising agency in Seattle. (Our office is under construction right now in the Pioneer Building.)

And we have an unusual approach to the work we do.

We stand behind it.

Chiat/Day's money back guarantee.

Some years ago, Jay Chiat and Guy Day made their unheard of guarantee to a prospective client who was looking for the right kind of agency. Chiat/Day got the account.

The account is still with us.

But Jay and Guy wouldn't leave well-enough alone. Over the years they've made similar guarantees to a number of other prospective clients. And not one has ever asked for his money back.

Now we're making the offer to you.

If you think advertising can increase your sales and we agree with you, together we'll set some goals. And then we'll guarantee the results.

Our guarantee is simple. After we've worked for you 90 days, you review our performance. If you don't think we've delivered what we both agreed on, we'll give all fees back to you.

We won't return money that was paid to media, but we will return every penny Chiat/Day made during our three months together. What can you lose?

What makes our ads guaranteeable?

They work.

Recently we were hired by Pacific Northwest Bell to handle their Yellow Pages advertising. You may have seen some of the TV commercials we did. The Yellow Pages open and out comes a showgirl, a magician's rabbit, a dancing moppet, a plumber, even a dragon.

Less than four weeks after the commercials went on the air, we hired a local research firm to check the results.

Completely unaided, 70% of the people who had seen our commercials correctly identified the sponsor. Some experts say that's about 40% better than we had any right to expect.

And we're willing to bet you it's better than your commercials are doing right now.*

About two years ago, Motel 6 came to us with a small budget and a chain of motels that had never been advertised nationally.

One year later their comptroller was all smiles. Motel 6 had rented an additional 80,000 rooms.

And this year they're setting a new occupancy record despite the energy crisis. If you don't think that's good, ask anybody in the hotel business.

Are your ads doing that well?

Four seasons ago Chiat/Day bet a race track in Southern California we could beat its attendance record. And we agreed to be paid solely on the basis of that increase.

We won the bet.

In fact, we increased the attendance so much our client asked us to go back to a

standard fee. We were making too much money.

Back in 1970 the word "Honda" meant motorcycles. But the Honda people wanted to gain acceptance (and a foothold) in the small car market too. They came to us. In less than

four years Honda has gone from no place on the chart to number 8 in imported small car sales.

They're selling every single car they can get off the boat. We think they'd be number 5 if they had more cars.

Did Honda accomplish this by out-spending the competition? Hardly. Honda has, by far, the smallest ad budget of the top 15 small car manufacturers.

ANNCR: Of all 1974 cars tested for gas mileage — by the U.S. Environmental Protection agency,

this car came in first. — The 4-speed Honda Civic.

Now you see why we believe in our work.

Face the facts. If we didn't think we could deliver, we wouldn't make the guarantee.

Is there a catch to all this?

Yes. It's you.

Chiat/Day is a special kind of agency that can produce results only when it's working with a special kind of client.

We don't work well if you're passive.

Or unaggressive.

Or have no goals.

We think of ourselves as the underdog's agency. What we do best is help a determined client who isn't on top get there.

If you're stuck with only half the budget your competition has, there is a solution. We make your ads twice as good. So they work twice as hard.

And it really is that simple.

To be continued...

After all this, you may think we expect you to grab the phone and call us.

We don't.

Chiat/Day is already talking to several clients here in Seattle and we're pretty sure we know the others we'd like to work for.

So we'll be calling you. (If you'd like to know more about us in the meantime, return this coupon and we'll send you the marketing stories we couldn't squeeze on this page.)

Name_____

Company_____

Address_____

City_____State_____Zip____

*Why not call our bluff? Duplicate our test using your own commercials. If yours score higher than ours did, send us the testing results and we'll send you a check for the research.

Chiat/Day, Inc.

600 First Avenue, Seattle, Washington 98104. (206) 682-4404.

"'The money back guarantee.' I cringed every time I said it."

76

PeoplesBank.
Member FDIC and the human race.

ANNCR VO: When we opened our bank we could have called ourselves something impressive like "The First Central Amalgamated Security Trust Exchange and Federal Mutual Bank."

PEOPLE: "Raspberry, yuk, raspberry, boo, raspberry, double boo, ha ha, ya know what I mean."

DOG COVERS EARS AND WHINES

ANNCR VO: But we didn't want to be just a bankers bank, we're People's Bank. Member FDIC and the Human Race.

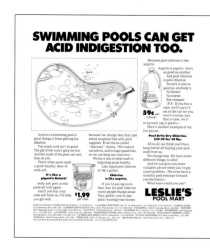

From the bonnie, bonnie banks of the Yamazaki.

IMPORTED

Suntory Royal
Special Reserve Whisky

A BLEND OF SELECTED WHISKIES
DISTILLED AND BOTTLED BY
4/5 QUART   **SUNTORY LTD.**   86.8 PROOF
DISTILLERY AT YAMAZAKI NEAR KYOTO, JAPAN
PRODUCT OF JAPAN

If Suntory Royal Whisky happens to taste like Scotch, we wouldn't be surprised.

Our misty Glen of Yamazaki looks much like those of Scotland. Our barley is fine, like theirs. Our peat fuel for drying the barley is theirs. And our white oak for ageing comes from the same forests as theirs.

In fact, some people believe our Suntory Royal is even smoother and lighter than Scotch. And from our point of view, that could be entirely possible.

Suntory Royal. Slightly East of Scotch.

86.8 PROOF. A BLEND OF RARE, SELECTED WHISKIES DISTILLED AND BOTTLED AT THE YAMAZAKI DISTILLERY NEAR KYOTO, JAPAN.

"I'm over at a casting session, right? We're sitting casting and I get this phone call. It's this young writer. And he's screaming and yelling that he's gonna call the police, that he's gonna press charges, someone assaulted him in the office. And I said, 'What are you talking about?' And he says, 'So and so didn't believe that there should be any radios in the office, because we're trying to do advertising and it should be a quiet environment.' So the kid had his walkman on, turned up where you could hear, you know, the sound coming out of his ears as he was sitting there typing. And he was in the office next door, and the other writer told him to turn it off, and he didn't. So this other writer came in and he ripped the earphones off of the kid and threw 'em on the floor, and smashed 'em. And the kid says, 'The man's crazy, he assaulted me, I'm gonna call the police, I'm gonna press charges.' And I say, 'Go on the other side of the office, don't go near him til I come back, and calm down.' Some days are like that."

Chiat/Day is looking for a good place to eat.

We're looking for a fast-food account with an aggressive mind, a good product, and a deep-seated abhorrence for schlock.

We've had an opening for one since the Sixties. And, frankly, this whole thing is really beginning to gnaw at our insides.

Not the hunger.

The frustration. Of having all these fast-food people at Chiat/Day, with no fast food to work on.

Why, there are people here who helped make Jack-In-The-Box a household word. People who helped Krystal increase sales 30% in one year. People who worked on McDonald's, Carl's Jr., der Wienerschnitzel, pizza, tacos, chicken, fish and chips, the works.

They're all here, waiting to be needed.

And to make sure they're needed soon, we'll offer you a money-back guarantee:

We'll rebate every media commission we earned on your account, if we don't meet the first quarter's objectives.

The last time we made an offer like this, it got us a food account. A good, but dormant, brand. And that brand is now enjoying a 36% sales increase. So maybe you should call Jay Chiat at (213) 381-7881 and discuss this thing. Who knows? He might even take you to lunch. At your place. Chiat/Day, Inc., Advertising. Los Angeles, San Francisco, Seattle.

"Every couple of weeks, Jay would have a meeting with the whole creative department and he would ask around the room, 'Who is having any problems with a partner, with a client, with an account guy?' And then if no one was having any problems, he would say, 'Okay, I just want it to be clear to you guys, work is what's important. Anybody gets in the way, I want to know. 'Cause we're going to have nothing getting in the way of doing good work.'"

Chiat/Day is starving.

We're hungry for a food account.

We want one so bad we can taste it.

For what? For greed, and avarice, and pride?

No.

We want it for the 1 out of every 4 people at Chiat/Day who have major food experience and miss it.

For the account supervisor who helped put the name of an unknown snack food on everyone's lips. For the media strategist who helped a me-too oral hygiene product dislodge the established competition. For the writer who helped a declining bakery product achieve an overnight 17% increase.

And for all the people at Chiat/Day who've worked on Borden's, on Campbell's, on Carnation, on Coca-Cola, on Falstaff, on Gallo, on Hills Bros., on Hunt-Wesson, on Laura Scudder's, on Lawry's, on Ore-Ida, on P&G, on Pillsbury.

Why, you can name virtually any product category on the shelf. And we've got someone who worked late for it, bled for it, made something happen for it.

If you're in the food business, you can understand what's in our blood. Why we've got this obsession to do it again.

To take a brand, think it out, and make it work.

So we'd like to make you an offer.

Call Jay Chiat at (213) 386-5528, collect. Give us a project involving any worthwhile brand that, for some reason, isn't making it. And if we can't turn that product around in 6 months, we'll rebate every media commission we earned on it.

This offer isn't based on misguided self-confidence.

It's based on the fact that Chiat/Day has people who've demonstrated their ability to make a product respond in the face of impossible odds.

Those are the people who'll work on your project.

Because they're the only kind of food people we have.

Chiat/Day, Inc., Los Angeles, San Francisco, Seattle.

Chiat/Day is airsick.

There are people at Chiat/Day who've worked on Air Siam, American, Bonanza, (remember them?) Continental, Eastern, Frontier, Golden West, JAL, Lufthansa, North Central, TWA, Texas International, UTA and Western.

So, to us, the airline business is home. And we miss it painfully.

Not for the romance of it all. But for the business of it all. For the challenge of marketing the most perishable commodity there is:

A seat that goes somewhere only once during a given period of time. And which, the minute it leaves the gate empty, becomes a worthless hunk of air.

We've seen these lost opportunities, on trips around the country. And while we know it's almost impossible to fill every plane on every trip, we look at those seats and wonder.

Could we make a difference like we did for a dying sport, an out-of-the-way amusement park, a once-obscure motel chain, and even a tree in Africa? Could we fill those seats?

Listen. If you can fill out this coupon, we can fill those seats.

Chiat/Day. In San Francisco, Los Angeles, Seattle. So far.

Chiat/Day, Inc. Advertising
1300 W. Olympic Blvd., Los Angeles, CA 90015
Gentlemen:
☐ I'd like to talk with you about recovering our seats with warm bodies.
☐ What I need is not more bodies in seats, but more friends in the CAB. When you work that out, let me know.

Name_____ Title_____
Airline_____
Address_____
City_____ State_____ Zip_____

Chiat/Day is still hungry, but no longer thirsty.

Last month, we ran an ad that said we were starving.

It said we were hungry for a packaged goods account because 1 out of every 4 people at Chiat/Day has major food experience and misses it.

It said we wanted such an account so bad, we'd even rebate media commissions if we couldn't turn the product around in 6 months.

It really said that.

And guess what happened.

We got a wine account. One of the largest and most desirable wine accounts an agency could ask for.

Obviously, we're pleased about it. Tickled rosé, as they say in the trade.

But there's still a lot of packaged goods experience around here, waiting to be needed.

There's dairy food experience, jams and jellies experience, canned goods experience,

soft drink experience, beer experience, coffee experience, sugar experience, spice experience, snack food experience,

H&BA experience, frozen foods experience, packaged mix experience, baked goods experience. More years of that than most of us like to think about.

And it's a shame to let all that go to waste.

So our offer still stands:

Call Jay Chiat at (213) 381-7881. Give us a project involving any worthwhile brand that, for some reason, isn't making it. And if we can't turn that product around in 6 months, we'll rebate every media commission we earned on it.

We know it's an ambitious offer.

But we also know we can deliver.

Because if anybody has people who can make a product respond, we do.

And it's not just the wine talking, either.

Chiat/Day, Inc., Advertising. Los Angeles, San Francisco, Seattle.

See Chiat/Day sit up and beg.

We want a pet food account.

We want a pet food account so much, we'll offer a money-back guarantee to get one.

All you have to do is call Jay Chiat at (213) 381-7881, collect, and give him a project involving any worthwhile brand that isn't making it.

And if we can't turn that product around in 6 months, we'll rebate every media commission we earned on it.

But let us warn you at the start.

We don't expect to lose.

Not after all those years we spent at other agencies working on Carnation, Jim Dandy, Kal-Kan, Kitty Salmon, Ralston-Purina, and Sergeants.

We've seen the competition, the proliferation of new products, the constant scrambling for awareness and share points.

We've seen it, and we've loved it.

If the truth be known, we've done our best work under marketing conditions exactly like yours. And we'd give our canine incisors to do it for any brand that wants to own the world.

We'll beg for it, bleed for it, slave for it, stay up nights for it, and worry over it.

We'll do anything except roll over and play dead for it.

Chiat/Day, Inc., Los Angeles, San Francisco, Seattle.

Chiat/Day wants to join a motorcycle gang.

It takes a tough bunch to handle a motorcycle account. But Chiat/Day has what it takes.

Speed. Balance. Savvy. Talent. Everything.

Except a client.

That's where Yamaha comes in. Between your innovative products, planning and marketing expertise; and our proven advertising and creative abilities, we can   sell motorcycles, accessories and snowmobiles like nobody else's business.

And if we can't, you'll get your money back.

That's right. You read it correctly. If we can't increase your sales, we'll refund the difference on a percentage basis from any media commissions or fees we may have earned.

Chiat/Day isn't afraid to join a motorcycle gang. Especially Yamaha's.

ⲻⲻⲻⲻ ‖‖‖‖

"Thank you, God of Advertising."

There is a God of Advertising. Even if he is a hideous, erratic, undependable god, there is a God of Advertising. That is what the full-time copywriter and part-time motorcyclist is thinking this morning. Twelve months ago, he wasn't so sure. That was the morning he found out Chiat/Day did not get the one account he really wanted to work on, the Yamaha account.

He thought the pitch went great. He thought the work they showed Yamaha was some of the best he and his partner had ever done. It was built around a strategy of which he had been a very vocal supporter: "We race, you win." The idea was to convince cyclists that if Yamaha could build a bike that satisfied professionals, they could build a bike that would satisfy the average street rider.

At first, Yamaha was skeptical about the strategy. All motorcycle companies had racing teams, but no mention of racing had ever been used in motorcycle advertising before. They felt that since people don't race motorcycles, people would see the ads and say, "Well, I don't race, I don't care about that, I don't need a motorcycle like that." Then Chiat/Day related the whole premise to tennis racquets, that if Mr. Smith sees a tennis racquet and thinks it's going to make him play a better game, even though he's not a professional, he will purchase the racquet that the professional is using. The same strategy that worked so successfully for tennis could also be applied to the motorcycle business.

By the end of the meeting, it seemed that Yamaha had really bought into the whole idea. The copywriter rode home that night thinking they had won the account. He didn't even mind that his boss had made him go out and buy a goddam suit for the presentation (although he did try to get reimbursed for it, listing it on an expense report as "wardrobe.") But two weeks later the Yamaha account went to another agency, and Chiat/Day lost what everyone recognized as its big chance to rebound from Honda.

In the following months, the copywriter did a lot of second-guessing. Even on the Sundays when he would go riding up to The Rock Store, this old liquor store made out of stone in the Santa Monica Mountains where motorcycle riders hung out on weekends, he couldn't stop thinking about it. He'd be riding up Mulholland for an hour, enjoying the scenery, and then he'd come around that last bend and see the flash of solid chrome, a couple of hundred bikes lined up near the old stone store, with bikers everywhere drinking beer and laughing, and it would remind him of Yamaha, if the work had been better, if the strategy had been better, on and on and on until he didn't want to look at another motorcycle.

All that, however, was before this morning, when the fickle God of Advertising reared up and made a true believer out of him. That was before Yamaha called Chiat/Day and asked if the agency would be interested in re-pitching the account.

All Yamaha wants now is a capabilities presentation to show them how Chiat/Day would run their business. Over the next week, the copywriter and his partner develop a booklet entitled "Why you should hire Chiat/Day—And why not." They go down to Yamaha with Jay and two account executives, and make the presentation. Yamaha thanks them, and the group returns to the office.

Two hours later, Jay's phone rings. Not only would Yamaha like to award their account to Chiat/Day, they would like to know if Chiat/Day would go ahead and start producing most of the advertising that they first showed to Yamaha in their pitch last year.

For Chiat/Day, it is the beginning of a new era, courtesy of Yamaha.

For the copywriter, it is Total Vindication, courtesy of the God of Advertising.

SFX: Rider's footsteps.
MUSIC: "SILVERBIRD" STARTS VERY LOW, BUILDS SLOWLY AND CONTINUES.
ANNCR VO: This on one of the five new Yamaha Specials...the most beautiful motorcycles we've ever built. With low-riding seat and handlebars that reach for you...instead of the other way around.
SFX: ENGINE SOUNDS, GEARS SHIFTING.
ANNCR VO: But looks aren't the only thing the Specials have going for them.
SFX: SOUND OF ENGINE WINDING HIGHER.
ANNCR VO: Just feel that four-stroke power.
THROUGHOUT THE REST OF THE SPOT THE SCENERY FLASHES BY AND THE HORIZON SHIFTS WITH EVERY TURN.
ANNCR VO: Now, the decision. Do you buy a Yamaha Special for the beauty...or the beast?

AERIAL OF ROAD RACE COURSE.
MUSIC: "Silverbird" throughout.
ANNCR VO: At Yamaha, we don't just have a little test track out behind the factory.
SFX: Sound of road racers, crowd.
ANNCR VO: We also test our engineering ideas wherever they race motorcycles.
ANNCR VO: Sound of motocrosser, crowd.
VIDEO OF NUMBER TWO YAMAHA IN FRONT.
ANNCR VO: From Carlsbad to Watkins Glen . . .
SFX: Sound of road racers.
VIDEO OF RACERS ROUNDING CORNER. NUMBER TWO YAMAHA IN FRONT.
ANNCR VO: From Daytona to Le Mans . . .
MOTOCROSSER TAKING CHECKERED FLAG.
ANNCR VO: In fact, Yamaha is the winningest racer in the world.
SUPER: Based on AMA Race results, 1972-1976.
VIDEO OF ROAD RACER TAKING CHECKERED FLAG.
ANNCR VO: And every time we race . . .
SOUND OF BIKES AND CROWD CHEERING.
ANNCR VO: . . . we learn more about how to build you a better motorcycle.
MUSIC: Up and out.

"When you go to these Motocross races, it's a big party. There are kids out there, women in tank tops, beer all over the place. A real family event."

INTRODUCING THE SECOND FASTEST MOTORCYCLE WE MAKE.

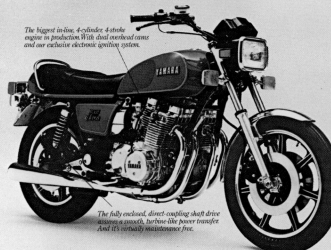

The biggest in-line, 4-cylinder, 4-stroke engine in production. With dual overhead cams and our exclusive electronic ignition system.

The fully enclosed, direct-coupling shaft drive assures a smooth, turbine-like power transfer. And it's virtually maintenance free.

We do make a motorcycle that's faster than our new XS Eleven four-stroke street bike.

Unfortunately, it's very expensive and you can only ride it on race tracks.

It's our TZ750, the number one road racer in the world. A motorcycle that so completely dominates Formula racing, few other bikes can even compete.

That puts the XS Eleven in pretty fast company.

THE UNDER 12-SECOND 4-STROKE.

In fact, with the Eleven's 1101cc, dual-overhead-cam, four-cylinder engine, it may just be the quickest production four-stroke motorcycle ever built.

Its unbelievable standing quarter-mile time: 11.73 seconds.

What does performance like that mean to you, unlikely as you are to be making quarter-mile runs?

It means a very impressive margin of power for high-speed cruising and touring. Plus unsurpassed acceleration and passing power whenever and wherever you need it.

Even with two passengers and a full load of touring gear, it has get up and go to spare.

SPEED ISN'T EVERYTHING.

But as proud as we are of the XS Eleven's speed and performance, that's not quite enough for us.

Comfort ranks pretty high, too.

That's why we hooked up the five-speed constant mesh transmission to one of the most sophisticated shaft drive systems available. Together they deliver an uncanny, turbine-like smoothness and quiet.

Actually, wherever you look on the XS Eleven you see evidence of Yamaha's innovative technology.

Our exclusive Transistor Controlled Ignition system, for example, uses precise electronic impulses instead of mechanical breaker points that wear out and need adjusting. And our unique vacuum advance system automatically senses and adjusts ignition timing for clean, efficient combustion at any speed. No other motorcycle has it.

As for extras, they're all there—without costing extra. Triple hydraulic disc brakes. Cast aluminum wheels. Three-way-adjustable front forks. Complete instrumentation, including electronic fuel gauge. Self-cancelling turn signals. And more.

The XS Eleven may be the second fastest motorcycle we make. But on the street, it's second to none.

YAMAHA
When you know how they're built.

HOW TO GROW UP TO BE A WINNER.

There comes a time in every young motocross rider's life when he feels like he's caught in the middle. Too big for a minibike. Not quite big enough for a full-size 125.

THE SHOCKING DIFFERENCE.

The Monoshock rear suspension found on the YZ100 is a Yamaha exclusive. Its single, adjustable, nitrogen/oil shock absorber provides control and response unmatched by any other system. Rear wheel wobble is eliminated while wheel travel is increased. Damping is consistent and, thus, predictable. Stability and traction are phenomenal.

The oil damped leading axle front forks deliver 5.5 inches of travel for precise and stable handling.

But if he races Yamahas right from the start, he'll never get that in-between feeling. Because we've got a system.

THE YAMAHA SYSTEM.

The heart of our system is the YZ100 you see pictured here.

When a youngster outgrows his YZ80, he moves quite naturally to the intermediate-size YZ100. It's a good deal longer, wider and taller than the 80, without going all the way to 125 dimensions.

Later, when his size and strength increase, the young rider can graduate to the YZ125. And at no point along the way will he find himself sitting on anything less than a genuine racing machine.

SMALL, BUT WIRY.

Reed valve Torque Induction gives the smaller displacement YZ100 engine loads of smooth usable power across a wide rpm range. And it's as rugged and dependable as any in the YZ line.

To lay that power down in the most efficient way possible, the YZ100 has a quick-shifting, six-speed racing transmission instead of a five-speed. Always the right gear at the right time.

Heavy-duty polypropylene tank, fenders and side covers keep weight down. A unique spring loaded chain tensioner assures a smooth power transfer. And a rugged double cradle, tubular steel frame holds the whole beautiful package together.

The YZ100 makes the Yamaha System the surest and most efficient way to start a winner and stay a winner.

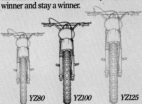

YZ80   YZ100   YZ125

Or, to put it another way, you can't beat The System.

YAMAHA
When you know how they're built.

Leading axle front forks for precise control.

Unique spring-loaded chain tensioner for smoother power transfer and less wear on chain and sprocket.

Exclusive nitrogen/oil Monoshock rear suspension. Spring preload is adjustable to track conditions.

Rugged, race-bred, two-stroke engine with reed valve Torque Induction. Six-speed short-throw racing transmission.

Mikuni carburetion is increased to 34mm this year. A new accelerator pump gives instantaneous throttle response.

A mark on the ball bearing-supported, overhead cam shows the exact position of the piston through the kick indicator window. This, together with a compression-release lever, makes starting easier.

U.S. Forestry approved exhaust system is tucked up, out of the way.

New larger fins on the head and aluminum cylinder keep the single running cool. Fin buttons keep the noise down.

Massive clutch has over 100 square inches of surface area for longer life.

9.0:1 compression ratio.

Five-speed, close ratio transmission to take advantage of the highest torque and broadest dual/dirt powerband in production.

Dry sump lubrication system provides a narrower engine and greater ground clearance. A full 9.2" on the TT500, 8.85" on the XT500.

HOW TO MAKE MOLEHILLS OUT OF MOUNTAINS.

When you tackle the great outdoors on a bike, it's more fun when the choice of going around or over an obstacle is left up to you. Not the bike.

Torque is what it takes.

And the off-road TT500 and dual-purpose XT500 have an abundance. The reason: one massive cylinder. The most powerful, big-bore, 4-stroke, single-cylinder motorcycle engine in production.

But incredible strength isn't their only strong point. They're also simple to maintain, very reliable, extra durable and down right frugal with fuel.

Both big singles have lightweight motocross

frames. A generous 7.7" of front fork travel and 6.4" in the rear from the laid-down nitrogen/oil shocks. Heavy-duty wheels and conical drum brakes. Plus an aluminum skid plate underneath.

And of course, the XT comes complete with street-legal lighting and instrumentation.

Our do-anything-in-the-dirt TT500. And the do-anything-anywhere dual-purpose XT500. Two big bores that are anything but boring.

TT500   *XT500*

YAMAHA
When you know how they're built.

THE YAMAHA IT'S: SOME OF THEIR BEST FEATURES ARE DESIGNED TO COME APART.

For a serious competition enduro rider like you, time is of the essence. A lost minute here, a few seconds there, can mean the difference between merely finishing and winning.

So every bike in the 1978 Yamaha IT line — 175, 250 and 400 — is equipped with quick-change features to save you time when you need it most.

Each wheel, for example, can be removed in just 30 seconds. And a flat tire repaired in as little as 90 seconds. (Cycle Magazine clocked a Yamaha ISDT rider at 89.4 seconds with a modified IT400.) The single-element foam air filter is so simple it can be changed with one hand. There's even a quick-release clutch cable.

As for the rest of the bike, neither rain, nor sleet, nor rocks, nor ruts, nor rivers can faze it.

A tough, motocross-bred engine

with reed valve Torque Induction gives you snappy low end response and smooth, dependable power across a wide rpm range.

Yamaha's exclusive Monoshock rear suspension, combined with long-travel, leading axle front forks, delivers extraordinary stability on any terrain, flat out or crawling.

Monoshock also qualifies as a quick-change feature, because you can adjust the damping to 17 settings with just a screwdriver. Spring preload and nitrogen pressure are fully adjustable, too.

The above features alone would be plenty to recommend our IT's to

any competitive rider. But the list goes on: a new, improved chain tensioner and chain guard. Chain adjusting cams. Complete tool kit. Large capacity, light-weight polyethylene gas tank. Extra-wide, extra-strong aluminum engine guards and flexible, polypropylene fenders. Hinged brake and shift levers that fold back in tight spots instead of bending.

The only thing missing from these outlandishly remarkable machines is the outlandishly high price you'd expect to pay for them.

And that, perhaps, is the best feature of the bunch.

The faster you get to your tools, the faster you make repairs.

Quick-release rear wheel.

Our exclusive nitrogen/oil monoshock can be adjusted to 17 damping settings with just a screwdriver. Spring preload, spring rate and nitrogen pressure are variable, too.

Chain adjusting cams, for rapid rear wheel alignment when adjusting chain or changing wheel.

Quick-change, single-element foam air filter can be replaced with one hand.

Quick-release front wheel.

IT 175

IT 250

IT 400

YAMAHA
When you know how they're built.

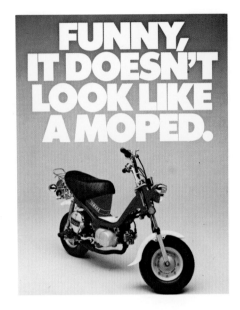

FUNNY, IT DOESN'T LOOK LIKE A MOPED.

The new Chappy Moped doesn't look much like the average moped because it's not the average moped.

It's a Yamaha.

And there are more than 20 years of two-wheel technology behind its design.

The sturdy frame, for instance, is strong and durable. The low center of gravity provides stability. And the wide tires improve handling.

For performance, there's a dependable two-stroke engine. For punch, our patented Torque Induction system. And for practicality, a kick starter, so you don't have to pedal your pants off to get it going.

And while all mopeds have automatic transmissions, ours has a convenient dual-range version for easier going. One speed for smooth travel on level streets. And another for smoothing out hilly areas.

There's Autolube, which automatically mixes gas and oil, so you don't have to. There's also a big, soft seat. Turn signals. Hydraulic/coil spring rear sus-

pension. And a lot more.

Like all mopeds, the Chappy is unbelievably economical. But unlike any other moped in the world, it's a Yamaha. So it comes with complete Yamaha parts and service to back it up.

All of which adds up to a funny looking moped that's really a very serious little machine.

The Chappy Moped.

Big, comfortable seat.

Full instrumentation, including turn signals.

Locking ignition switch.

Autolube mixes engine oil and fuel automatically.

Hydraulic/coil spring rear suspension.

Rigid frame and low center of gravity for stability.

Wide tires for easy handling.

Strong, dependable two-stroke engine with efficient dual-range final drive automatic transmission.

"Don't tell Jay we put this in the book. He never liked it."

YAMAHA
When you know how they're built.

To make sure you have the most fun on our moped, make sure you ride safely. Wear a helmet, proper eye protection and appropriate apparel.

"It was really exciting. The offices on Olympic were getting rundown. The neighborhood was so-so, you know, the middle of nowhere. It was okay, but it wasn't great. So to really move downtown and be at the beginning of downtown developing was exciting. And the Biltmore was at the forefront of it all."

Put this on your ceiling and pretend you're at the Biltmore.

SAN FRANCISCO PERSONALITIES SPEAK-
ING FOR BAY AREA RAPID TRANSIT.
ATTORNEY MELVIN BELLI STANDING IN
BART STATION.
BELLI: I have here before me unim-
peachable evidence that BART
now runs on Saturday.
TRAIN PASSES BEHIND HIM.
BELLI: The defense rests.

CAMERA OPENS ON RABBI STEPPING
OUT OF BART CAR.
ANNCR VO: For Bart, Rabbi
Herbert Morris.
RABBI: Bart's now running a Satur-
day Service. We've been doing that
for over 5,000 years.

*"We had a rabbi all lined up
and two days before the shoot,
he cancelled, said he just
couldn't do it. And so, I just
went through the Yellow Pages
and called up every synagogue
and finally found this rabbi.
He just showed up at the shoot,
and he was great."*

ⅢⅢ ⅢⅢ

"When do they put on my door?"

One morning, Jay Chiat gets off the elevator and takes a look around. He and Guy opened this office with thirty people. Now there are a hundred. On top of that, the building is falling apart.

It is time to move.

Somewhere in these crowded corridors sits an art director, frustrated. Honda is about to launch a new motorcycle campaign, he has been trying to do something great for Yamaha, and now he has to stop. He has to go down to one of the companies that prints up Chiat/Day's ads and check to make sure everything looks okay.

He gets there, and as he is looking down at his own work, something else catches his eye.

It is an ad that reads, "Honda. Follow the Leader."

By accident, he has fallen into Honda's new campaign. He goes back to the office a new man. He knows that in a month or so, Honda will have painted their new theme line all over the world. The only question is, how do you attack it?

He writes it on a piece of paper and stares at it and stares at it. He finally takes it to another art director and asks what he would say in response to "Follow the leader."

"How about 'Don't follow anyone'? Doesn't that make more sense?" the art director answers, simultaneously coming up with Yamaha's new battle cry, and disproving the notion that only copywriters can make up usable headlines.

They immediately shoot an outdoor board, and the media department spends an enjoyable week making sure that the Yamaha billboards are placed right behind the Honda billboards.

Within a month, everywhere you look is a smiling Honda guy with his bike and his girl and the line "Follow the leader." And right next to them, there is this balls-out, bad-ass looking bike, parked at this mean angle which makes the picture almost kind of evil, with the suggestion, "Don't follow anyone."

Honda executives are thrown into double apoplexy when "Don't follow anyone" billboards are erected on all roads leading to their offices.

Back at Chiat/Day, Jay has decided to open a branch office in San Francisco, mostly because National Semiconductor is moving its consumer products division there. It is called Novus, and it is a six million dollar account. He takes a small office situated over a European restaurant, and Chiat/Day San Francisco is born.

At the same time, he calls one of his new accounts, the Biltmore Hotel. It is a grand old hotel in downtown Los Angeles, both of which are in the midst of renovation. He has decided they both have the right feel to become Chiat/Day's new home.

The owner of the Biltmore is an architect, and at their first meeting, he asks Jay, "Do we really want to do offices with doors, or do we want to do something more exciting?" He has been reading about offices with no doors and low walls, where everyone is more or less out in the open. The idea is to create more interaction, less isolation, and more energy. "Let's try it," Jay says.

After the Biltmore, Chiat/Day will never build an office any other way.

FINALLY, AN ECONOMY BIKE YOU WON'T BE ASHAMED TO BE SEEN ON.

Pick up a free "How to buy a Motorcycle" booklet at your Yamaha dealer. Or write: Yamaha "How to buy" Booklet, 1349 West 166th St., Gardena, Ca. 90247.

The trouble with most economy motorcycles is that they look like economy motorcycles.

And they act like economy motorcycles.

Our new Exciter I, on the other hand, is as long on styling and performance as it is on economy.

The low, two-tier seat, for example, not only adds to an extra-comfortable ride, it allows you to put your feet squarely on the ground when you come to a stop. The graceful, pullback handlebars reach back to you. And the sleek, teardrop tank and chopped megaphone pipes make the Exciter's looks as impressive as its performance.

Speaking of which, the 249cc engine gives you all the muscle you can handle. But you don't need a lot of muscle to handle it. And the Exciter I sports a few amenities you might not expect to find on an economy bike. An electric starter. Transistor controlled ignition. Even a handy steering lock.

Maintenance is minimal. And gas mileage is phenomenal. Over 75 miles per gallon.* That's a long way to go on our good looks.

YAMAHA
When you know how they're built.

AFTER WE REFINED THIS MOTORCYCLE, WE REFINED THE REFINEMENTS.

While other motorcycle manufacturers have been busy imitating our Specials, we've been busy too.

Improving them.

And nothing demonstrates those improvements quite as dramatically as our 1980 XS Eleven Special. A shining example of Yamaha's exclusive "designed in" approach to the way a motorcycle looks. And feels. And performs.

While our competitors are content to take an existing frame, slap on a teardrop tank, stepped seat, pullback handlebars and call it better, we call it an imitation at best.

Our idea of improving the XS Eleven Special was to dedicate two years to altering its frame geometry. Then developing a unique mounting system to integrate seat with frame while reducing the seat height by a whole inch. Designing and re-designing its cast alloy grab rail to become an integral part of the bike's tail configuration. Including a twin bulb taillight to go with it.

We've added dual trailing-caliper, slotted disc brakes in front, with a single, fade resistant slotted disc in the rear. And a full, angled-back instrumentation panel.

What we couldn't improve, we've left well enough alone: our legendary 1101cc, four-cylinder engine. Still the biggest, most powerful four-stroke we make. With four, constant-velocity Mikuni carburetors, TCI, and our exclusive vacuum advance system.

Plus a fully enclosed, direct-coupling shaft drive and short-throw, constant-mesh five-speed transmission.

The result: a motorcycle that feels as good as it looks. And looks as good as it performs.

A motorcycle worthy of being called a Special. And a Yamaha.

YAMAHA
When you know how they're built.

INTRODUCING THE LATEST YAMAHA TECHNOLOGY MIXED WITH A LITTLE BLACK MAGIC.

What you see here is the incredible new Yamaha Midnight Special. The ultimate synthesis of styling and technical sophistication. A motorcycle, for the most part, built by hand, employing production innovations that have never been used before.

The frame, for instance, is hand welded using an argon process instead of conventional CO₂ gas welding. Smooth, even welds are the result.

To achieve the rich lustre of our black chrome and to keep the muffler from discoloring at normal operating temperatures, we developed a costly four-step plating process. The final step is cal polishing, again by hand, for a deeper, richer, blacker black.

From the black of the engine to the deep, glossy, triple-baked black that graces the tank, fenders, and side covers, a Midnight Special's finish is, quite simply, a labor of love.

What isn't meticulously black is meticulously gold. Gold gas cap, etched name plate, grab rail, and a pair of gold one-piece alloy wheels. Beautiful, durable gold plating that looks like the real thing because we used 24K gold as the standard.

The XS Eleven Midnight Special boasts a four-cylinder power plant that's the biggest we've ever put in a production machine. The XS850 Midnight Special sports our awesome three-cylinder engine. And both bikes offer the turbine-like propulsion of shaft-drive.

Hurry down to your Yamaha Dealer to see our most Special Specials, because they're very limited in quantity.

For a good reason.

When you take this much extra time and care to build a motorcycle, you just can't build that many.

YAMAHA
When you know how they're built.

"When Honda bikes were probably spending a lot more money, all of a sudden Yamaha would do a great eight-page insert and that might be the only ad that ran for three months. But everybody saw that insert."

"The funniest bit was every year they rented a track and held a ride day for the agency. The agency Ride Day. All the manufacturers held a similar day for their agencies. But they finally stopped it, because the day after there were so many people in the hospital. It would decimate the creative department. You'd look around and say, 'Where's so and so,' and they're off in a ditch someplace, moaning and groaning."

DT125/175

XT250/TT250

YZ490

SR500

TT500/XT500

XS650 SPECIAL

"Chiat/Day has always prided itself on the notion that no job was too big or too small for the senior people to work on, and that strategy was definitely put into play on those brochures."

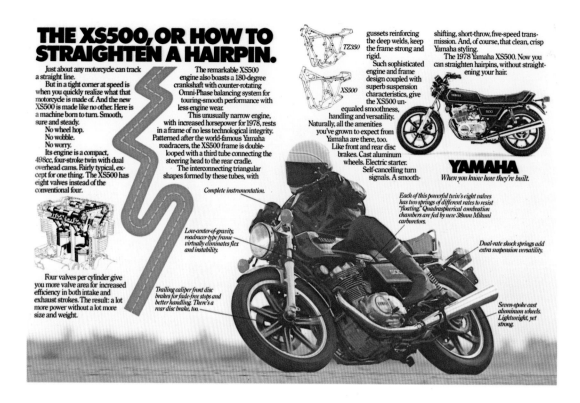

"It was a terrific account to work on. Their attitude was pretty much, 'You know the market, you convince me that you're right and I'll let you do it.' That was, I forget the man's name, but he was the very first Japanese man that we dealt with at Yamaha. He lasted three years, and when he left he told us that one of the things he enjoyed most about the relationship was that we didn't say 'yes.' We had a point of view and fought for it."

EVERY TIME WE RACE, YOU WIN.

At Yamaha our most important research and development work isn't done by theory-loving engineers in white lab coats. It's done by go-for-broke racers in helmets and leathers.

We believe the fastest, most thorough way to see if our R&D ideas work is to let the fastest riders test them. And the quickest way to come up with new ideas is to ask the men who want to be even quicker.

Like two-time World Grand Prix champion Kenny Roberts. No one can push a motorcycle to its limits like Roberts can. In one two-hundred-mile road race, he can prove more about the soundness of our engineering innovations than we can in two thousand miles of road testing.

And every time Kenny rolls into the pits he's got some ideas on how to make even better suspension systems, transmissions, brakes and engines.

Bob Hannah and Broc Glover run our YZ's into the ground every Sunday. Then, before they've even dusted themselves off, they suggest things that might make their motocross machines even better. Obviously they know what they're talking about. "Hurricane" Hannah has won three straight Supercross titles and two straight 250cc National championships. And Broc has raced his 125cc YZ Monoshocker to three straight National titles.

That's a lot of number one plates on Yamahas. Team Yamaha is the winningest combination of motorcycle racers one factory has ever had. And a very big reason why we build the most advanced motorcycles in the world.

At Yamaha we don't build great motorcycles just to win races. We win races so we can build great motorcycles.

YAMAHA
When you know how they're built.

FUNNY, IT DOESN'T LOOK LIKE A YAMAHA.

That's because Ron Teson, master builder of top-fuel drag bikes, got a hold of it.

When Ron came to us with a sound engineering proposal for a new dragster, we gave him a production-line XS11 engine and a plane ticket to the NHRA Nationals in Indianapolis.

He repaid us by building this track-scorching monster. And setting a new ET world record of 7.57 seconds at 183.67 mph.

Actually, it was rider Jim Bernard who piloted Teson's master-piece and won the record. (Ron has the good sense to build them, not ride them.) And he set the new ET mark in only the fourth competitive meet for the bike—long before most machines are close to being dialed in.

A SLICK INNOVATION.

Even though Jim is the brave one, Ron's idea to start with an XS11 was pretty daring in its own right. No one had ever before used one of our engines for the guts of a top-fuel dragster.

So the other manufacturers were a little surprised to see a bike with "Yamaha" on the side at the starting line. They were dumb-founded when it ran the quickest quarter-mile by a motorcycle. Ever.

But our XS11 seemed like a logical choice to Teson. First, it has a larger displacement than most of the engines usually used in drag bikes. Yet it's relatively light. Second, he thought the XS11's sturdy internal parts (one-piece crank, very strong stock valves, etc.) would stand up better to supercharged speeds and pressures.

WE'VE STOPPED SPINNING OUR WHEELS.

We're sure glad we listened to Ron when he came to us. Because of his inspired engineering and Jim Bernard's dare-devil riding, Yamaha has earned a name in the world of top-fuel drag racing.

The same name we've earned in motocross and roadracing: number one.

YAMAHA
When you know how they're built.

"With the incomparable flavor of honeydew."

The creative department is gathered in the conference room for a very exciting occasion. Suntory International, a Chiat/Day client and maker of the excellent Suntory Royal Whiskey, is ready to introduce a new product in America. It is a liqueur made from honeydew melons, which, the client explains, are very scarce and expensive in Japan, and are recognized as a delicacy.

Glasses are lined up, some bright green Midori Melon Liqueur is poured into each one, and they are passed out among the creative people. They all sample it at about the same time. The creative director is the first to speak.

"You know, this has quite an off-putting taste," he says, in fewer words.

The room concurs.

He tells the client that they are making a big mistake. Chiat/Day has marketed many new products, and this is one that the American public will simply not accept. Now everyone gives their opinions. It tastes like the stuff they put on snow cones. It is the worst drink they've ever tried. One copywriter, who wrote the headline "Slightly East of Scotch" for Suntory Whiskey, suggests the line "Slightly East of Scope."

The client insists that they are wrong. This is a wonderful, versatile liqueur, and if it is advertised well, it will be a success.

The agency goes to work, and comes up with this strategy: we've got to mix this stuff with something, because no one's going to drink it out of the bottle.

Thus, the birth of the Midori Melonball. Two parts Midori, one part vodka, four parts orange juice.

And the Midori Colada.

And the Midori/Milk.

And the Midori Margarita.

You can even send away for a recipe book to learn how to make a Midori Melon Cake.

The client is right, the creatives are wrong. Midori Melon Liqueur becomes a huge success.

Actually, it's bigger than that. It's a runaway success. A bonanza. Midori Melon climbs to number three in the entire liqueur category. It spawns so many imitators that within months, Midori adds the word "Original" to their label, and Chiat/Day begins to promote the drink as "The Original Melon Liqueur."

Up in San Francisco, Novus is a bust. National Semiconductor is closing their consumer products division, without whom the San Francisco office becomes a losing proposition. Plus, the place has roaches from the restaurant downstairs. The branch is closed.

Suntory, in the meantime, wants to move their account to New York. Jay goes to New York to check things out, and one night has dinner with one of Chiat/Day's art directors, who is in town on a shoot.

"What are you gonna do?" the art director asks.

Jay's downplaying the whole thing. He'll have to find a creative director, and he's having a hard time, because he doesn't wanna hire a guy from New York because, all of a sudden, it'll be a New York agency and that's not what we are and that's not how we'll succeed.

"I think I want to bring somebody from L.A. to New York," Jay says, chewing some food. "What about you?"

It is as close to a formal wooing as one gets at Chiat/Day, so the art director says, "I'll go if you go."

They return to Los Angeles, and start packing.

How to go through a bottle of Midori.

For starters, follow these tasty directions.

And when our unique flavor of fresh honeydew bewitches your imagination, write for our free recipe book. It will guide you in style through many bottles of imported Midori Melon Liqueur.

Midori Rocks
Pour Midori Liqueur over ice, add a squeeze of lime.

Midori Colada: 2 oz. Midori Liqueur 1 oz. Rum, 6 oz. Piña Colada Mix Mix in blender.

Midori Cooler
1 oz. Midori Liqueur 2 oz. Club Soda Pour Midori into tall glass filled with ice. Add soda and stir.

Midori Daiquiri
1 oz. Midori Liqueur ½ oz. White Rum 1 oz. Sweet & Sour Mix. Blend and pour.

Midori Sour
1 oz. Midori Liqueur 2 oz. Sweet & Sour Mix Blend and strain.

Melonball: 2 oz. Midori Liqueur 1 oz. Vodka Orange Juice In a tall glass, add Midori and Vodka over ice. Fill glass with orange juice and stir.

Midori. The Original Melon Liqueur.

OPEN ON PLANE CABIN CROWDED WITH PASSENGERS.

ANNCR VO: These days, a lot of airlines are crowding more seats into their planes.

PASSENGER LEANS BACK, SEAT LANDS IN THE LAP OF PASSENGER BEHIND HIM.

ANNCR VO: . . . less room for people.

PASSENGER LOWERS NEWSPAPER TO REVEAL HIS KNEES UNDER HIS CHIN.

CUT TO ALASKA AIRLINE PLANE, WHERE PASSENGER IS RELAXING IN COMFORT.

ANNCR VO: But at Alaska Airlines, we don't cramp your style. That way you can sit back, relax and fly with a happy face.

CUT TO AERIAL FOOTAGE, SUPER TITLES.

FLIGHT ATTENDANT: Munchie time!

FLIGHT ATTENDANT WALKS DOWN PLANE AISLE HANDING BOXES OF FOOD TO PASSENGERS. CUT TO PASSENGER #1 OPENING HIS BOX.

PASSENGER: This is it?

CUT TO PRIEST ALSO OPENING HIS BOX.

ANNCR VO: Has your airline lost its taste for food?

CUT TO PASSENGER #2 STEALING LUNCH FROM SLEEPING PASSENGER NEXT TO HIM. CUT BACK TO PASSENGER #1, STILL IN DISBELIEF OVER CONTENTS OF BOX.

PASSENGER: This is it?

CUT TO MAN #2 OPENING BOX HE HAS STOLEN. HE FROWNS IN DISGUST OVER CONTENTS. PRIEST OPENS HIS BOX, CLOSES IT. SIGHS AND PRAYS. CUT BACK TO PASSENGER #1, STILL IN DISBELIEF.

PASSENGER: Evidently, this *is* it.

CUT TO BEAUTY SHOT OF ALASKA AIRLINES FOOD.

ANNCR VO: Next trip, try Alaska Airlines' Gold Coast Service.

CUT TO AERIAL FOOTAGE OF PLANE, SUPER TITLES.

ANNCR VO: It'll leave a good taste in your mouth.

LANDESBERG: I know it's been a while since I started saying if you call someone long distance, right now, you can save plenty. Well, maybe you've been calling your friends more, but not here. But that's okay. I have another proposition for you. If you call someone long distance this minute, not only will you save plenty, but you'll avoid the Christmas rush. So call now, okay? 'Cause I'm going on vacation.

SFX: Telephone ring.

LANDESBERG: Hello? Hi Mom. Vacation. I'm going to Cleveland, you wanna come?

SFX: Jiggling dial tone button.

LANDESBERG: Hello? Mom?

LANDESBERG (TO TELEPHONE): Ring...! (TO CAMERA) Hello. For those of you who didn't get the message the first time, you can call long distance anywhere in the United States and save 40%. SPOKESMAN LIFTS RECEIVER OFF HOOK, HOLDS IT TOWARD CAMERA.

LANDESBERG: Call your Uncle Horace in Arkansas. (gruff Arkansas accent) Yeah, we got a good football team. A lot of these boys, though, are afraid of gettin' hurt. They're afraid of pain, I say you got to play with pain, so I smack some of 'em around, I, uh, use a mallet, give 'em a little taste of it. All right, I'm busy now, I gotta go. Call now.

SPOKESMAN FINALLY HANGS UP. LOOKS AT CAMERA.

₥₥₥₥₥₥ II

"Who the hell are these Artesians, anyway?"

The Olympia Brewing Company has asked Chiat/Day to send a few people up to their offices in Tumwater, Washington. Olympia is a local brand whose popularity once stretched up and down the western United States. Recently, they have failed in an attempt to rollout nationally, and in trying to reposition themselves as a national brand, they have lost their cachet as a good local beer.

The copywriter, art director, and account executive fly up to Tumwater, arrive a litle early, and stop to have some lunch in a local coffee shop. They start talking about what Olympia beer has going for it, and about the only thing they can come up with is its water—something called Artesian brewing water.

None of them know what Artesian brewing water is, who the Artesians are, if there actually are Artesians anywhere, and if there are, how they manage to brew up all that water.

None of them know, so they all start to make stuff up. Artesians. They're these mythical little creatures who come from Artesia. They drive on the Artesian freeway. They're big. They're little. They're mean. They're friendly.

Eventually, the check comes.

When they get to Olympia, they are shown a barrage of research. One graph looks more depressing than the next. In fact, the only category in which Olympia comes in first in is something like "Most Hated Beer." They want Chiat/Day to do something creative; anything, really, that will drive up awareness.

On the plane ride home, the copywriter, art director, and account executive keep coming back to the Artesians. And within a couple of days, they have a whole campaign. They call Olympia and say, "If you want to see something truly unusual, we're ready to have a meeting." Although they bring some backup campaigns, they propose the advertising that will be built around a group of mythical characters that will never be shown, will never even be described. Olympia buys it.

Chiat/Day produces the commercials, and what amazes everyone most when the campaign breaks isn't how the spots have turned out, but that the Artesians have seemingly taken on a life all their own.

The art director is the first to notice this, when he is driving home from work one night and spots an "I brake for Artesians" bumper sticker on the car in front of him.

Radio stations get phone calls with Artesian sightings. Draw-an-Artesian contests spring up. Tons of people send in letters with their artistic renditions. Comedians start making Artesian jokes.

The Artesians grow to be so popular that when the creative team shoots a commercial about a couple named Delbert and Martha Clow who claim to have been taken prisoner by Artesians, the commercial gets killed because focus groups are incensed that an ad agency would even think of accusing the Artesians of forcing people to live in captivity.

The success of the campaign is eventually the death of it, as the Olympia brand grows to the point where it is sold to a major beer company which does not believe in Artesians.

In New York, Jay finds a few empty rooms in the back of Bantam Books which will serve as a Chiat/Day office for a few months. At the same time, he buys a San Francisco ad agency called Hoefer, Dietrich, and Brown, which will become Chiat/Day San Francisco. He believes that the first office failed because San Francisco is in many ways an old school town, and that with the help of an agency that is already well connected, Chiat/Day will succeed there.

With three offices in place, Jay Chiat will spend most of 1980 in the air, traveling from office to office.

One morning, he will come down, and pick up an issue of Advertising Age. He will see that his agency has been named the 1980 Agency of the Year.

MOUNTAIN MAN: I've been drinkin' Olympia beer goin' on forty...oh, forty-one years now. Heard tell about that Artesian brewing water they use. Ain't never seen no Artesians. Don't know what they do...but whatever it is, sure makes that beer taste good. If I ever do meet an Artesian, I want to shake his hand...if'n, uh, he's got hands.

NIGHT MAN: Evenin.' I'm the night vatmaster here at the Olympia Brewery. I expect you've heard about the Artesian brewing water we use. Well...I seen 'em...the Artesians. They come up late at night. Little wet footprints all over. I let 'em be though. I figure...what...what those Artesians do for the taste Oly...I don't want to make 'em mad.

"One lady tried to sue us 'cause she said she'd thought of the Artesians first. I actually had to give a deposition saying that we never saw this woman before in our lives."

GARDENER: I'm your gardener here at the Olympia Brewery. You know that Artesian brewing water that makes Olympia Beer taste so good: Well, it, uh, hasn't hurt my begonias either. 'Course some folks don't believe in Artesians. But I do. I've talked to 'em. I like 'em. I like everything about 'em. SPRINKLERS COME ON, SOAKING HIM.

GARDENER: 'Cept their sense of humor.

DELMER: We are Delmer and Martha

MARTHA: . . . Clow . . .

DELMER: . . . Clow. In 1979, we were taken by the Artesians and spent sixteen . . .

MARTHA: . . . thirteen . . .

DELMER: . . . months living with them. They are an interesting people with rather large feet.

MARTHA: . . . small . . .

DELMER: When we left, we promised to always drink Olympia Beer because the Arteisan brewing water makes it taste so good.

MARTHA: Also, they still have our two children, Harold and Annette.

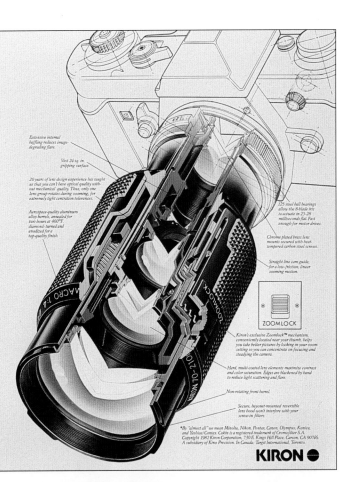

OPEN ON STREET CONSTRUCTION SITE IN WHICH WE SEE
A GROUP OF WORKERS. AN INTERVIEWER STEPS INTO
CAMERA AND ASKS THE WORKER IN FRONT A QUESTION.

INTERVIEWER: Excuse me, Sir. Excuse me, Sir. Uh,
hi. What do you do for a living?

CUT TO WORKER.

WORKER: I'm a brain surgeon.

BACK TO FULL SCENE.

INTERVIEWER: Ah, yes. Do you watch TV?

WORKER: Hey, fellas. Do I watch TV?

OTHER WORKERS: Yuck, yuck . . . Hey, hey . . .

WORKER: Only when I'm not brain surgeonon.

OTHER WORKERS DROP TOOLS AND MOVE UP BEHIND
MAIN WORKER

INTERVIEWER: Oh, ha-ha, that's very cute sir.
Anyway, we're asking TV experts, like yourself,
which of these color TV's you prefer.

A GIRL PULLS A DOLLY WITH THREE COVERED TELEVI-
SIONS ON IT INTO CAMERA.

WORKER: That one.

CUT TO WORKER AND INTERVIEWER.

INTERVIEWER: Because it doesn't take an electronics wizard to see the difference in ours.

WORKER: That one.

INTERVIEWER: Go ahead, sir, and please be honest.

CUT TO SHOT OVER TELEVISIONS OF WORKER AND
INTERVIEWER.

WORKER: That one!

INTERVIEWER: uh-huh, can you read the name
on the set?

GIRL LIFTS COVER OFF OF ONE OF THE THREE TELE-
VISION SETS.

WORKER: Sure I can read the name on the set.
There ain't no name on the set.

CUT TO WORKER AND INTERVIEWER.

WORKER: There's some kinda funny lookin' initials
on it though. Uh, M-G-A.

CUT TO FRONT VIEW OF WORKER AND INTERVIEWER.

INTERVIEWER: Right.

WORKER: Umga?

INTERVIEWER: uh, M-G-A.

CUT TO SHOT AS IF ENTIRE SCENE IS ON A MGA
TELEVISION.

INTERVIEWER: And another TV expert picks MGA
because seeing is believing.

WORKER: Hey-hey, what's a Umga?

INTERVIEWER: Ah, ha-ha...

WORKER: What's a Umga?

INTERVIEWER: Cut.

Welcome, IBM.

Seriously.

Welcome to the most exciting and important marketplace since the computer revolution began 35 years ago.

And congratulations on your first personal computer.

Putting real computer power in the hands of the individual is already improving the way people work, think, learn, communicate and spend their leisure hours.

Computer literacy is fast becoming as fundamental a skill as reading or writing.

When we invented the first personal computer system, we estimated that over 140,000,000 people worldwide could justify the purchase of one, if only they understood its benefits.

Next year alone, we project that well over 1,000,000 will come to that understanding. Over the next decade, the growth of the personal computer will continue in logarithmic leaps.

We look forward to responsible competition in the massive effort to distribute this American technology to the world. And we appreciate the magnitude of your commitment.

Because what we are doing is increasing social capital by enhancing individual productivity.

Welcome to the task. apple

Apple Computer Inc., 10260 Bandley Dr., Cupertino, CA 95014

⊬⊬⊬⊬⊬⊬⊬⊬ ⊬⊬⊬⊬⊬ |||

"Y'know, Apple didn't happen overnight. It took four years."

Jay Chiat sits in the New York office, spelling his name. He is on the phone like this a good part of every day, looking for new business in New York, listening to receptionists and secretaries and everybody else twist the name "Chiat" a hundred ugly ways, so he is constantly correcting, spelling, correcting, spelling.

So much for being a hot west coast shop. So much for being agency of the year. So much for thirteen years in the business.

An office away, on the other side of a partition, a young copywriter sits, listening to his boss spelling. He hears all the calls, knows the frustrations. When you told someone in L.A. that you worked at Chiat/Day, they were impressed. In New York, you tell someone you work at Chiat/Day, and before you know it, you're spelling.

Finding new business is one problem today; keeping new business is another. In San Francisco, they've had an account for only two months, and there are already complications: the client does not think any of the writers he has met are right for his business. Jay acquired the client, a company called Apple Computer, by purchasing the advertising department of a small Palo Alto public relations firm. Apple has a product that few people understand or have ever seen before. It is called a personal computer, and it can do so many things, it is almost impossible to find one simple way to describe it. It has been even harder to find a writer who understands computers well enough to write about them.

Even though Apple isn't a large account, it is a very important one. Apple is a company that might truly change the world, and its young president is someone who wants to do great advertising. If Chiat/Day is the ad agency that successfully introduces a new technology to America, then Chiat/Day could become one of the best known ad agencies in the country. If Chiat/Day becomes well known on any one account, all of its offices would benefit.

But before any of this can happen, what is needed is a copywriter.

An office away, the young copywriter is doing a trade ad for Fotomat. He has an enormous fondness for anything with batteries or a plug—stereos, cameras, pocket calculators, video games, remote-controlled tanks—if it's got current going through it, he likes it. Jay comes in and sits down. "What do you know about computers?" he asks. "I worked on Mits; I worked on Altair," the writer answers. Mits and Altair were trying to make personal computers back when Apple was still two guys working in a garage. The copywriter has also worked on everything from Bell and Howell remittance processing machinery to general automation computers to monogrammed chemical toilets for private aircraft ("Your head in the clouds.")

Jay decides this: he'll send the copywriter to San Francisco for a couple of weeks and let him do some ads. He still needs him in New York (except for a junior copywriter, he's the only writer there,) so he won't introduce him to the client. In the meantime, he'll find a new writer to work on Apple.

A couple of months go by. Apple is starting to buy the work, the copywriter is commuting between San Francisco and New York, Chiat/Day still hasn't found someone full time, and Apple's president says he wants to know who's going to be working on his advertising, and he wants to know now. So one day, Jay comes into the copywriter's office and says, I have to introduce you to the president of Apple. The copywriter says, I thought you wanted me in the background. Jay says, no, we haven't found anybody else, they're having an Apple show over at the Hilton, the guy is there, let's go over and meet him.

The New York Hilton. Hordes of people at the show. There is pushing. There is shoving. There is a fire in the hotel somewhere, so there are firemen. And in the middle of everything is Apple's twenty-five year old president, being jostled by the crowd, making small talk with the copywriter. They talk about Altair, they talk

113

about computers, they talk about classical music, and the next thing the copywriter knows, he's going to dinner that night at the Four Seasons with Jay and three people from Apple.

At dinner, the copywriter is nervous. He understands that this is The Dinner. He sits next to the president, who is a few years younger than he is, and lights a cigarette.

"If you're so smart, how come you smoke?" the president asks.

He takes a few puffs and puts out the cigarette. Then, the president says, "So, Jay tells me you're their best writer. Is that true?" Gee, the copywriter thinks, Jay never told me anything like that, they don't even let me out of the office. But he says, "If that's what Jay thinks," and smiles politely.

A few courses come and go, and dinner is going well. They are all talking about the potential of Apple, and Jay remarks on how amazing it is that Apple is already a 700-million dollar company with the eyes of the world upon it.

"Y'know, Apple didn't happen overnight," the twenty-five year old across the table explains to him. "It took four years."

At the end of the evening, the copywriter hails a cab while his boss and the Apple president exchange goodbyes. The cab comes, the copywriter gets in, and Jay slides in next to him. As they pull away from the curb, Jay turns to the young man and punches him in the arm.

"He likes you! He likes you!" he says. Then Mr. Chiat leans back and watches as the traffic lights of the city change from red to green, red to green, all the way home.

MALE ANNCR: If you do your business planning with pencil, paper and calculator, get a load of this . . . An Apple Personal Computer can be an electronic worksheet . . . you can change one figure and it automatically changes all the totals, so revisions are no problem . . . and it's easy to ask; what if? Always a magical question. For instance, uh . . . what if Apple sales don't go up after this commercial

SFX: Computer buzzes.

MALE ANNCER: Oh, I see . . .

ANNCR VO: Apple, the Personal Computer.

MALE ANNCR: I'm learning to use an Apple for text editing . . . which is useful . . . some of my texts could use some editing . . . You can edit right here on the screen . . . you can add words like this . . . or you can move paragraphs around to anywhere you want them . . . Amazing. You can use the very same Apple to do a zillion other things . . . You could say that the Apple is mightier than the pen . . . hmmmm . . .

ANNCR VO: Apple, the Personal Computer.

Baked Apple.

Last Thanksgiving, a designer from Lynn/Ohio Corporation took one of the company's Apple Personal Computers home for the holidays.

While he was out eating turkey, it got baked.

His cat, perhaps miffed at being left alone, knocked over a lamp which started

a fire which, among other unpleasantries, melted his TV set all over his computer. He thought his goose was cooked.

But when he took the Apple to Cincinnati Computer Store, *mirabile dictu,* it still worked.

A new case and keyboard made it as good as new.

Nearly 1,000 Apple dealers have complete service centers that can quickly fix just about anything that might go wrong, no matter how bizarre.

So if you're looking for a personal computer that solves problems instead of creating them, look to your authorized Apple dealer.

You'll find everything well-done.

The personal computer.

For the authorized dealer nearest you, call (800) 538-9696. In California, call (800) 662-9238. Or write: Apple Computer Inc., 10260 Bandley Dr., Cupertino, CA 95014.

"We had hired a new account supervisor on Apple, so I took him to Steve Jobs and said, 'I'd like you to meet your new account supervisor.' And Jobs looked at him and said, 'What do you do?' He said, 'Well I'm the management supervisor on the Apple account. I'm going to run your business.' Jobs says 'No, what do you do?' The guy says, 'Well I'm an account person basically. I, um… I….' Jobs says, 'No, you don't understand. What do you do? Do you draw pictures? Do you write copy? Do you do music? What are you gonna do for me?' And the guy says, 'Well, uh, I'm uh, uh, I'm an account manager. I make sure everything runs smoothly for you.' And Jobs looks at him and says, 'Oh, overhead,' and walked away."

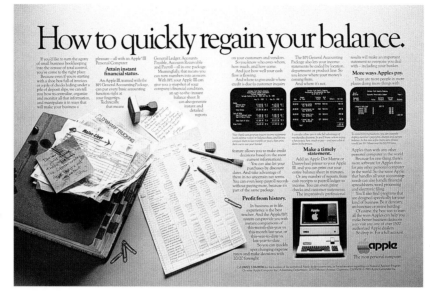

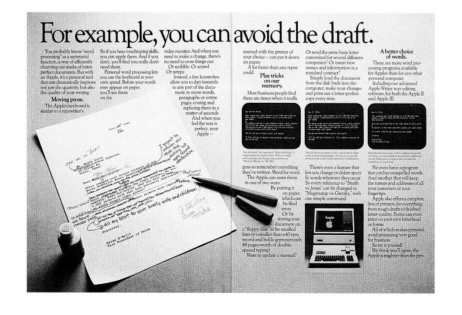

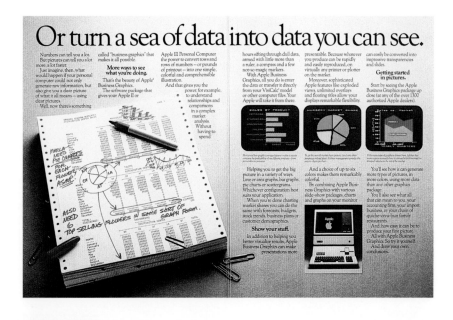

"My ice cream is a lot like me. Sweet but unrefined."
—Gilbert H. Brockmeyer

If you ask most ice cream experts what makes ice cream sweet, they'll say refined sugar. I say baloney.

Thanks to a special blend of orange blossom and clover honeys, my ice cream is the sweetest, smoothest, creamiest I've ever tasted. And it doesn't contain even a smidgen of refined sugar.

True, using only the most natural, best tasting ingredients makes my ice cream cost a little more than most. But if you love ice cream as much as I do, why scrimp?

I don't.

Gilbert H. Brockmeyer's Natural Ice Cream

My 100% natural ice cream contains absolutely no preservatives and no refined sugars.

"I can taste fake vanilla a mile away. And that's as close as it'll ever get to my ice cream."
—Gilbert H. Brockmeyer

They call it Vanillin. Might as well call it Charlie for all it tastes like real vanilla. You see, I use only real vanilla extract from bourbon beans like the ones you see here. Bourbon bean vanilla is the finest that money can buy.

And it tastes like it.

True, using no preservatives, no refined sugars and only the best tasting ingredients makes my ice cream cost a little more than most. But if you love ice cream as much as I do, why scrimp? I don't.

Gilbert H. Brockmeyer's Natural Ice Cream.

My 100% natural ice cream contains absolutely no preservatives and no refined sugars.

BAKED

Alaska Airlines to Los A

"If you like my Raspberry Swirl ice cream, pray for sun in Klamath Falls."
—Gilbert H. Brockmeyer

I take quite a razzing about my raspberries. Mostly from my friends in the ice cream business. They think I'm crazy to go clear to Oregon for raspberries when perfectly good crops grow a lot closer.

But as long as the sweetest, juiciest, best tasting raspberries grow in Oregon, I'll go to Oregon.

True, using only the finest, best tasting ingredients makes my ice cream cost a little more than most. But if you love ice cream as much as I do, why scrimp?

I don't.

Gilbert H. Brockmeyer's Natural™ Ice Cream

My 100% natural ice cream contains absolutely no preservatives and no refined sugars.

"Who says ice cream bars have to be junk food?"
—Gilbert H. Brockmeyer

. I'm appalled. And if you knew the things some people put in ice cream bars, you would be, too.

My ice cream bars are completely natural. They begin with my vanilla ice cream (made with only real Bourbon Bean vanilla). Followed by a thick, rich coating of real carob (from Cyprus, the world's finest). And topped off with a liberal sprinkling of granulated peanuts and crisped rice (my own tasty invention).

True, using no preservatives, no refined sugars and only the best tasting ingredients makes my ice cream bars cost a little more than most. But if you love ice cream as much as I do, why scrimp?

I don't.

Gilbert H. Brockmeyer's Natural™ Ice Cream Bars

My 100% natural ice cream bars are now on sale at Ralph's, Alpha Beta and other fine supermarkets.

ALASKA.

geles and Palm Springs.

WHAT'S A PLACE LIKE FOTOMAT DOING IN A MAGAZINE LIKE THIS?

It takes more than nerve to stand here in front of God and everybody and tell you we've got terrific film and developing.

It takes terrific film. And terrific developing.

The bigger. The better.

If you haven't been to a Fotomat Store since you retired your Brownie, you're in for a big surprise

Big prints. 4"x 6" to be exact.

We call them Series 35 Custom prints. Part of a special 35mm developing service designed to please people as picky as you are.

They're not only 37% bigger than our handsome standard prints. They're better looking, too.

Only our most experienced photofinishers do our Series 35 developing. In a special section of our own Fotomat labs. Taking all the time they need to coax every subtle detail from the best possible negative.

Then, our most finicky inspectors see that you get only the best possible print. In a choice of borderless glossy or studio finish.

And to make sure your negatives continue getting the same special handling we've given them, each strip is individually wrapped.

Series 35 Custom prints do cost a little more.

And it shows.

Film as good as you-know-who's.

For years now, finding good film has been as easy as pointing to little yellow boxes behind a counter.

Our Series 35 envelope is extra-special. It's extra-sturdy, with separate compartments for both negatives and prints.

A special timing matrix in the sensitive layer and interlayer allows our ASA100 film to give you an exceptionally sharp image.

PROFESSIONAL

SERIES35

Series 35 prints aren't just bigger. They're better looking. You'll get brilliant color and clarity. Optimum contrast and density.

In spite of its speed, our ASA400 film gives you an ultra-fine grain that bears up beautifully under enlargement.

Your negatives are individually wrapped. So they continue getting the same special handling we've given them.

Shot with Fotomat 400 ASA film using a Nikon F-3 camera. 58mm lens (F28 @ 1/1000 sec.) and natural North light.

But you can drive into any Fotomat Store and point with the very same finger to our Fotomat film boxes and get the same consistently brilliant, carefully balanced color. Remarkable clarity. Optimum contrast and density.

Both our ASA100 and ASA400 film produce an extremely fine grain. Thanks to something called "precursor" technology: our $10 word for overcoming the speed/granularity trade-off.

It means that a bit of fidgeting with the emulsion's interlayer effect has enabled even our high-speed 400 film to bear up beautifully under enlargement.

In short, our film gives you color prints every bit as good as you-know-who's.

For a price as good as you-know-ours.

Talk's cheap.

We could go on. And on. But if you're worth your weight in 35mm lenses, you won't take our word for the quality of our film and developing.

You'll try our film.

You'll try our developing.

And find out first hand what a place like Fotomat is doing in a magazine like this.

Fotomat
FILM · FOTOMAT · DEVELOPING

ARE YOU BEING TAKEN BY YOUR PICTURES?

Think about it.
Considering what some camera stores and photofinishing labs charge for custom color prints these days, picture taking takes on a whole new meaning.

And the more pictures you take, the more you get taken.

Unless, of course, you take your film to Fotomat.

Custom quality without the custom price.
Like those other places, Fotomat has an extra-special custom developing service called Series 35. But at an extra-special price called a bargain.

Short of exotic hand finishing, you can't get better looking prints.

With our Series 35 developing, your prints not only measure an extra-big 4 X 6 instead of the regular 3½ X 5 (37% bigger), but measure up to the custom quality you're accustomed to paying much more for.

Only our most experienced photofinishers do our Series 35 work. In a separate section of our own Fotomat labs.

They fuss a little more over your negatives. Over the detail. The color. The density. The contrast.

They have to.

Because behind every perfect print, there's an inspector waiting for a print that's less than perfect.

You get your choice of a borderless glossy or studio finish.

And to make sure your negatives continue getting the same special handling we've given them, each strip is individually wrapped.

Series 35 Custom prints do cost more than our regular 35mm prints.

A special timing matrix in the sensitive layer and interlayer allows our ASA100 film to give you an exceptionally sharp image.

Your negatives are individually wrapped. So they continue getting the same special handling we've given them.

Even our Series 35 envelope is extra-special. It's extra-sturdy, with separate compartments for both negatives and prints.

Series 35 prints not only measure an extra-big 4x6, but measure up to the custom quality you're accustomed to paying much more for.

In spite of its speed, our ASA400 film gives you an ultra-fine grain that bears up beautifully under enlargement.

Taken with Fotomat ASA400 film, using a Nikon F-3 camera, 58mm lens (F 4/5.6 @ 1/125 sec.) and natural North light.

And it shows.
But more important, they cost less than most other custom prints.

And it doesn't show.

Film as good as you-know-who's.
While we're on the subject, we'd like to remind you that there's more to picture taking than developing.

There's film. Our film.

The biggest difference between our Fotomat film and that other film you're used to using, is the color of the box.

Both our ASA100 and ASA400 film give your color prints the same brilliant, carefully balanced color, the same clarity, contrast and density as you-know-who's.

For a price as good as you-know-ours.

Don't take us at our word.
If you're worth your weight in 35mm lenses, you certainly won't take our word for the quality of our Series 35 Custom prints. Or our film.

You'll try both. And compare our custom prints to theirs.

But don't be surprised if you can't see a difference.

Because the difference isn't in the print.

It's in the price.

|||||| |||||| ||||

"They couldn't believe how bright we were."

It is December in New York, two weeks before
Christmas. As the year winds down, America's thirst for melon drinks is subsiding, and
Chiat/Day New York finds its back against the
wall. Two and a half years, and they still haven't
won the kind of account that makes people
think you're going to be staying for a while.

They are invited to pitch the ten-million
dollar Holland America cruise line account.
Twelve agencies have been invited to pitch.
Holland America lays the ground rules: The
agencies are to make three presentations. The
first one will be credentials. Several agencies
will be eliminated. The second one will be understanding of the marketplace. Then, more agencies will be eliminated. The third presentation
will be for strategy, positioning, and creative
work. Then, an agency will be chosen.

Jay, an account guy, and the creative director
go to the first presentation. They get by that one,
and soon they get a call telling them that there are
now five agencies left, including two of the biggest, oldest advertising agencies in New York. The
thought of competing with agencies that size is
not a pretty one.

Jay gets together with the people working
on the pitch, which is just about everybody in the
shop, and says this: Personally, I think we can
have a great second meeting. I don't know what
the hell we're gonna do at a third meeting. I mean,
what do you do?

Nobody else knows, either.

He says: Why don't we do this. Let's do the
third meeting at the second meeting. Do all the
strategy, all the positioning, everything at the second meeting. We'll do all the things that we're sup-
posed to be doing at the second meeting, but we'll
have everything else ready.

Well.

Everybody, everybody is working on this
presentation. They do all the ads, in fact, but they
don't want Holland America to know that, so their

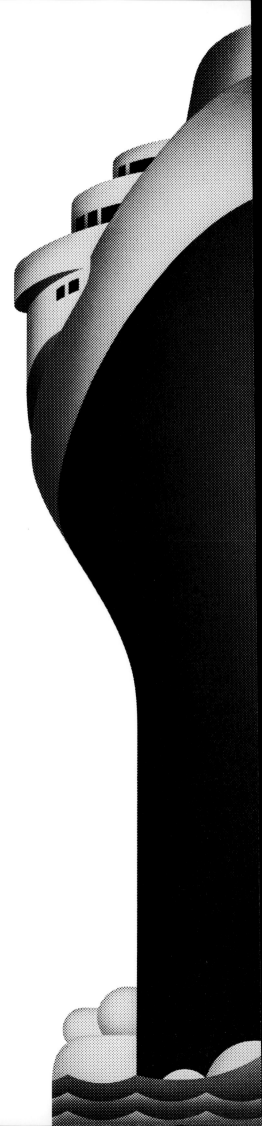

thing is, they're just going to draw magic marker ad ideas during the presentation, like the ads are a natural extension of the discussion.

The presentation comes, and as the meeting progresses, the walls of the room are slowly covered with these pages and pages of great ideas that seem to just keep coming, being drawn up as fast as the Chiat/Day team can think of 'em. The meeting ends politely, with a promise that Jay will be called soon one way or the other.

Now, it's Friday, and Christmas is approaching. The finals, if they make them, are scheduled for the first week in January, which will mean working straight through the holidays. It gives people mixed emotions about even wanting to still be in the pitch. Late in the afternoon, Jay gets the phone call. He sends out his assistant to gather everybody up in the conference room. He's talking to Holland America, she tells them, and she doesn't look too happy.

Everybody who works in the office, which is maybe twenty people, tops, is sitting there for ten, fifteen minutes. Then Jay comes strolling in.

He's got this dour look on his face, and he's talking real quiet, so quiet you can hardly hear him. He says, well, we got the phone call, and they said that they looked at all five presentations, and they were trying to figure out who should be in the finals, and they know that the work is going to have to be done over the holidays, and they feel really bad about doing that, so they decided one of the presentations was really so outstanding, they're not going to have the third meeting, they're just gonna give out the account. And they've decided to give the account to Chiat/Day.

They start to party, and keep going for three days straight.

A few months into the New Year, Jay gets a call from Guy.

"I'm getting bored at home. You need any help?" Guy asks.

"When can you start?" Jay answers.

The Ocean Liner™ vs. the Cruise Ship.

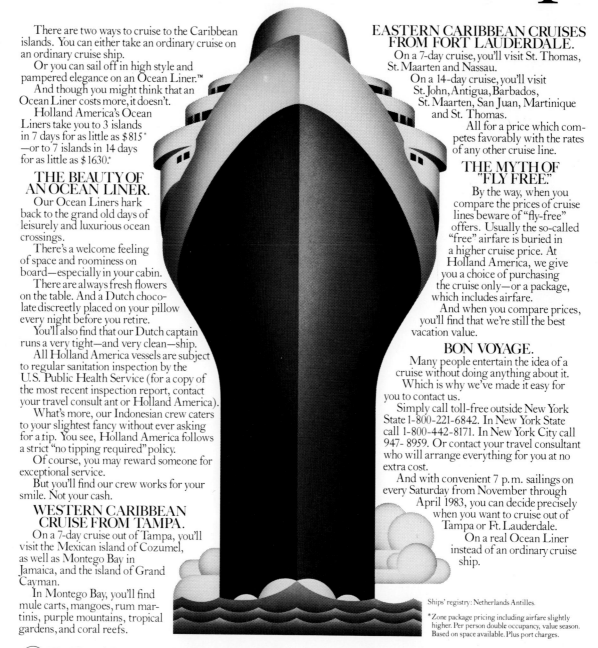

There are two ways to cruise to the Caribbean islands. You can either take an ordinary cruise on an ordinary cruise ship.

Or you can sail off in high style and pampered elegance on an Ocean Liner.™

And though you might think that an Ocean Liner costs more, it doesn't.

Holland America's Ocean Liners take you to 3 islands in 7 days for as little as $815* —or to 7 islands in 14 days for as little as $1630.*

THE BEAUTY OF AN OCEAN LINER.

Our Ocean Liners hark back to the grand old days of leisurely and luxurious ocean crossings.

There's a welcome feeling of space and roominess on board—especially in your cabin.

There are always fresh flowers on the table. And a Dutch chocolate discreetly placed on your pillow every night before you retire.

You'll also find that our Dutch captain runs a very tight—and very clean—ship.

All Holland America vessels are subject to regular sanitation inspection by the U.S. Public Health Service (for a copy of the most recent inspection report, contact your travel consultant or Holland America).

What's more, our Indonesian crew caters to your slightest fancy without ever asking for a tip. You see, Holland America follows a strict "no tipping required" policy.

Of course, you may reward someone for exceptional service.

But you'll find our crew works for your smile. Not your cash.

WESTERN CARIBBEAN CRUISE FROM TAMPA.

On a 7-day cruise out of Tampa, you'll visit the Mexican island of Cozumel, as well as Montego Bay in Jamaica, and the island of Grand Cayman.

In Montego Bay, you'll find mule carts, mangoes, rum martinis, purple mountains, tropical gardens, and coral reefs.

EASTERN CARIBBEAN CRUISES FROM FORT LAUDERDALE.

On a 7-day cruise, you'll visit St. Thomas, St. Maarten and Nassau.

On a 14-day cruise, you'll visit St. John, Antigua, Barbados, St. Maarten, San Juan, Martinique and St. Thomas.

All for a price which competes favorably with the rates of any other cruise line.

THE MYTH OF "FLY FREE."

By the way, when you compare the prices of cruise lines beware of "fly-free" offers. Usually the so-called "free" airfare is buried in a higher cruise price. At Holland America, we give you a choice of purchasing the cruise only—or a package, which includes airfare.

And when you compare prices, you'll find that we're still the best vacation value.

BON VOYAGE.

Many people entertain the idea of a cruise without doing anything about it.

Which is why we've made it easy for you to contact us.

Simply call toll-free outside New York State 1-800-221-6842. In New York State call 1-800-442-8171. In New York City call 947-8959. Or contact your travel consultant who will arrange everything for you at no extra cost.

And with convenient 7 p.m. sailings on every Saturday from November through April 1983, you can decide precisely when you want to cruise out of Tampa or Ft. Lauderdale.

On a real Ocean Liner instead of an ordinary cruise ship.

Ships' registry: Netherlands Antilles.

*Zone package pricing including airfare slightly higher. Per person double occupancy, value season. Based on space available. Plus port charges.

Holland America to the Caribbean

How to select your first cruise.

Everyone knows a cruise can be one of life's most romantic adventures.

But almost nobody knows it can cost less than an ordinary vacation. For as little as $760 per person double occupancy,* you can cruise to Bermuda from New York for 7 days.

All meals included.
All entertainment included.
All service included.

Everything—from moonlit strolls on deck to sun-drowsed days in Bermuda—included.

So now you know the first fact about your first cruise:

You can afford it.

START YOUR VACATION BEFORE YOU GET THERE.

If you ever felt you needed a vacation from a vacation, you're a candidate for a cruise.

It's the most hassle-free vacation on earth, air or sea.

It's also the only vacation that starts before you leave.

From the moment you step on board, you have nothing to organize. Nothing to carry.

All you've got is time to relax. And a willing crew to pamper you every minute you're awake.

So now you know the second fact about your first cruise:

It gives you more of what you take a vacation for. And less of what a vacation takes you for.

YOUR ROOM GOES WITH YOU.

Most vacations suffer from the pack-unpack-pack syndrome.

Not a cruise. You only pack once. Because your room goes with you. All your vacation time is spent having a vacation.

START WITH BERMUDA.

Bermuda is the ideal destination for your first cruise.

Because you can cruise there and back in the perfect time of 7 days.

With its pink sand and crystal water, Bermuda may be the reason the sun shines.

And a Holland America cruise is the best way to enjoy it, because your ship docks right beside Front

Street in the charming port of Hamilton.

A better location than any hotel in Bermuda.

You can shop, explore and disco. Or rent a moped and scoot off to countless beaches.

THE GOOD LIFE GETS BETTER ON BOARD.

People wonder what life is like on a cruise liner.

Think of it as an exciting resort. You dine like royalty. Course after delicious course. Five meals a day, including a Midnight Buffet.

You can play backgammon, bingo, bridge and ping-pong. You can shoot skeet and jog.

Work out in the gym.
Take a dip in the pool.
And drive golf balls off the deck into the sea.

By night, the ship comes alive in a different way.

You can get into the flash of the disco.

Have your own cabin party or join someone else's.

Watch a hit movie.
Try your luck in the casino.
Take a romantic stroll on deck under the stars.

And wake up the next morning in a totally different place.

That's one of the advantages a cruise has over a resort:

You're not stuck with the same view from your room all the time.

IT'S NICE TO HAVE A DUTCH UNCLE.

Our Dutch captain runs a tight ship.

Down to those little touches that make a big difference.

There are always fresh flowers on the table. A Dutch chocolate discreetly placed on your pillow before you retire.

And a standard of cleanliness upheld not only because we're Dutch, but because all Holland America vessels are subject to regular inspection by the U.S. Public Health Service (for a copy of the most recent inspection report contact your travel consultant or Holland America).

Our Indonesian crew is so warm and friendly, you'd swear they were born with smiles on their faces.

And despite the fact that they cater to your slightest fancy, they never ask for a tip.

Holland America follows a strict

"no tipping required" policy. Of course, you can reward someone for absolutely exceptional service.

But you'll find our crew works for your smile. Not your cash.

And our Dutch officers serve you in the great Holland America seafaring tradition of over 100 years.

WHAT TO WEAR ON YOUR FIRST CRUISE.

Plan for two formal evenings. Black tie is never mandatory, but if you're invited to sit at the Captain's Table, you'll want to look your best.

During the day you can wear your favorite casual clothes: bathing suit, shorts, slacks, lightweight cottons, whatever you like.

Since there are no restrictions on luggage, and since you only pack once on a cruise (your room goes with you), feel free to bring your whole wardrobe.

CRUISES END, FRIENDSHIPS DON'T.

What happens to people brought together on a cruise? Amazing things.

We've lost count of the number of marriages made at sea. Or romances that started on board.

New friendships are created every day, because cruise people are so diverse: the marrieds and the singles, the widowed and the young, the retired and the divorced.

Whether you're on your first or second

honeymoon, or looking for a great time, or just want to relax for a week, you'll find who and what you're looking for, even if it's yourself.

THE BEST RESORT IN BERMUDA LEAVES NEW YORK EVERY WEEKEND.

Holland America cruise ships leave New York for Bermuda on Saturdays and Sundays.

The ss Volendam leaves on Sundays and stops at Hamilton and St. George's. Choose from 27 sailing dates, April through October.

The ss Veendam leaves on Saturdays and sails straight to Hamilton, where it docks 4 days. Choose from 30 sailing dates, April through October.

BON VOYAGE.

Many people entertain the idea of a cruise without doing anything about it.

They don't realize how easy it is to call or visit a travel consultant and arrange everything. At no extra cost.

The dates. The times. The rates. All the details. It's as easy as making one phone call—which is the last thing you should know about your first cruise.

Holland America to Bermuda

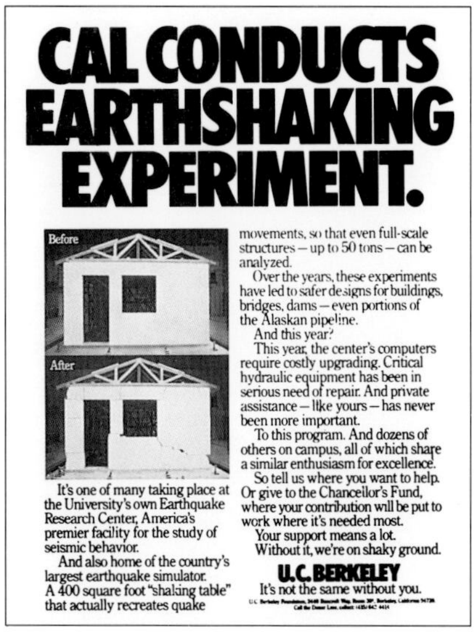
CAL CONDUCTS EARTHSHAKING EXPERIMENT.
Before
After
It's one of many taking place at the University's own Earthquake Research Center, America's premier facility for the study of seismic behavior.
And also home of the country's largest earthquake simulator. A 400 square foot "shaking table" that actually recreates quake
movements, so that even full-scale structures — up to 50 tons — can be analyzed.
Over the years, these experiments have led to safer designs for buildings, bridges, dams — even portions of the Alaskan pipeline.
And this year?
This year, the center's computers require costly upgrading. Critical hydraulic equipment has been in serious need of repair. And private assistance — like yours — has never been more important.
To this program. And dozens of others on campus, all of which share a similar enthusiasm for excellence.
So tell us where you want to help. Or give to the Chancellor's Fund, where your contribution will be put to work where it's needed most.
Your support means a lot.
Without it, we're on shaky ground.
U.C. BERKELEY
It's not the same without you.

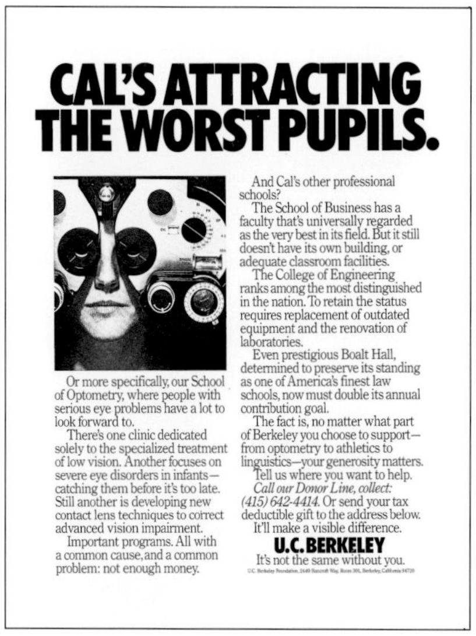
CAL'S ATTRACTING THE WORST PUPILS.
Or more specifically, our School of Optometry, where people with serious eye problems have a lot to look forward to.
There's one clinic dedicated solely to the specialized treatment of low vision. Another focuses on severe eye disorders in infants — catching them before it's too late. Still another is developing new contact lens techniques to correct advanced vision impairment.
Important programs. All with a common cause, and a common problem: not enough money.
And Cal's other professional schools?
The School of Business has a faculty that's universally regarded as the very best in its field. But it still doesn't have its own building, or adequate classroom facilities.
The College of Engineering ranks among the most distinguished in the nation. To retain the status requires replacement of outdated equipment and the renovation of laboratories.
Even prestigious Boalt Hall, determined to preserve its standing as one of America's finest law schools, now must double its annual contribution goal.
The fact is, no matter what part of Berkeley you choose to support — from optometry to athletics to linguistics — your generosity matters.
Tell us where you want to help.
Call our Donor Line, collect: (415) 642-4414. Or send your tax deductible gift to the address below.
It'll make a visible difference.
U.C. BERKELEY
It's not the same without you.

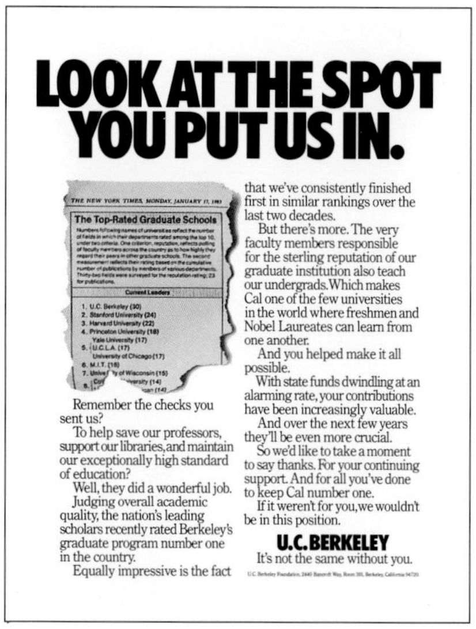
LOOK AT THE SPOT YOU PUT US IN.
The Top-Rated Graduate Schools
Current Leaders
1. U.C. Berkeley (30)
2. Stanford University (24)
3. Harvard University (22)
4. Princeton University (18)
Yale University (17)
5. U.C.L.A. (17)
University of Chicago (17)
6. M.I.T. (16)
7. University of Wisconsin (15)
Remember the checks you sent us?
To help save our professors, support our libraries, and maintain our exceptionally high standard of education?
Well, they did a wonderful job.
Judging overall academic quality, the nation's leading scholars recently rated Berkeley's graduate program number one in the country.
Equally impressive is the fact that we've consistently finished first in similar rankings over the last two decades.
But there's more. The very faculty members responsible for the sterling reputation of our graduate institution also teach our undergrads. Which makes Cal one of the few universities in the world where freshmen and Nobel Laureates can learn from one another.
And you helped make it all possible.
With state funds dwindling at an alarming rate, your contributions have been increasingly valuable.
And over the next few years they'll be even more crucial.
So we'd like to take a moment to say thanks. For your continuing support. And for all you've done to keep Cal number one.
If it weren't for you, we wouldn't be in this position.
U.C. BERKELEY
It's not the same without you.

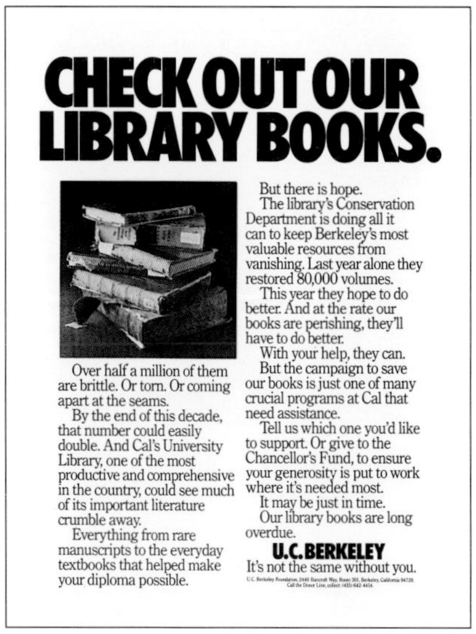
CHECK OUT OUR LIBRARY BOOKS.
Over half a million of them are brittle. Or torn. Or coming apart at the seams.
By the end of this decade, that number could easily double. And Cal's University Library, one of the most productive and comprehensive in the country, could see much of its important literature crumble away.
Everything from rare manuscripts to the everyday textbooks that helped make your diploma possible.
But there is hope.
The library's Conservation Department is doing all it can to keep Berkeley's most valuable resources from vanishing. Last year alone they restored 80,000 volumes.
This year they hope to do better. And at the rate our books are perishing, they'll have to do better.
With your help, they can.
But the campaign to save our books is just one of many crucial programs at Cal that need assistance.
Tell us which one you'd like to support. Or give to the Chancellor's Fund, to ensure your generosity is put to work where it's needed most.
It may be just in time.
Our library books are long overdue.
U.C. BERKELEY
It's not the same without you.

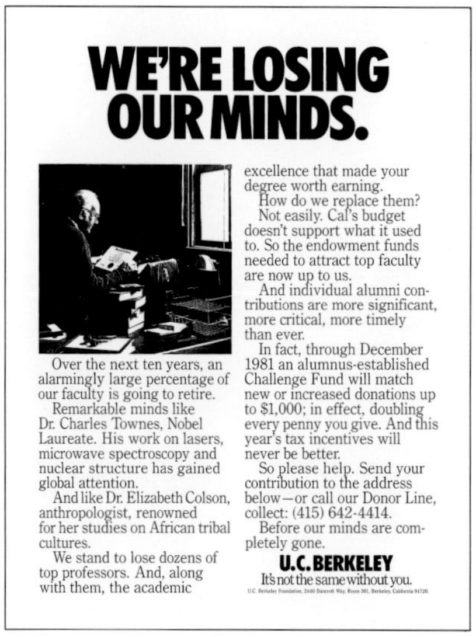
WE'RE LOSING OUR MINDS.
Over the next ten years, an alarmingly large percentage of our faculty is going to retire.
Remarkable minds like Dr. Charles Townes, Nobel Laureate. His work on lasers, microwave spectroscopy and nuclear structure has gained global attention.
And like Dr. Elizabeth Colson, anthropologist, renowned for her studies on African tribal cultures.
We stand to lose dozens of top professors. And, along with them, the academic
excellence that made your degree worth earning.
How do we replace them?
Not easily. Cal's budget doesn't support what it used to. So the endowment funds needed to attract top faculty are now up to us.
And individual alumni contributions are more significant, more critical, more timely than ever.
In fact, through December 1981 an alumnus-established Challenge Fund will match new or increased donations up to $1,000; in effect, doubling every penny you give. And this year's tax incentives will never be better.
So please help. Send your contribution to the address below—or call our Donor Line, collect: (415) 642-4414.
Before our minds are completely gone.
U.C. BERKELEY
It's not the same without you.

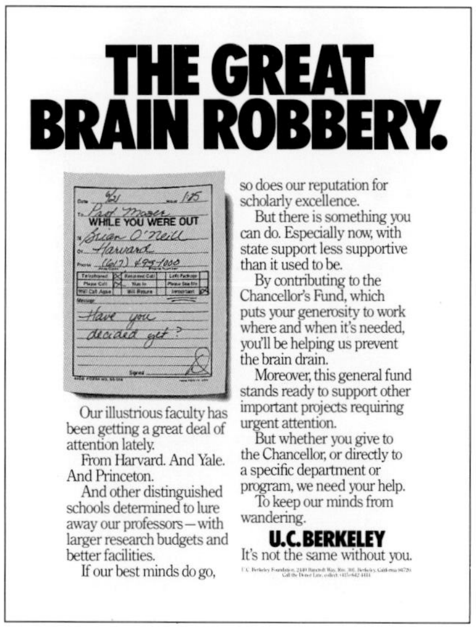
THE GREAT BRAIN ROBBERY.
WHILE YOU WERE OUT
Our illustrious faculty has been getting a great deal of attention lately.
From Harvard. And Yale. And Princeton.
And other distinguished schools determined to lure away our professors — with larger research budgets and better facilities.
If our best minds do go, so does our reputation for scholarly excellence.
But there is something you can do. Especially now, with state support less supportive than it used to be.
By contributing to the Chancellor's Fund, which puts your generosity to work where and when it's needed, you'll be helping us prevent the brain drain.
Moreover, this general fund stands ready to support other important projects requiring urgent attention.
But whether you give to the Chancellor, or directly to a specific department or program, we need your help.
To keep our minds from wandering.
U.C. BERKELEY
It's not the same without you.

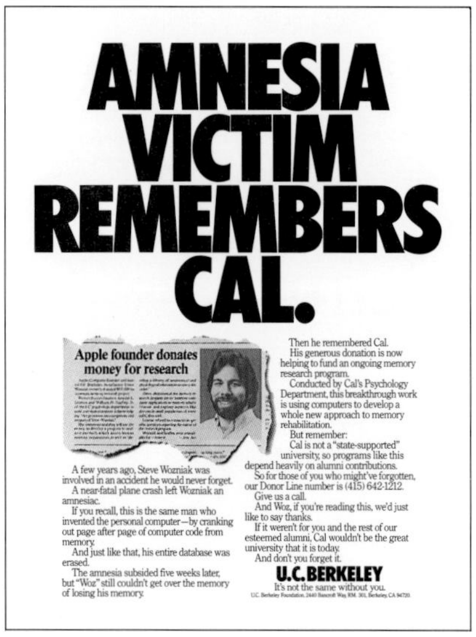
AMNESIA VICTIM REMEMBERS CAL.
Apple founder donates money for research
A few years ago, Steve Wozniak was involved in an accident he would never forget.
A near-fatal plane crash left Wozniak an amnesiac.
If you recall, this is the same man who invented the personal computer — by cranking out page after page of computer code from memory.
And just like that, his entire database was erased.
The amnesia subsided five weeks later, but "Woz" still couldn't get over the memory of losing his memory.
Then he remembered Cal.
His generous donation is now helping to fund an ongoing memory research program.
Conducted by Cal's Psychology Department, this breakthrough work is using computers to develop a whole new approach to memory rehabilitation.
But remember:
Cal is not a "state-supported" university, so programs like this depend heavily on alumni contributions.
So for those of you who might've forgotten, our Donor Line number is (415) 642-1212.
Give us a call.
And Woz, if you're reading this, we'd just like to say thanks.
If it weren't for you and the rest of our esteemed alumni, Cal wouldn't be the great university that it is today.
And don't you forget it.
U.C. BERKELEY
It's not the same without you.

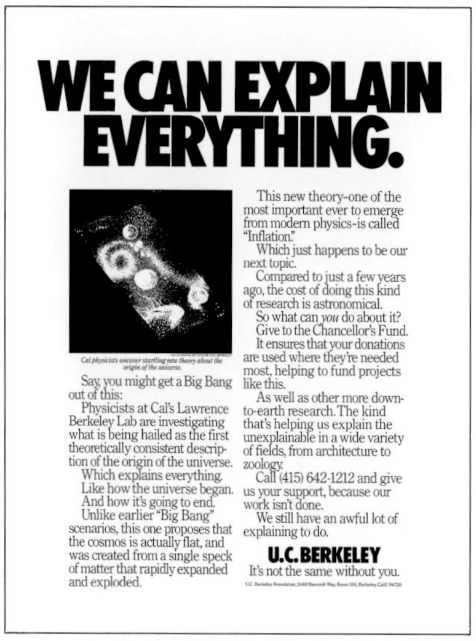
WE CAN EXPLAIN EVERYTHING.
Cal physicists uncover startling new theory about the origin of the universe.
Say you might get a Big Bang out of this:
Physicists at Cal's Lawrence Berkeley Lab are investigating what is being hailed as the first theoretically consistent description of the origin of the universe.
Which explains everything.
Like how the universe began.
And how it's going to end.
Unlike earlier "Big Bang" scenarios, this one proposes that the cosmos is actually flat, and was created from a single speck of matter that rapidly expanded and exploded.
This new theory-one of the most important ever to emerge from modern physics-is called "Inflation."
Which just happens to be our next topic.
Compared to just a few years ago, the cost of doing this kind of research is astronomical.
So what can you do about it?
Give to the Chancellor's Fund.
It ensures that your donations are used where they're needed most, helping to fund projects like this.
As well as other more down-to-earth research. The kind that's helping us explain the unexplainable in a wide variety of fields, from architecture to zoology.
Call (415) 642-1212 and give us your support, because our work isn't done.
We still have an awful lot of explaining to do.
U.C. BERKELEY
It's not the same without you.

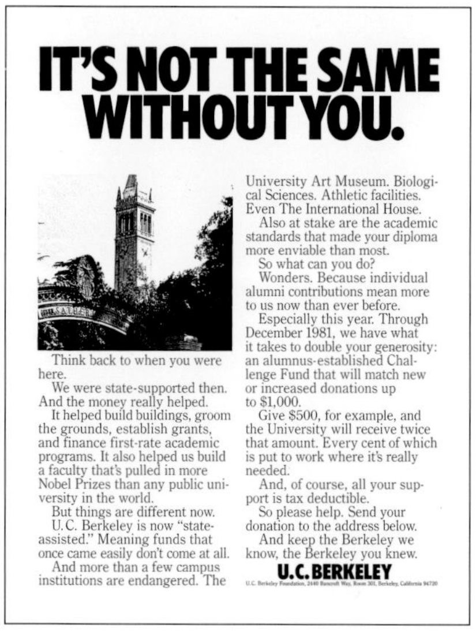
IT'S NOT THE SAME WITHOUT YOU.
Think back to when you were here.
We were state-supported then. And the money really helped.
It helped build buildings, groom the grounds, establish grants, and finance first-rate academic programs. It also helped us build a faculty that's pulled in more Nobel Prizes than any public university in the world.
But things are different now.
U. C. Berkeley is now "state-assisted." Meaning funds that once came easily don't come at all.
And more than a few campus institutions are endangered. The
University Art Museum. Biological Sciences. Athletic facilities. Even The International House.
Also at stake are the academic standards that made your diploma more enviable than most.
So what can you do?
Wonders. Because individual alumni contributions mean more to us now than ever before.
Especially this year. Through December 1981, we have what it takes to double your generosity: an alumnus-established Challenge Fund that will match new or increased donations up to $1,000.
Give $500, for example, and the University will receive twice that amount. Every cent of which is put to work where it's really needed.
And, of course, all your support is tax deductible.
So please help. Send your donation to the address below.
And keep the Berkeley we know, the Berkeley you knew.
U.C. BERKELEY

HELP UNCOVER UNDERWORLD FIGURES.

Like this bronze statuette, over 20 centuries old.

Years of research and hard work have enabled archaeologists from U.C. Berkeley to recover this important Greek artifact, along with other historical treasures. A temple. A stadium. Even a vaulted tunnel, the first physical proof that Greeks, not Romans, invented the arch.

Several hundred miles away, another Berkeley team is busy uncovering startling new facts about ancient Egypt.

And still another is digging in Virginia, where discoveries are now revealing what life was like in America—11,000 years ago.

Not your ordinary field trips.

But then Berkeley is no ordinary school. And it is achievements like these—in virtually every field—that have traditionally defined its greatness.

Your diploma says it all.

What it doesn't say is that Cal's budget is shrinking. And your role is crucial. Especially now, when contributions mean so much.

We need your support. *Call our Donor Line, collect: (415) 642-4414.* Or send your tax deductible gift to the address below.

And help all you can.

The deeper you dig, the more we uncover.

U.C. BERKELEY
It's not the same without you.

THIS BUILDING IS FILLED WITH MAD SCIENTISTS.

They're some of the most respected scientific minds in the country.

They're also mad.

You would be too if you had to teach and conduct critical research in Cal's Life Sciences building.

There are cracks in the ceilings and cracks in the walls.

And leaks in all the cracks.

Because of the rotten plumbing. Which may be what's causing those terrible odors.

The ones that won't go away, on account of all the ventilation problems.

And it won't be long before we'll have to put laboratories in the lavatories. (We've just about filled up the halls.)

Despite these and other hardships, our Biosciences departments continue to achieve world acclaim for breakthrough research in cancer prevention, brain development, and many other areas.

But the fact remains, Nobel Prize winners and Guggenheim Fellows don't grow on trees. In order to hang on to those we have—and continue to attract top faculty—we need more than a few new beakers and Bunsen burners.

We need your support.

Because largely through private contributions, we hope to begin building a Biological Sciences facility befitting a world class university.

So please call the number below.

And help us put a stop to this madness.

U.C. BERKELEY
It's not the same without you.

HELP US TIE A PROFESSOR TO THIS CHAIR.

It's called an endowed chair.

And it's only $400,000.

Which may seem a bit steep, considering the fact it doesn't recline. Or vibrate. Or even have arms.

But compared to the price of endowed chairs at other major universities, it's a respectable bargain.

And how is an endowed chair any different from the one in your dining room?

For one thing, it'll last forever.

Because your $400,000 establishes a perpetual endowment fund that covers everything but faculty salary (a state responsibility).

So year after year, an outstanding Cal professor will receive research assistance, equipment and other crucial support services.

And year after year, the generous donor—be it an individual, class or corporation—will receive well-deserved recognition.

Most importantly, endowed chairs enable Cal to attract and retain preeminent faculty, in virtually any field of learning you choose.

Or you can even choose to have us choose.

But the fact remains, without the support of a "chair," many of our top scholars are sitting targets for rival recruiters.

Call Vice-Chancellor Curtis R. Simic at (415) 642-1212, and tell him you want to help Cal meet its critical goal of 100 new endowed chairs by 1990.

Now's the time to take a stand.

And have a seat.

U.C. BERKELEY
It's not the same without you.

THE EYES OF TEXAS ARE UPON US.

University of Texas to use $32 million fund to lure top scholars

The University of Texas recently got some impressive new furniture.

32 "chairs" worth a million dollars apiece.

Now they're looking for 32 professors worth a million dollars apiece—to occupy those endowed chairs.

And that's just the tip of the oil well.

In the last 4 years alone, the University of Texas has established over 600 endowed faculty positions, part of an unprecedented effort to attract the finest minds in the country.

How does that affect Cal?

If we're not careful, many of our top scholars may soon be wearing cowboy hats.

And with nearly half of our distinguished faculty retiring in the next decade, we must do everything possible to retain and recruit promising young minds.

There's something you can do, too.

Simply by contributing to the endowment of faculty chairs, you can play an important role in helping Cal reach its goal of 100 new chairs by 1990.

These chairs will provide outstanding professors with equipment, research assistance and many other critical support services.

And also ensure that Cal's great tradition of scholarship continues to thrive.

Right here.

Not deep in the heart of Texas.

U.C. BERKELEY
It's not the same without you.

WE'RE PROTECTING YOUR FOOD WITH ALL OUR MITES.

They're called predator mites.

And they eat spider mites.

And *they* eat apples and almonds and peaches and cost California growers $75 million a year in crop damage.

Yet thanks to breakthrough research by Cal scientist Marjorie Hoy, the dreaded spider mite can now be controlled by these genetically improved predators.

This important work could soon enable growers all over the world to drastically reduce their use of pesticides.

But Professor Hoy isn't the only one on campus involved in a food fight.

Another Cal scientist recently discovered a way to prevent frost damage in lettuce fields. Still another has isolated the bacteria that's causing severe blight in our grape crop.

These and numerous other achievements have helped Cal's revitalized Biosciences program receive global attention.

Now we need your attention.

Lacking adequate facilities and equipment, our gifted scientists are relying more than ever on private contributions.

So please, call the number below, because our work isn't finished.

We're still trying to get all the bugs out.

U.C. BERKELEY
It's not the same without you.

THE HOPE DIAMOND.

We hope to turn this blueprint into a softball field.

And the sooner the better.

Come next year, our existing women's diamond will be declared unsuitable for conference play.

Guess somebody noticed the broken bleachers.

The funny little scoreboard.

And most embarrassing, the fact that our right field is 35 feet shorter than everyone else's (which makes it nonregulation).

To make matters worse, our funds are in a terrible slump. Which is also why, every Fall, our women's basketball team has no place on campus to practice.

And why our women's locker room is still shy a few amenities. Like lockers.

Fortunately, these and other hardships haven't seemed to hurt Cal's trophy collection.

Last year eight of our women's teams were among the top twenty in the country. This year, a few of the same athletes have a shot at winning Olympic gold medals.

But if we're to continue this tradition, we need more than an occasional pep rally.

We need equipment, facilities and scholarships competitive with those schools out to devour our reputation.

In short, we need your help. Your donation to Bear Boosters can help ensure that *all* our athletes have a sporting chance.

We may even be able to give our women what they deserve.

A diamond big as a softball field.

U.C. BERKELEY
It's not the same without you.

THIS IS YOUR LIFE.

Cal scientists have discovered that life is no bowl of cherries.

It's actually more like a pretzel.

By coating strands of DNA with a special protein, Prof. Nicholas Cozzarelli and his researchers have revealed for the first time the complex coiling process that occurs when a living cell is reproduced.

It's a whole new way of looking at life.

More importantly, this new technique has enabled Cozzarelli and his team to precisely predict when genetic material will be exchanged.

But these Cal scientists aren't the only ones preoccupied with life.

Take the extraordinary achievements of Professor Robert Tjian, who recently isolated a protein that actually triggers gene expression.

Or the pioneering work of Professor Gerald Rubin, whose studies have shed light on how DNA molecules affect vision.

Oh, here's another fact of life. If we're to continue to make advances in DNA and gene research, we need to replace our existing outdated facilities. The answer is Cal's proposed Genetics and Plant Biology building.

The question is, can we come up with the private funding necessary to match state money?

Call Vice-Chancellor Curtis R. Simic at (415) 642-1212 and tell him you want to contribute.

How much?

Well, how much is life worth to you?

U.C. BERKELEY
It's not the same without you.

BERKELEY THREATENS RUSSIA.

NOBEL PRIZES

U.C. Berkeley (14)	U.S.S.R. (8)

It's true, Cal's faculty has won almost as many Nobel Prizes as the entire Soviet Union.

Fourteen, to be exact.

That's four more than all of Italy. Five more than Japan and Canada combined.

But hey, who's counting?

Certainly not our professors, they've been too busy.

Helping discover plutonium. Pioneering the first laser beam. Isolating the virus that would play a key role in conquering polio.

These and other prize-winning achievements reflect an overall academic standard that has for over half a century been consistently phenomenal.

And for that, we deserve a medal.

Your contributions have provided our great minds with the resources needed to do great work.

However, now is not the time to rest on our Laureates.

Just ask our latest Nobel winner, economist Gerard Debreu. Upon receiving his award, he had this to say: "The magnificent research environment I have known at this university during the past 20 years ...is threatened by very lean budgets."

So please, contribute all you can. Our professors will gladly repay you. In gold.

U.C. BERKELEY
It's not the same without you.

"The 'Berkeley Threatens Russia' ad ran in Time as a public service announcement. And that week, a Berkeley professor happened to be going to Russia. When he got there, they were going through his things in Customs, they found the magazine with this ad in his suitcase, and they didn't let him in the country."

"Also, these ads were kind of hard to write because my partner was a real fanatic about type breaks, and the print was real big."

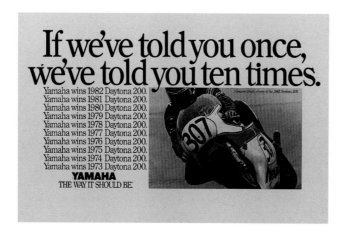
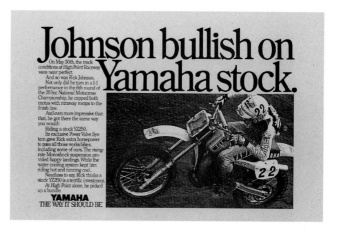

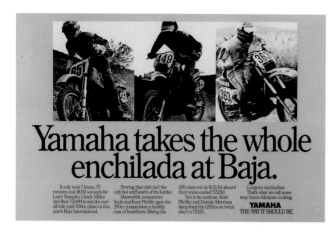

INTRODUCING A YAMAHA THAT'LL OUTRUN INFLATION. BRAVO.

In an economy where even regular gasoline is at a premium, Yamaha engineers were faced with a big challenge.

To design and build a totally new snowmobile that weighed less, cost less and consumed less. All without being any less of a

Yamaha. Their solution was a little something that's really something.

We call it the Bravo. And you'll understand why the first time you ride it.

The Bravo weighs in at a remarkable 281 lbs. Yet it's every bit as much fun for a sizable adult as a sizeable sled. And at $1348* you sure can't beat the size of its price.

It's 246cc, single cylinder engine is as simple as they come. For instance, the cylinder and head are one piece to reduce weight. But don't confuse simple with unsophisticated. It also has

high-tech Yamaha innovations like Autolube and CDI. Plus the most advanced carburetion set-up known to snowmobiles.

With that kind of engineering going for it, it's no surprise that the Bravo's economical. The surprise is that it doesn't look like an economy sled. Or handle like one. Or perform like one.

Not that the Bravo is about to take on our red-hot SRX, mind you. But it is fast enough to stay one jump ahead of inflation. And these days, that's fast.

YAMAHA
THE WAY IT SHOULD BE

LAST YEAR, WE MADE IT LAND LIKE A JET. THIS YEAR, WE MADE IT TAKE OFF LIKE ONE.

Two years ago, while searching for a better front suspension system for Yamaha's high-performance snowmobiles, our engineers looked to the heavens.

And there, attached to the nose landing gear of a low-flying jet, was the answer.

Telescopic Strut Suspension.

And since its introduction on the Yamaha SRV a year ago, TSS has become the standard of the industry.

Because TSS lets you take every dip, bump, rut or mole hill or mountain Mother Nature can dish out. Flat out.

Which on last year's SRV meant faster than any other fan-cooled sled on snow. And, believe it or not, this year's is even faster.

With over sixty horse-power, the new SRV is a fan-cooler that'll give a lot of liquid-cooled sleds a run for their money.

To make sure all that new-found power reaches the snow where it belongs, we gave the SRV our new extra-strong, extra-durable Yamaha drive clutch.

And to make sure

there's no mistaking what you're riding, we also gave it the kind of looks that let every one know this could only be the 1982 Yamaha SRV.

And the horsepower to make history of the competition.

YAMAHA
THE WAY IT SHOULD BE.

WHY YOU SHOULD TAKE A SLED THAT LOOKS THIS GOOD WHERE NO ONE ELSE WILL SEE IT.

Once your friends and neighbors have stopped oogling at your new SS440 take it out to show Mother Nature.

Because the farther you get from humanity, the more you'll appreciate the 440's real beauty: getting all

the way home again. And again. And again.

The 440cc, fan-cooled engine is flat-out the fastest in its class. And it's uniquely positioned to give the SS more positive steering, easy handling and uncanny maneuverability. Not to mention a lower center of gravity for added stability.

So you don't have to sneak quick peeks at the speedometer through the handlebars, we

mounted the instrumentation right into the handlebars. Which, by the way, are fully adjustable.

And by moving the storage compartment up front, under the hood, we made room for a longer, more comfortable seat. For longer, more comfortable rides.

Still, the most comforting feature we build into the SS440 remains the same as always.

Its unrivaled round-trip reliability.

And that you don't get from the pretty paint job.

YAMAHA
THE WAY IT SHOULD BE

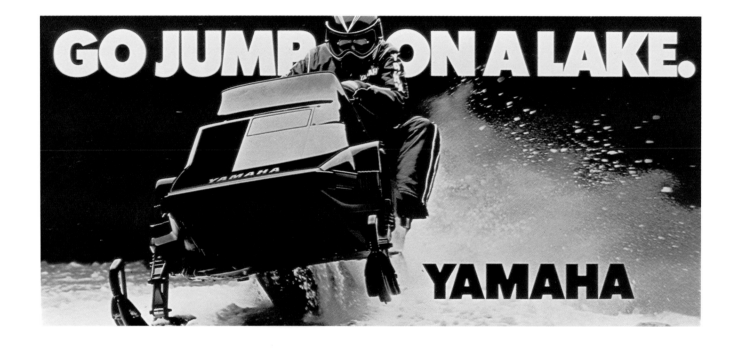

"That was truly a lot of fun to work on, 'cause you would go for a month to a city in Montana, right outside of Yellowstone, and they would have all these sleds lined up, and all the engineers, and all you did was ride Snowmobiles for two weeks and shoot pictures. Hard work, but it was just—you can't imagine how pretty it is up there. It's truly God's country. We're at ten thousand feet in the Beartooth Mountains, this funky little town, there's like eight people that live there, a big lodge and us."

225 MILLION AMERICANS UNDERSTAND HIM PERFECTLY.

He's got awful diction. A terrible temper. And a fanatical following.

Because to the millions upon millions of people who've hugged him at Disneyland and Walt Disney World, chuckled at his antics in cartoons, and made platinum records out of what has to be one of the worst singing voices in history, Donald Duck is saying something loud and clear.

Simply that basic human emotions speak to everyone.

And now, Donald is ready to get his message across in a new medium.

On The Disney Channel. Where the same magical Disney presence will be translated into 16 hours per day of the highest quality family entertainment.

Entertainment unlike anything cable subscribers will be able to find in theaters or anywhere else on television. Programming to engage the mind and the heart. New series like Contraption, Dreamfinders and Wish Upon A Star to get families laughing and talking with each other.

Films and cartoons from the vast Disney library that communicate in the universal language of imagination. Dramatic series. True Life Adventures. Wonder and science. The nostalgia of Zorro and the futureworld of Epcot Center.

It's a programming concept that reflects sixty years of experience in understanding what audiences want. Which may be why The Disney Channel could turn out to be one of the few things in this country 225 million people agree on.

For more information on The Disney Channel, call our toll-free number: 1-800-832-4636.

THE DISNEY CHANNEL

WHY IT'S SMART TO MAKE FRIENDS WITH DUMBO.

When Dumbo comes to town, he's accorded a hero's welcome.

Because he represents something there never seems to be enough of: wholesome, high quality entertainment for the whole family.

With the advent of The Disney Channel, the special blend of magic and wonder will now be available 16 hours a day. A happy alternative for subscribers concerned with pay T.V.'s increasingly "R" rating. And a viable solution for city councils under pressure to do something about it.

There are other areas, too, where Dumbo can really throw his weight around. Take basic lift, for example.

In a recent survey,(Decision Research

Corporation, August 1982)14% of families with children under 18 said they would add basic cable in order to get The Disney Channel.

However, Dumbo's more than just a good friend. He's also a pretty convincing salesman.

Because every time someone sees a Disney film, or visits Disneyland or Walt Disney World or listens to a Disney record or tape, another potential subscriber for the channel has just been sold.

So it's not only smart to make friends with Dumbo. It's smart to put him to work for you, too.

For more information on The Disney Channel, please call us at our toll-free number: 1-800-832-4636.

THE DISNEY CHANNEL

© 1983 Walt Disney Productions

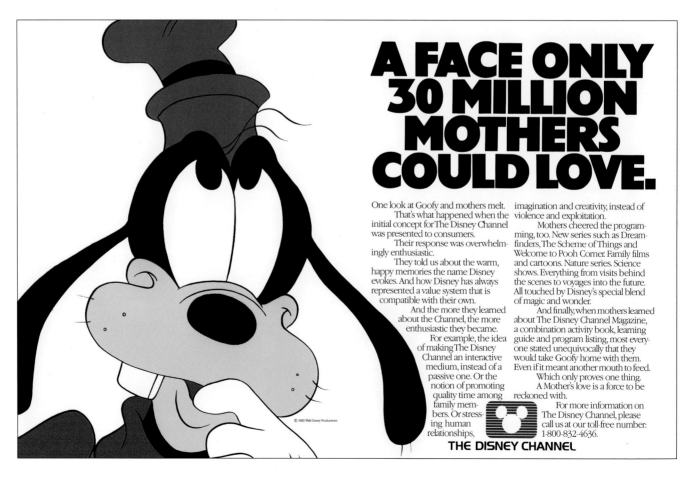

A FACE ONLY 30 MILLION MOTHERS COULD LOVE.

One look at Goofy and mothers melt.

That's what happened when the initial concept for The Disney Channel was presented to consumers.

Their response was overwhelmingly enthusiastic.

They told us about the warm, happy memories the name Disney evokes. And how Disney has always represented a value system that is compatible with their own.

And the more they learned about the Channel, the more enthusiastic they became.

For example, the idea of making The Disney Channel an interactive medium, instead of a passive one. Or the notion of promoting quality time among family members. Or stressing human relationships,

imagination and creativity, instead of violence and exploitation.

Mothers cheered the programming, too. New series such as Dreamfinders, The Scheme of Things and Welcome to Pooh Corner. Family films and cartoons. Nature series. Science shows. Everything from visits behind the scenes to voyages into the future. All touched by Disney's special blend of magic and wonder.

And finally, when mothers learned about The Disney Channel Magazine, a combination activity book, learning guide and program listing, most everyone stated unequivocally that they would take Goofy home with them. Even if it meant another mouth to feed.

Which only proves one thing.

A Mother's love is a force to be reckoned with.

For more information on The Disney Channel, please call us at our toll-free number: 1-800-832-4636.

THE DISNEY CHANNEL

© 1983 Walt Disney Productions

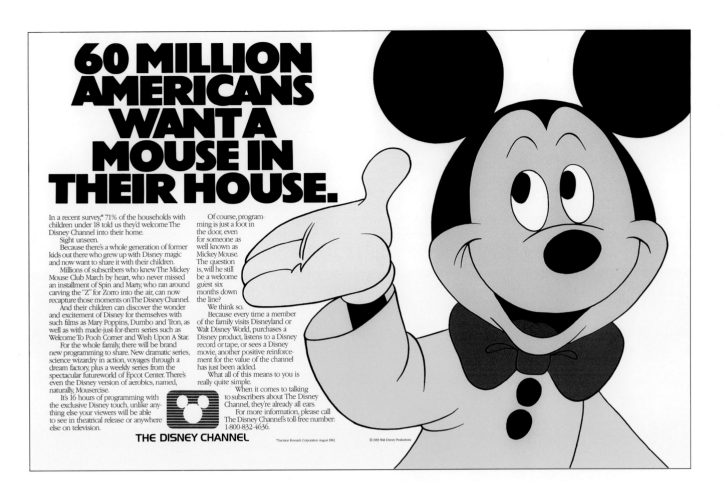

60 MILLION AMERICANS WANT A MOUSE IN THEIR HOUSE.

In a recent survey,* 71% of the households with children under 18 told us they'd welcome The Disney Channel into their home.

Sight unseen.

Because there's a whole generation of former kids out there who grew up with Disney magic and now want to share it with their children.

Millions of subscribers who knew The Mickey Mouse Club March by heart, who never missed an installment of Spin and Marty, who ran around carving the "Z" for Zorro into the air, can now recapture those moments on The Disney Channel.

And their children can discover the wonder and excitement of Disney for themselves with such films as Mary Poppins, Dumbo and Tron, as well as with made-just-for-them series such as Welcome To Pooh Corner and Wish Upon A Star.

For the whole family, there will be brand new programming to share. New dramatic series, science wizardry in action, voyages through a dream factory, plus a weekly series from the spectacular futureworld of Epcot Center. There's even the Disney version of aerobics, named, naturally, Mousercise.

It's 16 hours of programming with the exclusive Disney touch, unlike anything else your viewers will be able to see in theatrical release or anywhere else on television.

Of course, programming is just a foot in the door, even for someone as well known as Mickey Mouse. The question is, will he still be a welcome guest six months down the line?

We think so.

Because every time a member of the family visits Disneyland or Walt Disney World, purchases a Disney product, listens to a Disney record or tape, or sees a Disney movie, another positive reinforcement for the value of the channel has just been added.

What all of this means to you is really quite simple.

When it comes to talking to subscribers about The Disney Channel, they're already all ears.

For more information, please call The Disney Channel's toll-free number: 1-800-832-4636.

THE DISNEY CHANNEL

*Decision Research Corporation. August 1982.

© 1983 Walt Disney Productions

WHAT FAMILY PROGRAMMING NEEDS IS A GOOD WATCHDOG.

To the rescue.

The answer to endless hours of cat chases and car crashes in the corridors of network kid-vid.

The answer to critics of the cable industry who are giving pay T.V. an increasingly "R" rating.

The Disney Channel.

The Disney Channel is a whole new concept in pay T.V.

Sixteen hours a day of the Disney magic formula of fun and learning, unlike anything viewers will be able to find in theatrical release or anywhere else on television.

The watchword is involvement. Interactive shows like You and Me, Kid and Mousercise that encourage family participation. Fresh new series such as Welcome

© 1983 Walt Disney Productions

To Pooh Corner and Wish Upon A Star. Specials from Disneyland and Walt Disney World. Programming of the future from Epcot Center. Flights of fantasy, daring quests, soaring adventures that engage the heart and involve the mind at the same time. A library of more than 50 years of unforgettable films, from Dumbo and Mary Poppins to Tron.

There's even a high degree of involvement in The Disney Channel Magazine, a cut-out, fill-in, put-together adventure all of its own.

But in addition to our innovative programming, there's something else. A trust from the public that associates the name Disney with nothing but the highest quality family entertainment. A trust we take quite seriously.

Maybe that's why being a watchdog could become Pluto's finest role.

To become part of The Disney Channel, call our toll-free number: 1-800-832-4636.

THE DISNEY CHANNEL

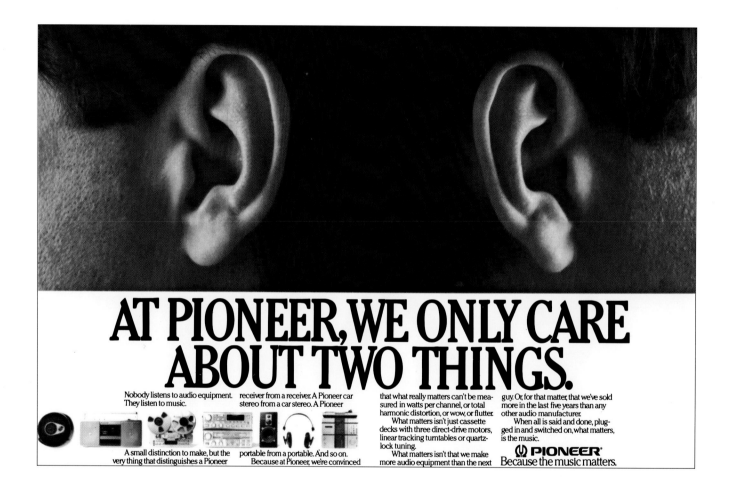

AT PIONEER, WE ONLY CARE ABOUT TWO THINGS.

Nobody listens to audio equipment. They listen to music.

A small distinction to make, but the very thing that distinguishes a Pioneer receiver from a receiver. A Pioneer car stereo from a car stereo. A Pioneer portable from a portable. And so on.

Because at Pioneer, we're convinced that what really matters can't be measured in watts per channel, or total harmonic distortion, or wow, or flutter.

What matters isn't just cassette decks with three direct-drive motors, linear tracking turntables or quartz-lock tuning.

What matters isn't that we make more audio equipment than the next guy. Or, for that matter, that we've sold more in the last five years than any other audio manufacturer.

When all is said and done, plugged in and switched on, what matters, is the music.

(Ͻ) PIONEER®
Because the music matters.

OPEN WITH A SHOT OF THE STEREOTYPICAL UNCLE SAM MAN WEARING A LARGE TOP HAT THAT'S RED, WHITE, AND BLUE.

VO: In 1967 General Electric lost 30% of it's audio market to foreign competition.

SFX: Hand slapping face.

VO: In 1977 steel production in America went down 15%.

SFX: Hand slapping face.

VO: In 1979 Foreign competition captured 80% of America's microchip market.

MUSIC: Chariots of Fire.

SFX: Hand slapping.

VO: In 1980 Imported cars took 27% of American car sales.

SFX: Airswish.

VO: In 1981, 20,000 American factories closed down.

SFX: Door slam.

VO: In February 1982, 9.5 million Americans were out of work.

SFX: Hand slap.

VO: Tonight General Electric announces its commitment to take on the biggest job in America. To bring new life to our country's factories. Read the full story in your Newspaper Monday morning.

"This spot never ran, although it's one we were very proud of. I guess GE didn't think it was, 'We bring good things to life.'"

SHOT OF (LEGS ONLY) DRUNK DRIVER TRYING TO WALK A STRAIGHT LINE AIDED BY A COP.

MAN: . . . drunken laughter

COP: Walk . . . Put your hands on the car . . .

CUT TO COP LEANING DRUNK MAN AGAINST CAR AND FRISKING HIM.

MAN: Is this really necessary? (still laughing)

COP: Let's go sir . . .

COP PUTS HANDCUFFS ON DRUNK MAN AND PUTS HIM IN THE BACK OF SQUAD CAR. CUT OF DRUNK MAN'S FACE AS HE SUDDENLY SOBERS UP A BIT REALIZING WHAT'S HAPPENING TO HIM.

COP: Hey, Connie . . . open up.

CUT TO JAIL WHERE COPS ARE LEADING MAN INSIDE. ELECTRONIC SECURITY DOORS OPEN UP.

CLERK: Empty his pockets. Got any jewelry?

COP CHECKS DRUNK MAN'S POCKETS, SECURITY CLERK TAKES VALUABLES.

COP: Yeah, he's got his wedding ring. Look at the camera.

MUG SHOTS TAKEN . . . CUT TO STREET PUNK BEING HAULED IN—PUNK IS CAUSING PROBLEMS AND OTHER COPS TRY TO SUBDUE HIM.

PUNK: (shouts) Hey . . . don't touch me!

DRUNK MAN MAKES PHONE CALL (AIDED BY COP) . . . HE IS SHOCKED BY THE PUNK'S OUTBURST AND LOOKS FRIGHTENED. COP LEADS DRUNK MAN TO HIS CELL.

ANNCR: Last year in California 350,000 people were thrown in jail for drunk driving.

CELL DOOR OPENS WHERE SEVERAL UNSAVORY CHARAC-TERS ARE BEING HELD. COP GUIDES DRUNK MAN INTO SAME CELL.

ANNCR: This year, the police are cracking down even harder. So, if you're caught driving drunk. Rest assured . . .

CELL DOOR SLAMS SHUT AND MAN LOOKS VERY SOBER NOW, FRIGHTENED.

ANNCR: you're going to jail.

"We went down to the Oakland Jail and said, 'What's it like?' And so they took us from step one all the way through. They said, 'We try to keep the hard criminals, the guys who are murderers and that kind of stuff—we separate those guys out. All the rest of them, they're in the cell with the driver.'"

Yamaha

Fine Art Dealer, Singapore.

Apple

Wienerschnitzel

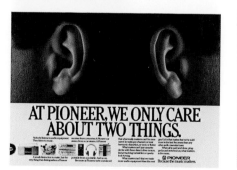

How to tell Chiat/Day from an ad agency.

There are advertising agencies. And then, there are advertising agencies.

We're the second kind.

Our unique approach to the business, simply stated, is this: the work comes first.

Not the balance sheet. Or how many offices we have. Or any of the other outward signs of success agencies get hung up on.

But the work.

Bold, daring, different, exciting, memorable, startling, unexpected, persuasive work.

We figure if the advertising we create does its job, the client will prosper. And if the client prospers, we will.

And we have.

Chiat/Day is now the largest West Coast-bred agency in the United States. We have full-service offices in Los Angeles, New York, San Francisco and Seattle.

And we're pleased to say that much of that growth was a direct result of the work we produced. It increased our clients' sales. And they increased their ad budgets.

Our pursuit of new business—you, for example—is much less concerned with the immediate bump in billings as it is with establishing that same kind of agency/client relationship.

One in which we can help you grow.

And you can do the same for us.

Chiat/Day

Los Angeles, New York, San Francisco and Seattle.

Even If You Can't Have The Best Of Everything, You Can Have The Best Of Something.

It's only human nature to want the best. Rolls Royces, chinchilla coats, villas on the Riviera, Renoirs on the wall.

Realistically, few of us can afford the best of everything. Most must settle for the best we can afford. And live with the compromises.

But for something as important in day-to-day life as a television set, there is a strong temptation to indulge oneself in

the best. Which makes a Mitsubishi TV well worth your consideration.

An elegant example is this model CK-2582 25-inch diagonal measure Mitsubishi color console with full-function wireless remote, state of the art random access tuning, and complete built-in cable reception capability.

It features a cabinet made not of genuine oak-grain plastic, but of genuine oak-grain oak. It also features one of the two most important innovations in color television tubes ever: Diamond Vision. (The other was the black matrix screen developed in the early 1970's.)

UP TO 40% WIDER COLOR RANGE WITH DIAMOND VISION.

Diamond Vision was developed initially to solve the problem of sun glare on our outdoor electronic scoreboards. Our solution was a special glass treatment that actually absorbs sunlight rather than reflecting it. Incorporated into our home picture tubes, it has the same effect on the sunlight or other ambient light you may have in your TV viewing room.

Conventional screen reflects most ambient light.

Diamond Vision absorbs most ambient light.

Further experimentation led to other treatments designed to filter out the undesirable light elements from those emitted by the phosphors of the picture tube itself.

The result was not only a picture relatively unaffected by ambient light, but a dramatically improved picture overall. A picture with better, richer, truer colors. Blacker blacks. Bluer blues. Greener greens.

Comparison of the color range reproduced by Diamond Vision and conventional TV tubes under ambient light.

Compared to the conventional TV tube, the range of colors that can be reproduced is wider by 15% to 40%, depending on the amount of ambient light present. For example, crimson rose can be reproduced exactly, something no other television can do. Marine blue, sky blue and green are also truer.

And since the colors themselves are more accurately reproduced, the various shades are differentiated as well. So instead of the flat, homogenized picture you're used to, you get one that's more three dimensional.

Speaking of which, there's yet another dimension to this Mitsubishi color console, one your ears will enjoy:

Two separate amplifiers and speaker systems.

Together they produce an exciting stereo effect even from regular mono television transmissions. And they deliver the real thing from stereo video discs, stereo videocassettes, and (with our built-in FM tuner) FM simulcasts.

This broadened range of capabilities is not a difference you have to take our word for. You can see and hear it clearly in a side-by-side comparison at your Mitsubishi dealer.

And there you will find that while you may never have the best of everything in this world, you can at least have the best of television.

▲ MITSUBISHI

Her Teeth Are 50% Brighter Thanks To A Tube Of Mitsubishi.

Have you ever looked at projection television and decided that the picture size was awesome but the picture wasn't?

What was doubtless dimming your enthusiasm was the lack of brightness, a traditional problem with projection TV.

For which Mitsubishi now introduces the solution. A major projection TV breakthrough that delivers 180 foot Lamberts of brightness on our over 4-foot-diagonal of screen. No other front-projection TV has over 120 foot Lamberts.

And this 50% improvement in brightness was achieved without sacrifice to picture sharpness.

This translates into a projection TV picture as bright as that on a conventional 25-inch set.

For those of you who like to know the whys and wherefores, read on.

Each of our lens systems contains six lens elements instead of the usual three offered by every other leading front-projection TV. This results in a sharper, higher-contrast picture.

6 glass elements vs. 3 plastic elements. There's no comparison.

But even more revealing is what those lenses are made of.

Ours are fine precision ground optical glass, the kind you find in the most expensive cameras.

Theirs are plastic.

Glass possesses some inherent technical advantages over plastic.

Glass can be coated, reducing light reflections within the lens barrel for improved picture contrast. This coating also improves lens transparency, which allows more light through, resulting in a brighter picture.

Our most impressive representation of these technological advancements is the model VS-522R you see before you.

Close its doors and the screen is discreetly hidden from view.

How to hide a Mitsubishi.

Open them and you open up a whole new dimension in home entertainment: twice the diagonal measure and four times the square footage of a conventional 25-inch television screen.

It's analogous to having a movie theater screen in front of your easy chair. An appealing idea in a world of five-dollar movie tickets.

All of the above notwithstanding, you may prefer to trust your own eyes rather than any advertising claim. In which case, we confidently invite you to visit your Mitsubishi dealer and see for yourself.

And if you think it looks good, wait till you hear how it sounds.

Because the VS-522R also features two separate amplifiers and speaker systems. Together they produce an exciting stereo effect even from regular mono television transmissions. And they deliver the real thing from stereo video discs, stereo video-cassettes, and (with our built-in FM tuner) FM simulcasts.

And if you think that sounds good, wait till you see how it looks.

▲ MITSUBISHI

Even If You Can't Have The Best Of Everything,
You Can Have The Best Of Something.

OPEN WITH A CLOSE-UP OF MAN
STRAINING TO CHEW A PIECE OF GUM.
SFX: Man grunting loudly.
VO: Bazooka bubble gum. If you're tough enough
to chew the hard stuff.

OPEN WITH A CLOSE-UP OF MAN STRAINING TO CHEW
A PIECE OF GUM.
SFX: Of car trying to start then stalling out.
VO: It's harder to get started, but once it gets
going, it never stops.
Bazooka bubble gum. If you're tough enough to
chew the hard stuff.

*"I worked on the account,
chewed their gum for months,
and wound up having to go
for a root canal the day of
the shoot."*

The mouse that roared.

"The age of friendly computing has begun."
— *Newsweek*

"The key to Lisa's charms is the mouse...
Anyone who can push a button can use Lisa."
— *Fortune*

"After Lisa the professional computing world
will never be the same again."
— *The Seybold Report on
Professional Computing*

"With the announcement of Apple's Lisa, the
era of the easy computer has gained another
benchmark with which to measure future
machines." — *Personal Computing*

"The Lisa system is the most important
development in computers in the last five
years." — *Byte*

"I have seen the future and it is Lisa."
— *Computer Dealer*

"Lisa will become the standard of comparison
to all other personal computer products."
— *Business Week*

"I was blown away." — *Infoworld*

Soon there'll be just two kinds of people.
Those who use computers and
those who use Apples.

Think of it as a Maserati for your mind.

It's been said personal computers are at the same stage of development as the automobile in 1921.

They'll get you there. But you have to have a tolerance for crank-starting, flat tires and bugs in your teeth.

Now comes the next generation from Apple: Lisa."

And it's as if everything from self-starting to turbocharging had been perfected overnight.

Lisa's powerplant is the 32-bit MC68000 microprocessor, capable of screaming through information at speeds once reserved for the mainframe that runs your bank.

Each system comes standard with a whole workbench of business tools for shaping information in any form: words, numbers, graphs, even pictures.

Each program works the same intuitive way, replacing complex commands with familiar symbols that simulate the way you work at your desk. And you can work with several programs on the screen at once.

It's like automatic transmission. For ideas. So you can concentrate on what you want done. Not on how to get the computer to do it.

And learning time is reduced from days. To minutes.

All of which makes Lisa the fastest you can go, sitting at a desk.

Soon there'll be just two kinds of people. Those who use computers and those who use Apples.

It took 200 years to draw this picture.

This cheery little doodle represents 432,000 hours of work by some of the brightest minds in computer design.

And yes, they actually got paid for it.

Because it also represents a whole new way for humans to interact with computers on more human terms:

Lisa" from Apple."

With its unique 32-bit design and 1 million characters of internal memory, it's the most powerful personal office computer ever developed, capable of a lot more than doodling. Each system gives you a whole workbench of powerful business tools, from word processing to electronic project management.

But the real story is the way we used that power — not to make electrons go faster, but to help you go faster.

Because Lisa is the first (and only) computer that works in a visual way. It replaces complex computer commands with pictures familiar to anyone who's ever worked at a desk.

File folders look like file folders. Memos like memos. There's a clipboard, a calculator, even a wastebasket.

To tell Lisa what to do, you simply point to the appropriate symbol.

So you can actually learn to use Lisa in minutes. Instead of days.

And that's the bigger picture.

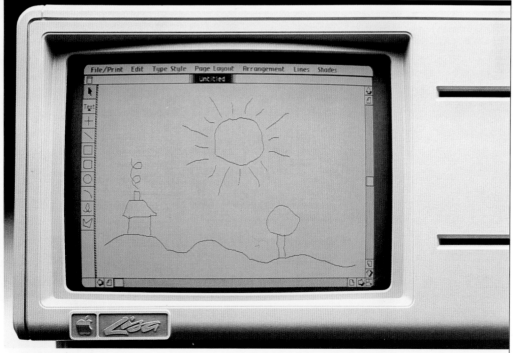

Soon there'll be just two kinds of people. Those who use computers and those who use Apples.

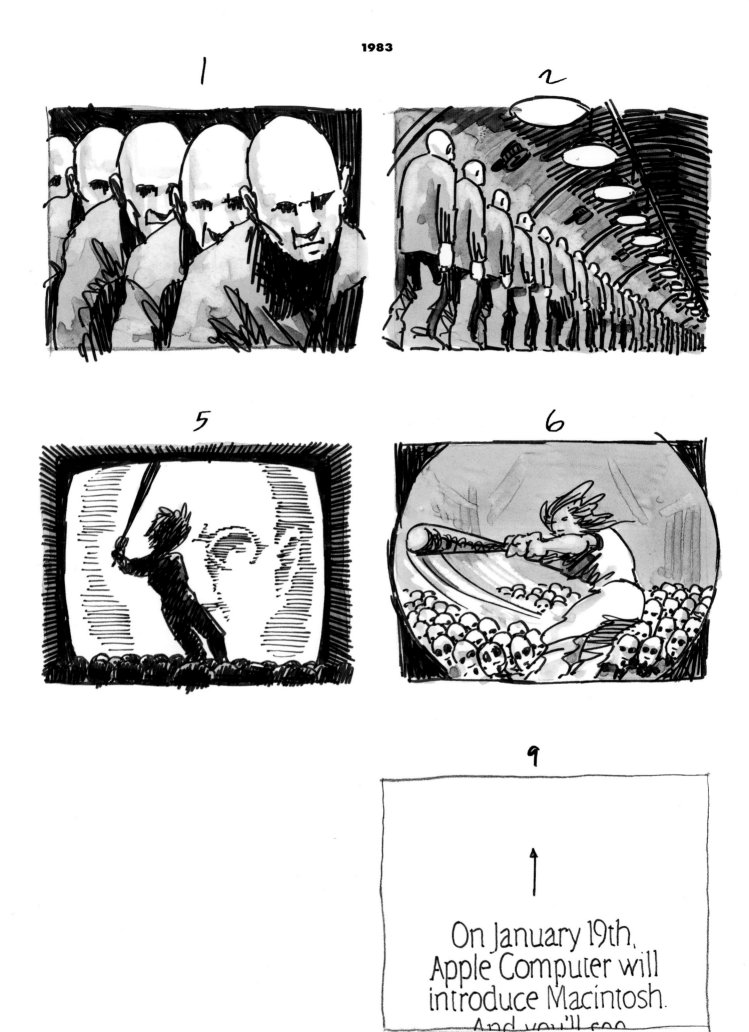

3

4

1

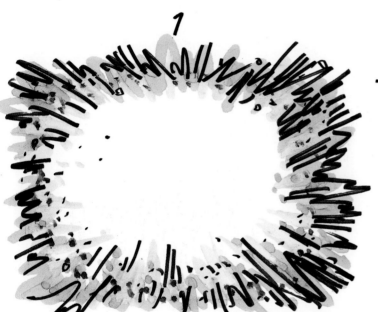

8

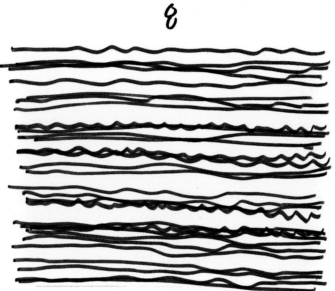

10

On January 19th,
Apple Computer will
introduce Macintosh.
And you'll see
why 1984 won't
be like "1984."

"Do you think we can do something with this headline?"

For the art director, it is just one more thing to do.

Up at Apple, they have been working on this new computer called Macintosh. They think it is more than just another product; they think it will change the world. They want to do a big introduction, maybe throw simultaneous parties across America with the most famous rock bands in the world, people dancing in the street, the heralding of a new age. After a brief cost analysis, they realize they can either throw the parties or make the computer. They tell Chiat/Day, "Well, do us a TV commercial or something."

The art director, who works in Los Angeles, is looking through a three-foot pile of dead Apple ads from the San Francisco office. With Apple, it is not unusual to do thirty or forty ads in order to sell one or two. As he thumbs through the work, he sees a print piece with a headline that reads: "Why 1984 won't be like 1984." It is part of a series of proposed newspaper ads that will help define Apple's corporate mission.

The ad argues that computers will add another element of democratization to society. Rather than having some big computer in a basement somewhere which only a few people would have access to, Apple's hope was to take that power and put it on the desk of every individual, giving everyone the same access to information.

The art director thinks this is exactly the point of Macintosh. So he goes to his copywriter, shows him the headline, and says he thinks it might make a good TV spot.

The copywriter says, I've got this great idea. We'll satirize all the things people were afraid 1984 would be. And it starts off kind of humorous, with ray guns and space suits and people talking gibberish—go to level nine, section nine—that kind of stuff. They have Big Brother on a huge TV screen, and men marching down dark halls, and when they think they

have enough, they take the idea over to the creative director.

He likes it, but he says, basically, you've got to break this image somehow. Let's have somebody come in and blow up the screen, get a girl to run in with a baseball bat and throw it at the screen, and that will burst this bubble of totalitarian control.

Now, everybody's happy. The whole thing takes about fifteen minutes. The art director takes the board to the artist who's almost always around, who has been drawing Chiat/Day's storyboards since there's been a Chiat/Day. When the storyboard is finished, the art director knows that this is a commercial that will make his career. All he has to do now is sell it.

At Apple, the board keeps getting presented in meeting after meeting, and everything else keeps getting killed, and this board keeps making it through. Not that everybody loves it, but they kind of think it's interesting, and they don't want to kill it straight off. Boards all around it are getting shot down, and "1984" is still alive.

Now the art director thinks the board has a chance. Now, he is fixated.

And now, Apple decides what they really want is a commercial for a computer that is coming out before Macintosh, called Lisa.

So Chiat/Day works on a new spot, which Apple loves, and "1984" becomes merely an afterthought. But not to the art director. He and a Chiat/Day producer are meeting with the director of "Alien" and "Bladerunner," whom they feel is the man to shoot "1984." The creative director is excited, and now he decides to try and sell "1984" all over again.

The creative director, the copywriter, and the art director go back to Apple. They show the director's work, which Apple thinks is great, and they say this: We can do a great job on Lisa, but this guy'll only shoot Lisa if he can also shoot "1984"—and it won't be too much more money.

It is agreed that the famous director will do two spots—the Lisa commercial, and that other one.

Apple signs the budget, and the art director flies up to Cupertino to watch them do it, just to make sure that nothing goes wrong.

A couple of weeks later, the art director is off to London to shoot the spot. He gets there eight days ahead of time to do preproduction, and he can't believe he's really there, he's really going to do it.

The day before the shoot, Apple calls with a question: How much would it cost if we pull the plug right now?

The shoot is off.

The Chiat/Day producer tells Apple that all the money's been spent, but they can still save the cost of lunch.

The shoot is on.

The first day of the shoot, the director gives two suggestions: He thinks the girl should be throwing a sledgehammer instead of a bat, and he feels that Big Brother should really be saying something. The art director phones the copywriter in Los Angeles, and asks, can he write something overnight? The copywriter calls his brother, a fellow student of history. They go to a local bar and throw around all the jingoistic Marxist phrases they know—the running dogs of imperialism, the wreckers have been cast out—that sort of thing. The copywriter goes back to the office, writes the speech, and sends it off to London.

The commercial is shot. The art director does some editing there, then brings it back to Chiat/Day, and with the creative director and Chiat/Day's most trusted editor, does some editing here. Finally, they have a rough cut for initial approval, which they take to Apple.

The first screening takes place in a janitor's closet that they roll a tape machine into. It is the art director, the creative director, the president of Apple, and one of the key people on the Macintosh project. The two men from Apple are ecstatic, and give their approval.

The art director is happy. It's really going to get finished. It's really going to run.

The spot does get finished, and time is

bought to show it on the Superbowl, early next year. They send the finished spot up to Apple, where it is screened for the board of directors. After it is shown, one of the men raises his hand and says, "Shall we vote on finding a new agency now?"

"You don't understand," the president of Apple says, "We're showing you this spot because we *like* it." For weeks, to air or not to air is the topic of many a heated discussion between Chiat/Day and Apple, and within Apple itself.

The week before Super Sunday, the art director is told that Chiat/Day has been instructed to try and sell off the time that has been bought during the Superbowl. Apple doesn't want to run the spot.

Monday, Tuesday, Wednesday, Thursday, it is now Friday, noon, two days before the Superbowl, two hours before the deadline for selling off Superbowl airtime. So far, no takers. The art director goes to the account executive and says, "If I hear that you sell this time after two-o-clock, if I find out you sold it at two-o-five, I'll kill you." He then goes to the creative director's office, sits on the couch, stares at his watch, and waits.

They can't sell the time.

Superbowl Sunday. The 49ers are playing the Dolphins. Everyone has gathered at one of the copywriters' homes to watch the game. The first half goes on forever, and then it's half time, and then it's third quarter. One commercial goes by, then another, then another. And then, he hears the marching footsteps that are the beginning of "1984."

The room cheers. He closes his eyes.

Epilogue: It is midnight in Los Angeles. The copywriter gets a phone call from New York. It's Jay.

"How does it feel to be a fucking star?" he asks.

卌卌卌 I

"We don't do anything bad here."

"1984" is only the beginning of 1984. The introduction of Macintosh is accompanied by a twenty-four page magazine insert that introduces "The computer for the rest of us" and the result is a barrage of media interest in Apple, and then, Chiat/Day. If 1984 had ended in February, it would still have been a banner year.

But it doesn't. There is still Nike.

Last summer, a letter came from the athletic footwear company in Beaverton, Oregon. They were searching for an ad agency to do something special for the 1984 Olympics. The letter said things like, we don't want any pin-striped, zoot-suited account executives. We wanna deal with the guys who do the shit. We want people who'll do cool stuff for Nike. Chiat/Day sends a numbered, gift-wrapped brick to every employee in their company. When they assemble the bricks, they have built a wall painted with a picture of L.A. Laker Michael Cooper bent over, stretching.

Now, Nike is a client, and they have gotten the non-traditional agency-client relationship they sought. They sit around a table at Chiat/Day with the creative director and a creative team. They are all yelling their heads off. Nike wants to be outrageous, and Chiat/Day says you can do outrageous advertising, but you must return to your roots as an authentic athletic brand. You must say that you understand the work ethic, the sweat and sacrifice that goes into being an athlete.

From this discussion, they evolve a campaign that uses no words. The feeling is: why say it when you can show it? The plan is to have athletes working out at their respective sports and paint them on outdoor boards and buildings everywhere.

To translate the work to television, the copywriter goes around the country and interviews some of the best athletes in their fields—Moses Malone, Lester Hayes, Joan Benoit, Carl Lewis. When he hears the passion with which they speak about what they do, he is convinced that it must be the athletes themselves who tell their stories. He distills the interviews to twenty seconds or so, writes the scripts, and he and his partner shoot commercials which, like the boards, are as simple and spare as possible— there is not even a mention of who the athlete is; they not only want Nike to be identified with the athlete, but also, with the kind of sports buff who would know the athlete.

Summer comes, and the campaign breaks. Everywhere you look, there is Nike. One day, the copywriter picks up the newspaper, turns to the sports section, and reads this: I hate television commercials, but there is one commercial that is so good I have to talk about it. The columnist is referring to the Moses Malone spot. Over the next month, the copywriter finds himself in an interesting position. Without writing a word, he will have become one of the most famous copywriters in America.

By the time the Olympics begin, Nike's "I Love LA" commercial has become the unofficial anthem of the games. Within weeks, Chiat/Day wins both the Porsche and Pizza Hut accounts. The agency will have to start hiring new creative people.

In one such transaction, the head of the Apple account will be interviewing a junior copywriter. The junior talks about not wanting to work on small projects, on coupons, on brochures, on trade ads—you know, the bad stuff.

"You don't understand," the man replies, "We don't do anything bad here."

WE OPEN ON A FUTURISTIC BUT GRITTY SCENE—
A MONUMENTAL STRUCTURE WITH THE LOOK OF
FAILED SOCIALISM.

BIG BROTHER VO (ON HUGE TV SCREEN): For today
we celebrate the first glorious anniversary of the
Information Purification Directives.

CUT TO SHAVED-HEADED AUTOMATONS MARCHING
IN LOCK STEP AS THE OMNI-PRESENT "BIG BROTHER"
HARRANGUES THEM OVER COUNTLESS VIDEOSCREENS.

BIG BROTHER VO: We have created for the first time
in all history, a garden of pure ideology, where
each worker may bloom secure from the pests of
contradictory and confusing truths.

CUT TO A GREAT HALL WHERE THE AUTOMATONS ARE
SITTING, ROW AFTER ROW, LISTENING TO "BIG BROTHER"
ON A HUGE SCREEN.

BIG BROTHER VO: Our Unification of Thought is
more powerful a weapon than any fleet or army
on earth.

INTERCUT SEQUENCES OF A BRIGHTLY-CLAD YOUNG
WOMAN BEING PURSUED BY SINISTER "THOUGHT
POLICE."

BIG BROTHER VO: We are one people. With one
will. One resolve. One cause.

WOMAN RUNS TO THE CENTER OF THE GREAT HALL,
HER PURSUERS CLOSING ON HER. SHE SWINGS A HEAVY
SLEDGEHAMMER AROUND AND OVER HER HEAD LIKE
AN OLYMPIAN AND HURLS IT AT THE VIDEO IMAGE OF
BIG BROTHER.

BIG BROTHER VO: Our enemies shall talk themselves to death. And we will bury them with their
own confusion. We shall prevail.

THE SCREEN EXPLODES. THE CAMERA PANS DOWN ROWS
OF AWED AUTOMATONS.

ANNCR VO: On January 24th, Apple Computer
will introduce Macintosh and you'll see why 1984,
won't be like 1984.

On January 24th,
Apple Computer will introduce
Macintosh.
And you'll see why 1984
won't be like "1984."

"The reaction was tremendous,
as I recall."

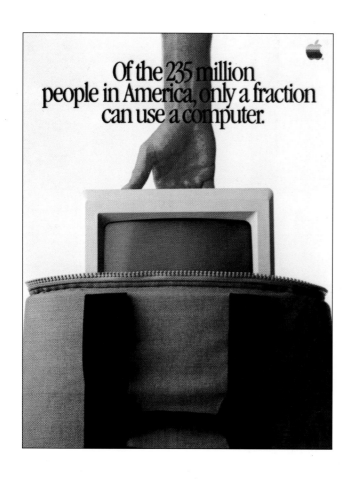

"The original line was 'Macintosh. The computer for the rest of you.' That was my line. Luckily a designer at Apple suggested changing it to 'the rest of us.' We had, 'Of the 235 million people living in America, only a fraction can use a computer—here's the computer for the rest of you.' And he said, 'I don't mean to criticize, but don't you think it'd be a little friendlier with us?' We said, 'Oh, yeah. How about that.'"

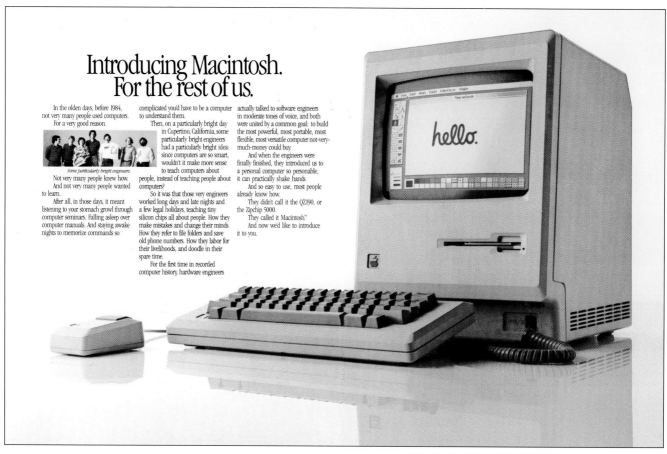

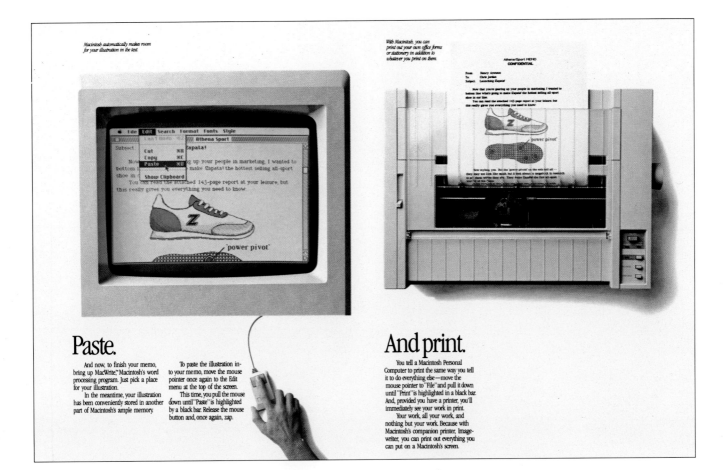

Macintosh automatically makes room for your illustration in the text.

With Macintosh, you can print out your own office forms or stationery in addition to whatever you print on them.

Paste.

And now, to finish your memo, bring up MacWrite," Macintosh's word processing program. Just pick a place for your illustration.

In the meantime, your illustration has been conveniently stored in another part of Macintosh's ample memory.

To paste the illustration into your memo, move the mouse pointer once again to the Edit menu at the top of the screen.

This time, you pull the mouse down until "Paste" is highlighted by a black bar. Release the mouse button and, once again, zap.

And print.

You tell a Macintosh Personal Computer to print the same way you tell it to do everything else—move the mouse pointer to "File" and pull it down until "Print" is highlighted in a black bar. And, provided you have a printer, you'll immediately see your work in print.

Your work, all your work, and nothing but your work. Because with Macintosh's companion printer, Imagewriter, you can print out everything you can put on a Macintosh's screen.

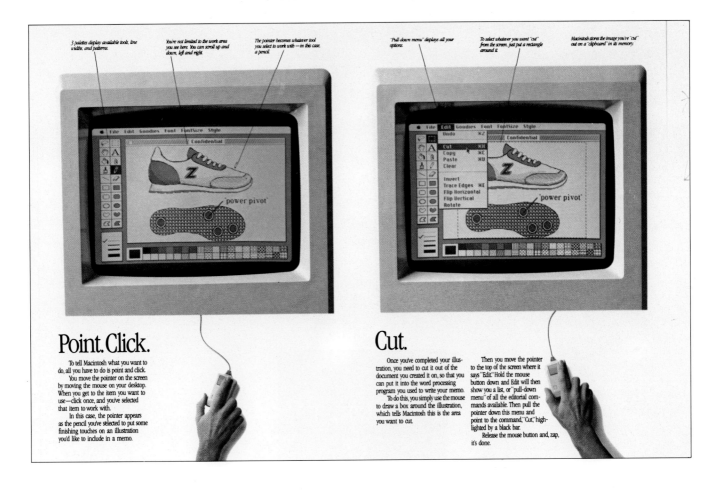

3 palettes display available tools, line widths, and patterns.

You're not limited to the work area you see here. You can scroll up and down, left and right.

The pointer becomes whatever tool you select to work with—in this case, a pencil.

"Pull-down menu" displays all your options.

To select whatever you want "cut" from the screen, just put a rectangle around it.

Macintosh stores the image you've "cut" out on a "clipboard" in its memory.

Point. Click.

To tell Macintosh what you want to do, all you have to do is point and click.

You move the pointer on the screen by moving the mouse on your desktop. When you get to the item you want to use—click once, and you've selected that item to work with.

In this case, the pointer appears as the pencil you've selected to put some finishing touches on an illustration you'd like to include in a memo.

Cut.

Once you've completed your illustration, you need to cut it out of the document you created it on, so that you can put it into the word processing program you used to write your memo.

To do this, you simply use the mouse to draw a box around the illustration, which tells Macintosh this is the area you want to cut.

Then you move the pointer to the top of the screen where it says "Edit." Hold the mouse button down and Edit will then show you a list, or "pull-down menu" of all the editorial commands available. Then pull the pointer down this menu and point to the command, "Cut," highlighted by a black bar.

Release the mouse button and, zap, it's done.

STACK OF MANUALS DROPS INTO FRAME.

ANNCR VO: This is a highly sophisticated business computer. And to use it . . . all you have to do is learn this . . .

SINGLE MANUAL DROPS INTO FRAME.

ANNCR VO: This is Macintosh from Apple. Also a highly sophisticated business computer. And to use it, all you have to do is learn this . . . Now . . . you decide which one's more sophisticated.

ANNCR VO: Macintosh. The computer for the rest of us.

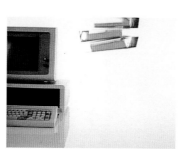

"Jay said at the time, 'This could be the next Volkswagen campaign. Don't you want to do that? This is the greatest thing that ever happened. Don't you understand how big this is?'"

Macintosh™

1984

ANNCR VO: With Macintosh from Apple . . . you can do all of this . . .
VARIOUS SHOTS OF DIFFERENT SCREENS BEING GENERATED ON THE COMPUTER.
HAND PUSHES BUTTON ON MOUSE.
ANNCR VO: . . . by simply doing this.
DISSOLVE TO LOGO.
ANNCR VO: Macintosh.

ANNCR VO: Using Apple's new Macintosh.
OPEN ON BEAUTY SHOT OF MACINTOSH COMPUTER.
ANNCR VO: does require some . . .
CUT TO SHOT OF PLUG.
ANNCR VO: . . . technical skill.
CUT TO SHOT OF SOCKET. HAND PUTS PLUG IN SOCKET.
DISSOLVE TO LOGO.
ANNCR VO: Macintosh.

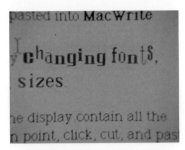 

.-- .... -.-- .- .-. . -. - -.-- --- ..- .-. . .- -.. .. -. --. - .... . --- - .... . .-. ... .. -.. . --- ..-. - .... . .--. .- --. . ..--..

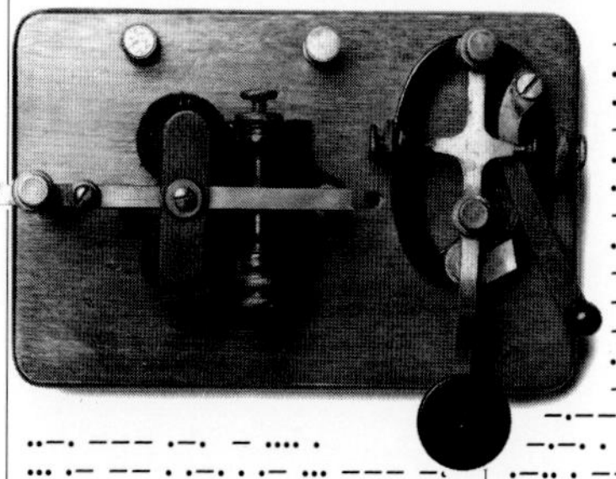

Why aren't you reading
the other side of the page?

For the same reason, we suspect, that nine out of ten people in your office can't get a computer to do anything but confuse them.

To explain, we really have to go back a hundred years, when Western Union dominated the communications industry with a handy little device called the telegraph key. First demonstrated by Samuel Morse and Alfred Vail at Vail's shop in 1838, it linked America coast-to-coast in just 23 years. By 1861, you could send a message from New York to San Francisco, via relays, in just a few hours.

In fact, if you used a highly skilled telegraph operator, he might relay your message at the incredible speed of 30 words per minute.

And you might have twirled your handlebar mustache in amazement, thinking you would most certainly use a device like the telegraph key, if only you could.

Of course, learning how would mean spending hours memorizing that complicated system of dots and dashes known as Morse Code. About the same amount of time people spend today, memorizing the "Q-Z-Control-A" keystroke commands that compose the code of conventional business computers.

But fortunately, while the use of telegraphy was still limited by the handful of key operators who could converse in its code, a strange little man with whiskers saved the rest of us the bother of learning it.

On February 14, 1876, Alexander Graham Bell patented the telephone.

The genius of the telephone wasn't just that it allowed anyone who could speak instant access to anyone who could listen. Or that now a simple appliance could transmit the smile in a voice, the hesitation in a question.

The real genius was that now people could communicate the way they always have: via the human voice.

Such is the nature of a technological breakthrough. It changes the way we do things by not changing the way we do things.

With that little bit of history in mind, we at Apple took a look at current generation business computers and said to ourselves, as Bell must have, "there must be an easier way."

We dreamed of making the technology of computing as accessible as the telephone.

So, while the computer establishment flatly accepted people having to invest 20-40 hours learning to use their computers, we invested hours, nights, and a few weekends investigating ways to make computers easier to use.

And it paid off.

In the form of a whole new family of compatible 32-bit computers we call the Apple® 32 SuperMicros™ Macintosh™ Lisa™ 2, Lisa 2/5 and Lisa 2/10.

Simply put, our SuperMicro technology does for computing precisely what the telephone did for communicating.

And, like the telephone, its real genius isn't that it allows anyone who can point to use a computer. But that it allows writers to write, composers to compose, and tinkerers to tinker, in the time it takes to think about it.

Thanks to a small rolling box called a mouse, your mind is free to concentrate on what you're doing, instead of how to do it.

Which makes all the difference.

The difference between computers that are history, and computers that change history. The difference between 1983 and 1984.

The difference between the left side of the page and this one.

"What we learned from Planning on Macintosh was that it was so inherently revolutionary, so inherently important as a product launch, that it couldn't just be hidden in a kind of generic ease of use strategy. So the key point was adding the concept of 'radical.' And the concept of 'radical ease of use' shaped the whole development of the campaign."

MUSIC: "I Can See Clearly Now".

A MONTAGE OF SHOTS TAKEN IN AND AROUND THE BLIND
CHILDRENS CENTER. ALL SITUATIONS SHOW THE LOVING,
SUPPORTIVE ENVIRONMENT OF THE CENTER AS WELL
AS THE CHILDRENS' POTENTIAL FOR REAL GROWTH
AND ACHIEVEMENT.

LYRICS: I can see clearly now, the rain is gone. I
can see all obstacles in my way. Gone are the dark
clouds that had me blind . . . Gonna be a bright,
bright, sunshiny day. Gonna be a bright, bright
sunshiny day. Look all around, there's nothing
but blue skies...look straight ahead nothing
but blue skies . . .

SHOTS SHOW VARIOUS BLIND CHILDREN INTERACTING
WITH EACH OTHER AND THEIR TEACHERS, BOTH
IN CLASSROOM SITUATIONS AND OUTSIDE ON PLAY
EQUIPMENT.

ANNCR.: With the extra love, care and support of
the Blind Children's Center, you'd be amazed at
how much a blind child can see.

SUPER: Serving visually handicapped children,
regardless of race, color, national or ethnic
origin, sex or religion. A project of the Southern
California Delta Gamma Alumnae.

LYRICS: Gonna be a bright, bright, sunshiny day.

"On the drive over, I was thinking about being surrounded by all these pre-school blind kids, and I said to my partner, "I don't know if I'm ready for this," and he said, "I don't know if I am either." But when we got there, it was the warmest, neatest place, and a very happy place. When the spot was done, we brought it to the school, and they were all happy, I turned to my partner and said, 'Hey, maybe we will go to heaven after all.'

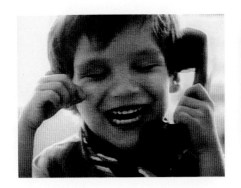  

"The Carl Lewis board where
he's jumping off the end. I
walked into my partner's
office, he was laying it out,
and he had Carl in the middle of the board, jumping,
but the tissue overlay was
jarred to the side, so that
when I walked in and looked
at it, I said, 'Hey it's great,
the way he's going off the
edge there.' My partner looked
at me and said, 'What the hell
are you talking about it?'"

OPEN ON CARL LEWIS AT BACK OF LONG JUMP RUNWAY.
HE IS CONCENTRATING ON JUMPING.
LEWIS VO: My first jump was a joke. Nine feet
even. But I said to myself "don't give up."
HE STARTS TO RUN IN VERY SLOW MOTION.
LEWIS VO: In high school, I kept coming in second.
I could have called it quits.
HE HITS BOARD AND JUMPS IN SLOW MOTION.
LEWIS VO: But I believe you should never give up.
THE CAMERA HOLDS AS HE GOES OUT OF FRAME, SO YOU
NEVER SEE HIM LAND.
LEWIS VO: When that's your philosophy, there's no
telling how far you can go.
CAMERA HOLDS ON SKY.

"I went and interviewed him up in Oregon. I asked him, 'What would you tell a kid, what's your philosophy?' And he said, 'My philosophy is to always keep trying.'"

"Nike was very vocal, a lot of arguing and screaming and yelling. They were an authentic athletic brand and that was their strength and their roots. And yes, you could be cool and yes you could even be unexpected and do neat stuff, but it had to come from your roots."

"I'm talking to some guy at UCLA, and he said, 'What do you do?' And I said, 'I work for an advertising agency.' He said, 'You know, I was just driving here on the 405, and I saw a billboard, and I've never done this in my life before, I got off at the exit, 'cause I really, it just went by so fast that it caught me. I went back so I could see it again, and it was a billboard for Nike.' And he said, 'I didn't know what it was at first, 'cause the logo was so small.' He said, 'Do you have any idea who's doing that?' I said, 'Yeah, that's the agency that I work for.' That's when it occurred to me that something I'd done was striking a chord."

OPEN ON FOOTBALL FIELD. NO PLAYERS.

SFX: Crowd. Quarterback calling signals.

LESTER HAYES STALKS INTO HIS AREA.

HAYES VO: By the time I hit the field, I've already worked overtime.

HAYES PROWLS AROUND WAITING TO START.

HAYES: Studying films of the guy across the line, for hours a night.

HE GETS DOWN IN HIS CORNERBACK STANCE.

HAYES: Because I believe in doing my homework.

CAMERA STARTS MOVING AT HAYES LIKE IT IS A RUNNING BACK TRYING TO AVOID HIS TACKLE.

HAYES: And people wonder how come I'm always in the right place . . .

HE MOVES AFTER THE CAMERA AND TACKLES IT.

SFX: Crunch.

IT GOES TO BLACK.

HAYES VO: . . . at the right time.

THE FOLLOWING PAGES ARE A MONTAGE OF
IMAGES FROM THE NIKE "I LOVE L. A." TELEVI-
SION COMMERCIAL. THIS IS THE SCRIPT OF THE
COMMERCIAL.

VARIOUS VIGNETTES OF LA PEOPLE, NIKE PEOPLE AND
RANDY NEWMAN
MUSIC: "I Love LA" throughout.
RANDY NEWMAN: Rollin' down Imperial Highway.
A big nasty red-head at my side. Santa Ana winds
blowin' hot from the north. We was born to ride.
From the South Bay, to the Valley. From the West
Side, to the East Side. Everybody's very happy
'cause the sun is shining all the time. It's like
another perfect day. I love LA!
CHORUS: We love it!
RANDY NEWMAN: We love it!
CHORUS: Ah, ah, ah, ah . . .
RANDY NEWMAN: I love LA!
CHORUS: We love it!

This year the Chiat/Day
Christmas Party will be held during
our regular business hours.

6:30pm to 1:30am.

You and a guest are cordially invited
to attend the
Chiat/Day Christmas Party
on Wednesday, December 19th.
It will be held at The Palace,
1735 N. Vine, in Hollywood
(across from Capitol Records).
We are enclosing
a ticket for each of you
for free admission to the
parking lot and to the restaurant.

CHIAT/DAY IS LOOKING FOR TWO GREAT ACCOUNT EXECUTIVES. WE'RE ALSO LOOKING FOR A UNICORN, THE TREASURE OF SIERRA MADRE AND THE HOLY GRAIL.

We know good AE's really do exist. We actually have a few around here already.

If you have two years experience, some on financial accounts, or five years experience, some on automotive/motorcycle accounts, write (don't call) Barbara Stolar, Chiat/Day, 517 So. Olive Street, Los Angeles, California 90013.

CHIAT/DAY

̶H̶H̶T̶ ̶H̶H̶T̶ ̶H̶H̶T̶ II

"It's not a bear, it's an iliop."

It goes something like this: In San Francisco, the copywriter and art director are waiting in the conference room. A client, Worlds of Wonder, would like to meet with the creative team who will be doing their new advertising campaign. The client wants to introduce them to Teddy Ruxpin. Everyone at Chiat/Day has heard about Teddy. He is going to be the world's first talking teddy bear.

Three people arrive. The founder of Worlds of Wonder, his associate, and a gentle, quiet looking man, wearing a backpack that you might carry a child in. Sitting in the backpack, watching the world go by him, is Teddy Ruxpin.

"We would never keep Teddy in a box," the inventor says, setting the doll on the table.

The founder is a super salesman, and he is talking up a blue streak about the World of Teddy Ruxpin. Teddy is not a toy for children, he will be a friend; he will be as much a part of their lives as a brother or sister, and Worlds of Wonder has created an entire universe for him. As the founder is saying this, the inventor touches Teddy somewhere on his back, at which point Teddy starts talking and singing and playing music and just generally starts having a marvelous time.

"That's the most incredible teddy bear I've ever seen," the art director says.

"Oh, he's not a bear," the founder says, "He's an iliop."

"Pardon me?"

"IL-EE-OP," the man repeats.

The art director looks at the copywriter.

The copywriter looks at the art director.

And before they know it, the man rolls out this big map and is off into the incredible world of Teddy Ruxpin, a world of iliops and fobs and mugwumps and god knows what else, the land of the greebs, or something like that, there are stories about them all, and Teddy will tell them. Teddy is privy to these stories, of course, because he is not a bear, but an iliop.

"I don't think we can call it an iliop," the copywriter says. "People won't know what we're talking about."

Well, you don't have to call him an iliop, the founder says, but we don't want you calling him a bear. See what you can do.

The creative team creates two commercials, one for children, one for adults. The commercial for adults is a parody of Frankenstein which shows a mad doctor bringing the, um, unnamed bear-like creature to life.

The commercials start running in late November, and by early December, the Teddy Ruxpin doll is a sellout. By Christmas, stores are issuing Teddy Ruxpin rainchecks which can be redeemed in April. It is one of those times when it is hard to say how big a role advertising has played in a product's success. For Teddy had the kind of personality that was probably going to succeed no matter what.

During the following twelve months that the creative team works on Teddy Ruxpin's advertising, they will not refer to him as a bear.

At least, not to his face.

SFX: Storm.

OPEN THROUGH WINDOW OF GREY CASTLE, MAD SCIENTIST-STYLE LABORATORY BELOW. HUNCHBACK BECKONS WITH LANTERN.

HUNCH: Follow me, sir.

LITTLE BOY FOLLOWING, LOOKS DOWN TO LAB.

BOY: Hi, Dad!

PROFESSOR, STANDING IN LAB WITH CLIPBOARD, LOOKS UP AND SEES BOY.

PROF: Ah, my son!

PROF PULLS SHEET OFF TABLE TO REVEAL TEDDY RUXPIN STRAPPED DOWN.

PROF: Now we are ready.

HUNCHBACK AND BOY COME NEAR TABLE. BOY SEATS HIMSELF AND REMOVES CAP.

PROF: It's bound to work this time.

PROF PULLS LEVER.

SFX: Light travels up and down wires.

PROF DIRECTS HUNCHBACK TO PULL SOME LEVERS AT ANOTHER BLINKING SWITCHBOARD. PROF PULLS LEVER BACK, GOES TOWARD TEDDY RUXPIN AND FEELS FOR A PULSE.

PROF: I've failed again.

HUNCHBACK LEANS IN SYMPATHY AGAINST PROFESSOR.

HUNCH: Awww.

HUNCHBACK PULLS OUT A HANDFUL OF BATTERIES. CUT ON BATTERIES. HUNCHBACK OFFERS BATTERIES.

HUNCH: How about these, master?

CUT OF TEDDY'S FACE. BEGINS TO MOVE.

TEDDY: Hi there. My name is Teddy Ruxpin. How are you today?

CAMERA PULLS BACK TO REVEAL STUNNED SON AND HUNCHBACK.

BOY: Fine.

PROF REACHES FORWARD TO FEEL PULSE. TEDDY KEEPS TALKING.

TEDDY: Well then. I would like to tell you a story . . .

SUPER: Additional storybook cassettes available.

ANNCR VO: Teddy Ruxpin . . .

PROF THROWS UP ARMS IN GLEE. STORM SOUNDS, CONTINUES THROUGHOUT.

PROF (SHOUTING): It's alive!

ANNCR VO: The world's first animated story-telling bear.

CAMERA IS PULLING BACK TO INCLUDE LAB SCENE, AS VIEWER IS TAKEN UP AND OUT THROUGH GREY STONE WINDOW, LOOKING DOWN AT JUBILANT PROFESSOR.

PROF: It's alive!

ANNCR VO: Now available at stores everywhere.

SUPER: Teddy Ruxpin a friend for life has come to life.

PROF (STILL SHOUTING): It's alive! Haha!

"Teddy Ruxpin. Very easy to work with."

Over one million Teddy Ruxpins® will disappear from toy shelves by the end of our first year. And like Teddy, the new products from Worlds of Wonder will be disappearing just as quickly. Because they're based on the same simple promise: Give people more than they can imagine. A promise that's anything but empty.

W•W
WORLDS OF WONDER®

OPEN ON OVERHEAD VIEW, INTERIOR OF FUTURISTIC STADIUM INNARDS.

MUSIC: Momentous score throughout.

WOMAN DRAWS BLACK SLASH MARKS ON HER CHEEKS. PLAYERS, IN SILVER SUITS, RECEIVE LAZER GUNS FROM CHECK-OUT COUNTER. CLOSE-UP TO BATTERIES INTO LAZER GUN. CUT TO GIANT LOUDSPEAKER. PLAYERS REACT, LOOKING GRIM.

METALLIC VOICE: Players to stadium now. Players to stadium now.

PLAYERS EXCHANGE SIGNIFICANT LOOKS. CROWD CHEERING IN BACKGROUND: LAZER! LAZER! PLAYERS HEAD TOWARD DOOR INTO THE LIGHT ARENA. DOOR SLAMS SHUT TO BLACK.

SFX: Crowd cheering throughout.

OPEN ON OVERHEAD VIEW OF ARENA. FANS LOOK DOWN INTO PIT WHERE PLAY TAKES PLACE. REFEREE, MOUNTED IN SPACE-AGE MOTORIZED CART, COMES SWOOPING BETWEEN TEAM CAPTAINS, WHO COME FORWARD TO FACE EACH OTHER. CLOSE-UP, THEY SNEER AT EACH OTHER.

REFEREE: On my signal, begin. Now!

PLAYERS DART, AIM, SHOOT, LEAP, ETC.

REFEREE: Out! you're out! Out!

VIEW FROM CROUCHING PLAYER'S POINT OF VIEW, AS LAST PLAYER HOVERS ABOVE, LAZER IN HAND. HE SHOOTS, SCREEN GOES BRIGHT TO PRODUCT SHOT. PACKAGE WITH CONTENTS ON TOP.

ANNCR VO: Lazer Tag. The game that moves at the speed of light. From Worlds of Wonder. Stadium not included.

"The director thought seeing some blood might be nice. But we talked him out of it."

Stadium not included.

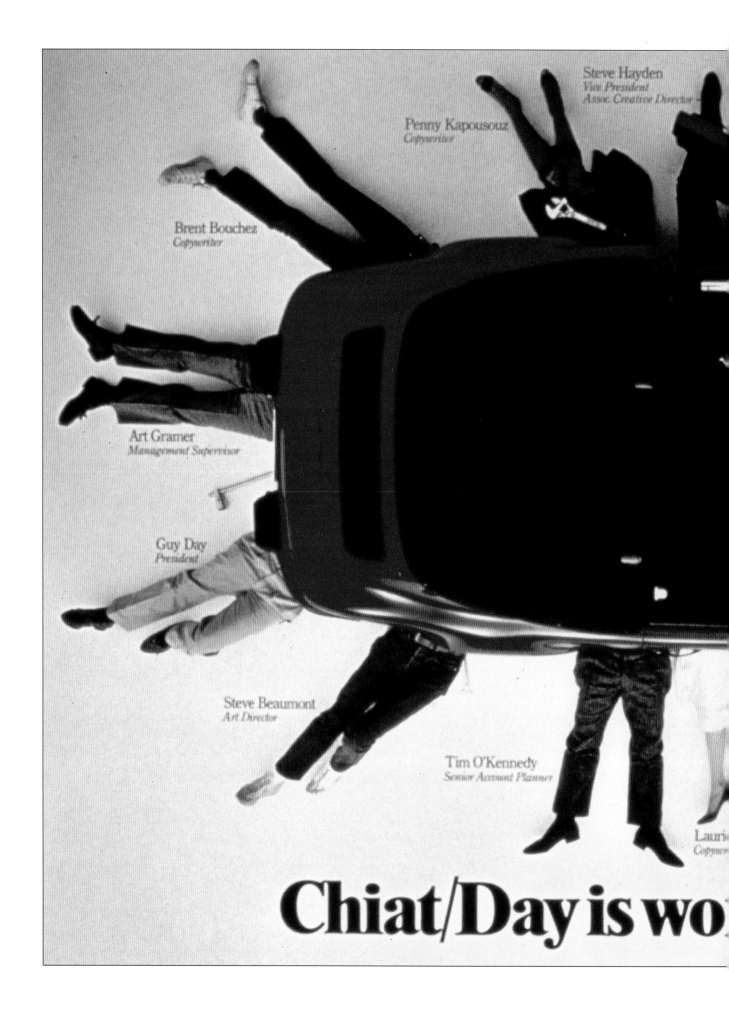

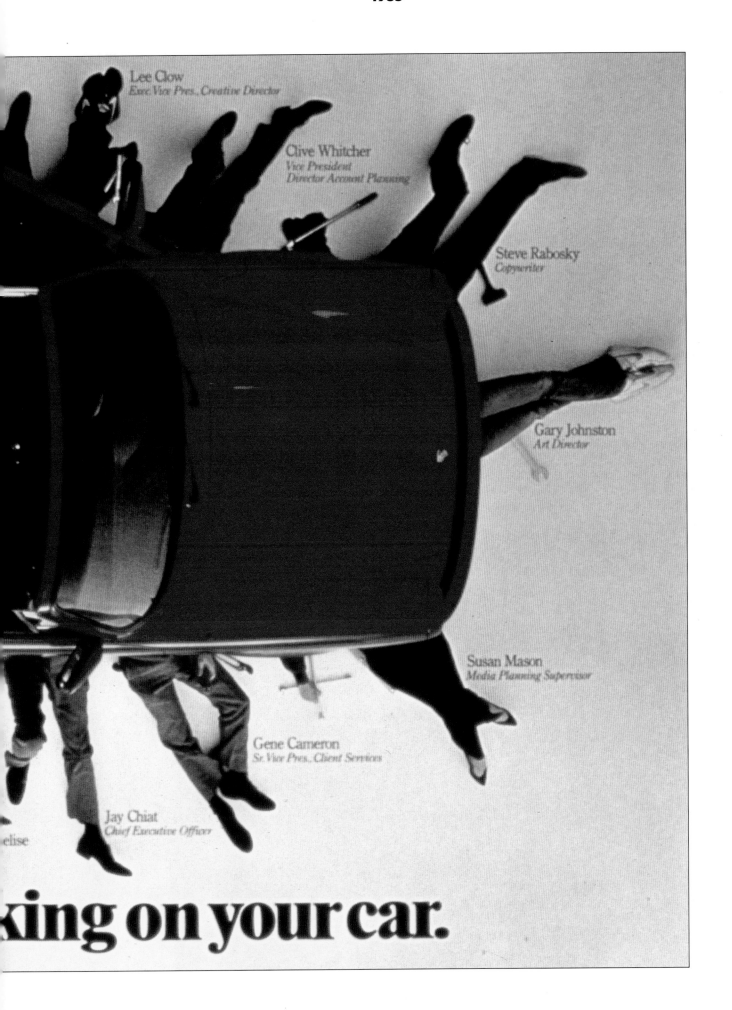

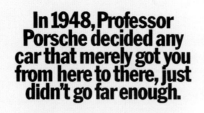

In 1948, Professor Porsche decided any car that merely got you from here to there, just didn't go far enough.

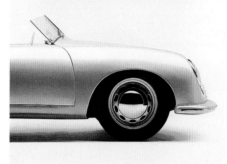

In 37 years, nothing has changed.

There's a restlessness about Weissach.

Even in winter.

The bitter cold that keeps more reasonable Germans inside, only means Helmuth Bott and Helmut Flegl will wear fur-lined gloves to the test track this morning.

The snow has been plowed against the catch-fences.

The tarmac, freshly salted, is safe enough to test a suspension system. If everyone is careful.

Bott, head of Research & Development, and Flegl, Director of Research, will do today what men with such titles usually prefer leaving to men without such titles.

Risk a good deal more than cold hands to do what Porsche engineers have done since the beginning.

Discover.

Discover the same kinds of things that, for 37 years, have helped build cars like the 911.

A car that is not only immediately recognizable as a Porsche, but also universally recognized as a phenomenon.

Its basic shape and 6-cylinder, air-cooled, rear-engine design have remained essentially unchanged since the 911 was introduced in 1964.

But under that apparently familiar exterior lies 20 years of new car.

Horsepower has been increased 54%. Stroke lengthened. Wheelbase lengthened. Grills added. 5-mph bumpers and front air dams incorporated.

Grills removed. Heating improved. Sound deadening increased. Suspension modified. Gearbox improved.

Catalytic converters have replaced thermal reactors. And Quartz-Grey Metallic has replaced Anthracite.

Otherwise, the Porsche 911 remains the same study in simplicity it has always been.

Reliable. Revered. And most important, the best 911 it can possibly be. This year.

911 Carrera 6-cylinder horizontally opposed, two overhead camshafts, air-cooled, rear engine, 3164cc's, 200 hp. Weight: 2756 lbs. Top speed: 146 mph.

Fun may be the most important discipline of all.

When Roland Kussmaul is tired of meetings, tired of wearing a tie, tired of hearing his phone ring, he leaves his office in the racing compound a few hundred yards west of the test track, to do the one thing he never gets tired of doing.

Driving.

Not driving as people who wear ties know it. But driving as Kussmaul knows it.

Putting the car a little bit sideways.

Kussmaul is a professional test driver. Which means he can detect a millimeter's difference in the thickness of a sway bar or a 5% adjustment in a spring rate. In a single test lap.

Kussmaul was Project Leader for our customer-owned 956 race cars. Project Manager on our SCCA 944

racer. And when he isn't helping tune the suspension of the Paris/Dakar 4-wheel drive car, he's out crossing African deserts in one.

Needless to say, a man like Roland Kussmaul isn't easily entertained.

Which says something about the Porsche 944.

A car Kussmaul drives not

because it can do 0 to 60 mph in 7.2 seconds.

Not because its transaxle design helps make it the best handling production sports car on the market. Even when driven to Kussmaul's limit.

And no, not for its newly designed, 928-like interior.

But for what may be the best reason of all to drive any Porsche.

The fun of it.

944 4-cylinder in-line, single overhead camshaft, liquid-cooled, front-engine, 2479cc's, 143 hp., transaxle. Weight: 2778 lbs. Top speed: 130 mph.

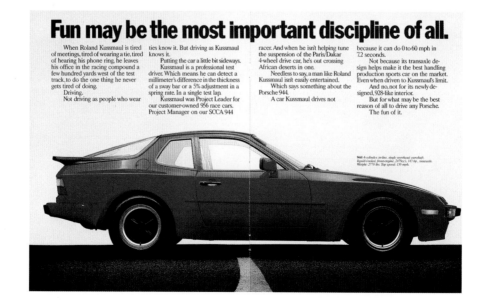

And Professor Porsche expects still more.

The windows in Professor Porsche's office in Zuffenhausen overlook a courtyard.

A courtyard lined with Porsches parked in a patchwork of colors and model designs.

Not shiny new cars, but the ones that have already met foul weather and potholes. Survived the winding kilometers between summer picnics and winter ski trips.

To Professor Porsche, these are very important Porsches.

Because when he stands at this window, hands crossed behind his back, rocking from toe to heel, and looks down at the cars in the courtyard, he imagines.

He is reminded of how much is yet to be accomplished.

It is the reason Professor Porsche drives his company much the same way one drives his cars.

With passion. Respect. Conviction.

The result, cars that set new expectations of what a car ought to be. Cars like this one.

Porsche's latest project, the 959. Or, more affectionately known as the "Gruppe B" car.

A car powered by the same 6-cylinder, horizontally opposed, twin overhead cam engine used in Porsche's 956 race car. Producing 400 hp.

A car with such a sophisticated drive train you can actually dial in the power to each of the four wheels.

A car with a self-adjusting suspension system that automatically lowers it as speed increases.

Top speed: no one really knows. Yet.

And as far as Professor Porsche is concerned, it really doesn't matter. Because no matter how close to perfection the Gruppe B car comes, there will be another day when he stands at his window.

And imagines.

959 (Gruppe B) 6-cylinder horizontally opposed, four overhead camshafts, four valves per cylinder, water-cooled rear engine with twin intercooled turbochargers, 2850cc's, 400+ hp. Estimated top speed: 180+ mph.

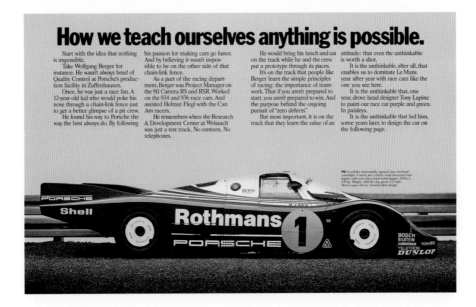

How we teach ourselves anything is possible.

Start with the idea that nothing is impossible.

Take Wolfgang Berger for instance. He wasn't always head of Quality Control at Porsche's production facility in Zuffenhausen.

Once, he was just a race fan. A 12-year-old kid who would poke his nose through a chain-link fence just to get a better glimpse of a pit crew.

He found his way to Porsche the way the best always do. By following

his passion for making cars go faster.

And by believing it wasn't impossible to be on the other side of that chain-link fence.

As a part of the racing department, Berger was Project Manager on the 911 Carrera RS and RSR. Worked on the 934 and 936 race cars. And assisted Helmut Flegl with the Can Am racers.

He remembers when the Research & Development Center at Weissach was just a test track. No canteen. No telephones.

He would bring his lunch and eat on the track while he and the crew put a prototype through its paces.

It's on the track that people like Berger learn the simple principles of racing: the importance of teamwork. That if you aren't prepared to start, you aren't prepared to win. And the purpose behind the ongoing pursuit of "zero defects".

But most important, it is on the track that they learn the value of an

attitude: that even the unthinkable is worth a shot.

It is the unthinkable, after all, that enables us to dominate Le Mans year after year with race cars like the one you see here.

It is the unthinkable that, one year, drove head designer Tony Lapine to paint our race car purple and green. In paisleys.

It is the unthinkable that led him, some years later, to design the car on the following page.

956 6-cylinder horizontally opposed, four overhead camshafts, 4 valves per cylinder, water-cooled mid engine with twin intercooled turbochargers, 2649cc's, 630 hp. Weight: 1848 lbs. Top speed: 217 mph. Monocoque chassis. Ground effect design.

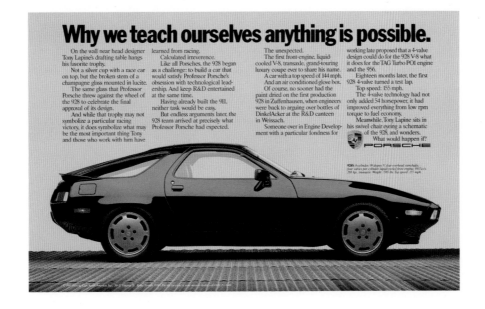

Why we teach ourselves anything is possible.

On the wall near head designer Tony Lapine's drafting table hangs his favorite trophy.

Not a silver cup with a race car on top, but the broken stem of a champagne glass mounted in lucite.

The same glass that Professor Porsche threw against the wheel of the 928 to celebrate the final approval of its design.

And while that trophy may not symbolize a particular racing victory, it does symbolize what may be the most important thing Tony and those who work with him have

learned from racing.

Calculated irreverence.

Like all Porsches, the 928 began as a challenge: to build a car that would satisfy Professor Porsche's obsession with technological leadership. And keep R&D entertained at the same time.

Having already built the 911, neither task would be easy.

But endless arguments later, the 928 team arrived at precisely what Professor Porsche had expected.

The unexpected.

The first front-engine, liquid-cooled V-8, transaxle, grand-touring luxury coupe ever to share his name.

A car with a top speed of 144 mph. And an air conditioned glove box.

Of course, no sooner had the paint dried on the first production 928 in Zuffenhausen, when engineers were back to arguing over bottles of DinkelAcker at the R&D canteen in Weissach.

Someone over in Engine Development with a particular fondness for

working late proposed that a 4-valve design could do for the 928 V-8 what it does for the TAG Turbo-POI engine and the 956.

Eighteen months later, the first 928 4-valve turned a test lap.

Top speed: 155 mph.

The 4-valve technology had not only added 54 horsepower, it had improved everything from low rpm torque to fuel economy.

Meanwhile, Tony Lapine sits in his swivel chair eyeing a schematic of the 928, and wonders.

What would happen if?

PORSCHE

928S 8-cylinder V-8 dopinc V, four overhead camshafts, four valves per cylinder liquid-cooled front engine, 4957cc's, 288 hp, automatic. Weight: 3385 lbs. Top speed: 155 mph.

"Before I had ever gotten to Germany, I thought, 'I'm gonna have to write about this stuff and I have no idea what these people are like or what Weissach is like,' and so I said to the guy from Porsche, 'Could you just sit with me for a while and tell me about Porsche and Germany?' And he sat down and just, he kind of thought in headlines, you know? And that was one of the first lines out of his mouth, 'There's a restlessness about Weissach, even in winter.' And I wrote it down and used it. That was the opening line of the insert. And he was also my interpreter, through the four days there, 'cause he spoke German, French and English. Very nice guy. Eventually, I married him."

MUSIC: THROUGHOUT

ANNCR VO: Imagine you were a car.

SFX: A generic car accelerating; continues.

ANNCR VO: What would you be?

SFX: Porsche 944 accelerating, without turbocharger.

ANNCR VO: You'd be a sports car.

SFX: Engine revs.

ANNCR VO: You'd be quick . . .

SFX: Continue.

ANNCR VO: . . . Agile.

SFX: Continue.

ANNCR VO: You'd be . . . turbocharged.

SFX: Engine sound increases, amplified by tunnel, as Turbocharger kicks in.

ANNCR VO: And, of course . . . You'd be a Porsche.

The New 944 Turbo

PORSCHE

"The area we wanted to shoot in still had snow on the ground, so we had to go down to a lower level where the snow had pretty much melted, but it was still very cold. The director wanted to hose down the road to make it look good, but as soon as we did that, the road turned to ice. We were driving in a van with a special rig on it to get the low point of view, and it started swerving all over the road. It wouldn't drive at a decent clip. And so we had to go out, the crew went out and got I don't know how many truckloads of salt, and the whole crew, including us and the account people, everybody, with a bag of salt under one arm, just walked up and down probably close to half a mile of road, salting it down, so we could get the shot."

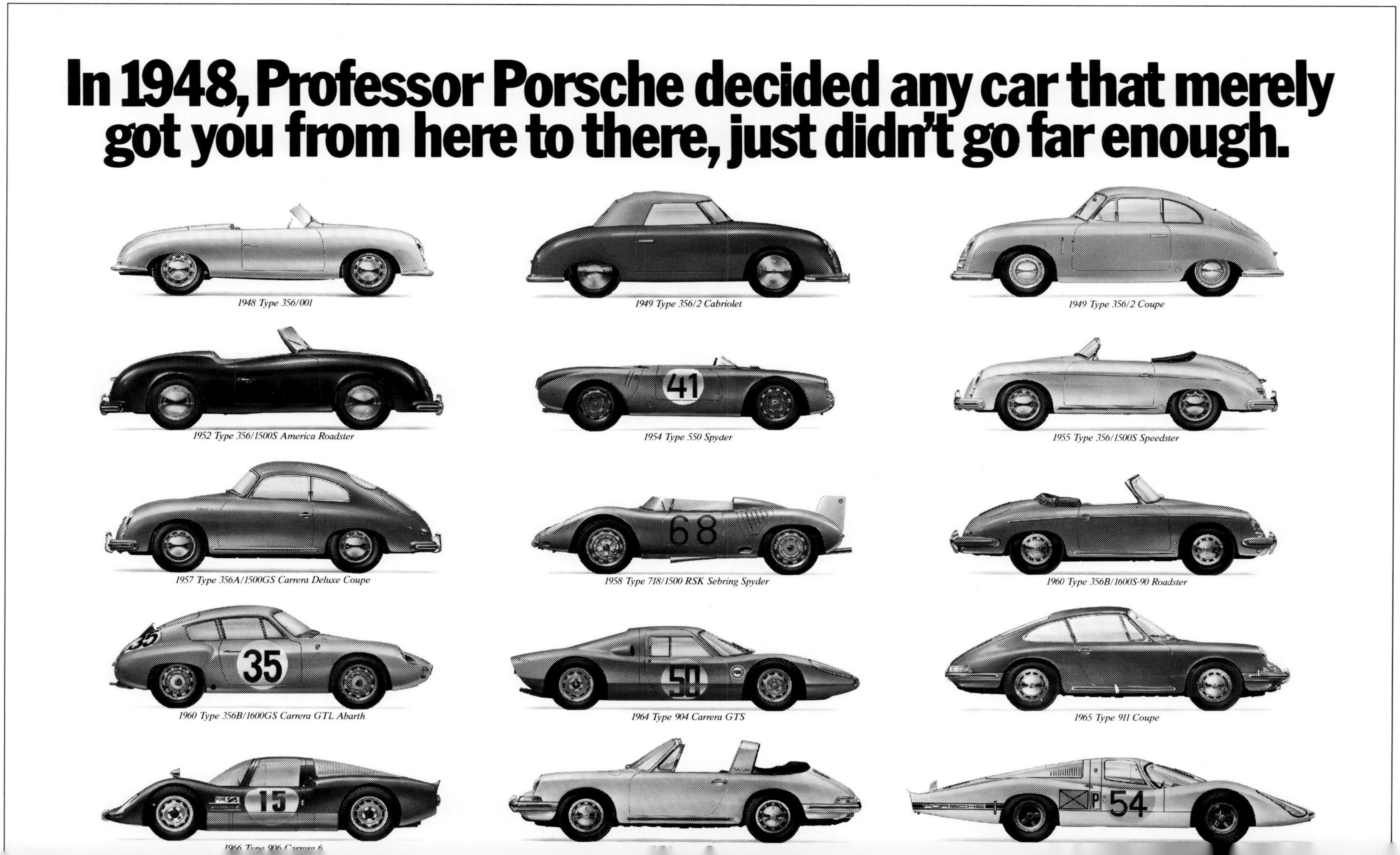

In 1948, Professor Porsche decided any car that merely got you from here to there, just didn't go far enough.

1949 Type 356/2 Coupe

1955 Type 356/1500S Speedster

1960 Type 356B/1600S-90 Roadster

1965 Type 911 Coupe

1949 Type 356/2 Cabriolet

1954 Type 550 Spyder

1958 Type 718/1500 RSK Sebring Spyder

1964 Type 904 Carrera GTS

1948 Type 356/001

1952 Type 356/1500S America Roadster

1957 Type 356A/1500GS Carrera Deluxe Coupe

1960 Type 356B/1600GS Carrera GTL Abarth

1966 Type 906 Carrera 6

1973 Type 911 Carrera RS

1976 Type 911 Turbo

1978 Type 936 Spyder

1985 Type 959 Gruppe B

1985 Type 928S 4-valve

1970 Type 914

1974 Type 911 Carrera RSR Turbo

1978 Type 928

1984 Type 962

1985 Type 944

1969 Type 908/02 "Flounder" Spyder

1973 Type 917/30 Spyder

1978 Type 935 "Moby Dick"

1980 Type 924 Carrera GT

1985 Type 911 Cabriolet

For Christmas 1920, Ferdinand Porsche Jr. received a toy car. Not the kind you push around on the floor or wind up and let go.

The kind you drive.

Fully operational, with headlights and an engine that would push it along at a brisk 30 miles per hour.

Of course, like most 11 year-olds, young Ferry had little understanding of the practical uses for the automobile. And cared even less.

Because his car provided him with countless hours of the one thing eleven year-olds value more than anything else.

Fun.

Twenty-eight years later, the first 356 Porsche was introduced. With 40 horsepower and a top speed of 84 mph. Ferry Porsche was now Dr. Porsche, but the thrill of his first days behind the wheel was etched clearly in his memory.

And with his new silver convertible, he played a strong hunch. That while everyone else was building utilitarian cars for the masses, there must be at least a few people like himself who still felt eleven years old. And who would want a car that did more than simply transport you from one place to another.

The kind of car you drive…just for the fun of it.

Thirty-seven years have passed since the car in the upper left hand corner of this page was introduced.

The hunch had become a legend. One that still thrives in the car in the lower right hand corner of this page.

The latest Porsche. Model 928S. With four valves per-cylinder, 288 horsepower and a top speed of 155 mph.

As for Dr. Porsche, he's now a professor.

On his 75th birthday, he was presented with another toy car. A scale model of the Le Mans winning 936 Porsche with a five horsepower engine and just enough room for an eager 75 year-old man to squeeze into the cockpit.

And before any pictures could be snapped or toasts proposed, the little car had disappeared.

Along with Professor Porsche. PORSCHE

OPEN WITH A CLOSE-UP MARCHING
FEET ON SURREALISTIC PLAIN
SFX: Wind.
WE SEE A LONG LINE SNAKING OFF
INTO THE DISTANCE. VERY FAINTLY, WE
HEAR A CHOIR OF WHISTLING.
SFX: Whistling to the tune of
"Hi Ho, Hi Ho, it's off to work
we go . . ."
DRAWING CLOSER, WE SEE THE LINE IS
MADE UP OF MEN AND WOMEN MARCH-
ING SINGLE FILE. ANOTHER ANGLE,
STILL CLOSER. ALL ARE IN BUSINESS
SUITS. ALL ARE BLINDFOLDED.
ANOTHER ANGLE. THE SINGLE LINE IS
MARCHING RIGHT OFF A CLIFF INTO
SPACE, ONE PERSON AFTER ANOTHER,
STILL WHISTLING. OTHER ANGLES. PEO-
PLE DISAPPEARING OVER THE EDGE,
THE WHISTLING DIMINISHES. WE FOCUS
ON THE LAST MAN IN LINE. HE NOTICES
THAT THERE ARE FEWER AND FEWER
PEOPLE WHISTLING WITH HIM. HE
NOTICES THAT HE'S COMPLETELY ALONE.
ANNCR VO: On January 23 Apple
Computer will announce the
Macintosh Office.
HE BREAKS PACE, UNCOMFORTABLE,
FALTERING. HE STOPS IN HIS TRACKS.
HIS WHISTLING TRAILS OFF TO SILENCE.
HE LIFTS HIS BLINDFOLD OVER ONE
EYE, WHICH BLINKS, ADJUSTING TO
THE LIGHT.
ANNCR VO: You can look into it.
CUT TO ANOTHER LINE OF BUSINESS
PEOPLE BLINDFOLDED AS THE FIRST
GROUP.
ANNCR VO: Or you can go on with
business a usual.

*"Some people didn't like
this spot, as I recall."*

IBM is finally talking to us.

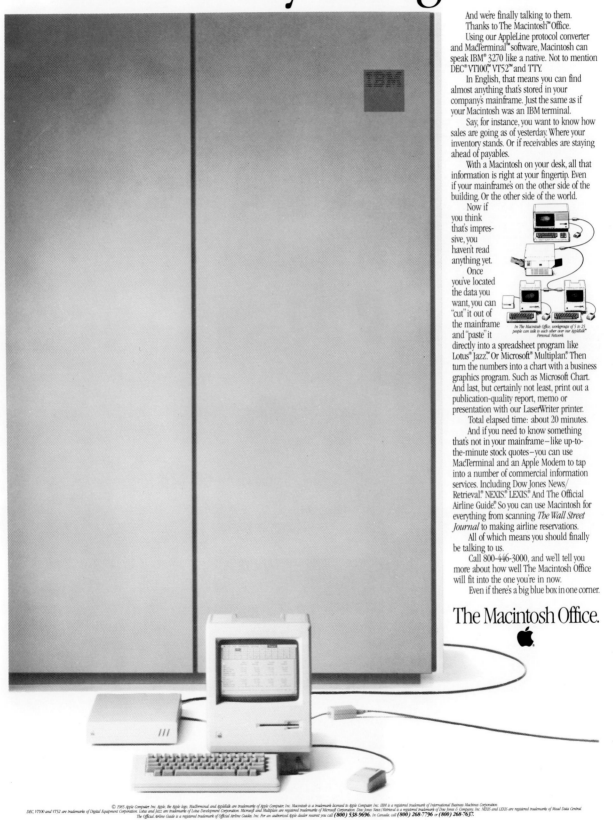

And we're finally talking to them.

Thanks to The Macintosh™ Office.

Using our AppleLine protocol converter and MacTerminal™ software, Macintosh can speak IBM® 3270 like a native. Not to mention DEC® VT100,™ VT52™ and TTY.

In English, that means you can find almost anything that's stored in your company's mainframe. Just the same as if your Macintosh was an IBM terminal.

Say, for instance, you want to know how sales are going as of yesterday. Where your inventory stands. Or if receivables are staying ahead of payables.

With a Macintosh on your desk, all that information is right at your fingertip. Even if your mainframe's on the other side of the building. Or the other side of the world.

Now if you think that's impressive, you haven't read anything yet.

Once you've located the data you want, you can "cut" it out of the mainframe and "paste" it

In The Macintosh Office, workgroups of 5 to 25 people can talk to each other over our AppleTalk™ Personal Network.

directly into a spreadsheet program like Lotus® Jazz.™ Or Microsoft® Multiplan.® Then turn the numbers into a chart with a business graphics program. Such as Microsoft Chart. And last, but certainly not least, print out a publication-quality report, memo or presentation with our LaserWriter printer.

Total elapsed time: about 20 minutes.

And if you need to know something that's not in your mainframe—like up-to-the-minute stock quotes—you can use MacTerminal and an Apple Modem to tap into a number of commercial information services. Including Dow Jones News/Retrieval.® NEXIS.® LEXIS.® And The Official Airline Guide.® So you can use Macintosh for everything from scanning *The Wall Street Journal* to making airline reservations.

All of which means you should finally be talking to us.

Call 800-446-3000, and we'll tell you more about how well The Macintosh Office will fit into the one you're in now.

Even if there's a big blue box in one corner.

The Macintosh Office.

ANNCR VO: This is Apple's
Macintosh.
CUT TO VARIOUS PROGRAMS ON
MACHINE.
ANNCR VO: And this is some of the
software that's being developed for
Macintosh.
CAMERA PULLS BACK TO SHOW
ADDITIONAL PROGRAMS.
ANNCR VO: At the rate of one new
program every business day.
Exactly how much software is
that?
CAMERA CONTINUES TO PULL
BACK REVEALING MORE AND
MORE PROGRAMS.
ANNCR VO: We'll give you a hint.

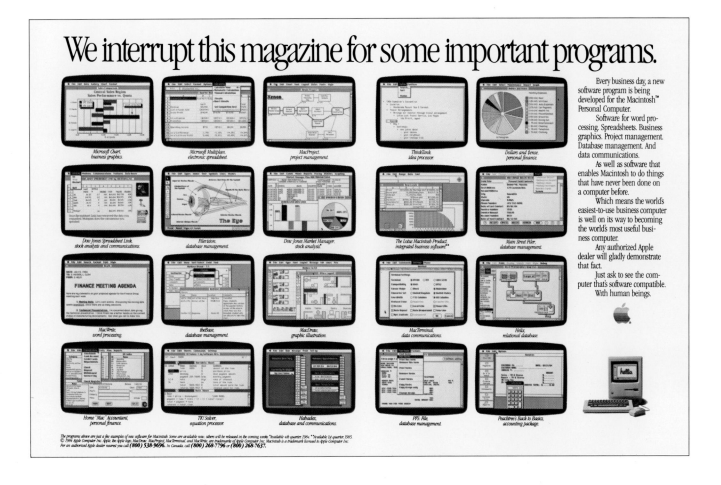

Take Mac
for a te

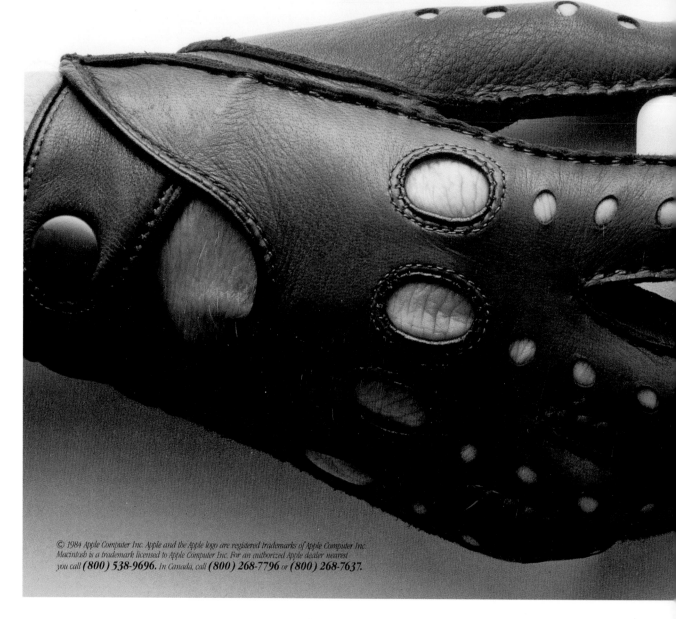

ntosh out st drive.

Since we introduced Macintosh,™ we've been telling you it's the first business computer anyone can learn to use overnight.

Now we're going to prove it.

By giving you a Macintosh to use. Overnight.

Right now, anyone who qualifies can walk into a participating authorized Apple dealer, and walk out with a Macintosh Personal Computer.

No purchase necessary.

It's our way of letting you test drive a Macintosh in the comfort of your own office, home, RV, hotel room, dorm room or whatever.

And really experience, first-hand, how much your finger already knows about computing.

Simply put, in less time than it takes to get frustrated on an ordinary computer, you'll be doing real work on Macintosh.

Because the hard part of test driving a Macintosh isn't figuring out how to use it.

The hard part is bringing it back.

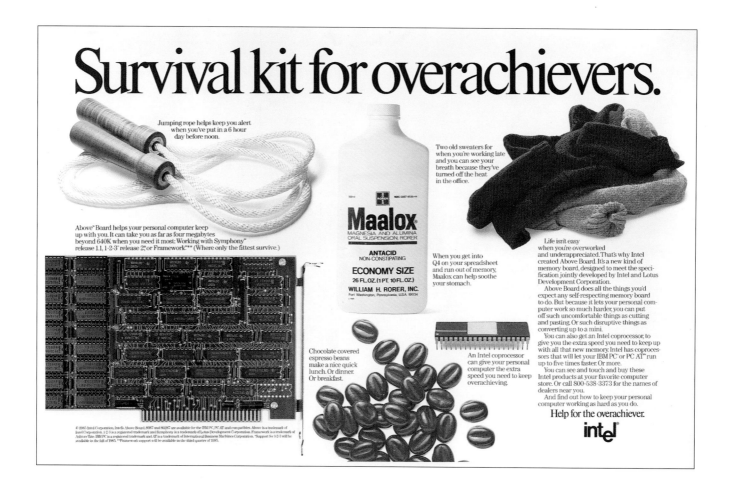

Intel announces the end of computer generated graphics.

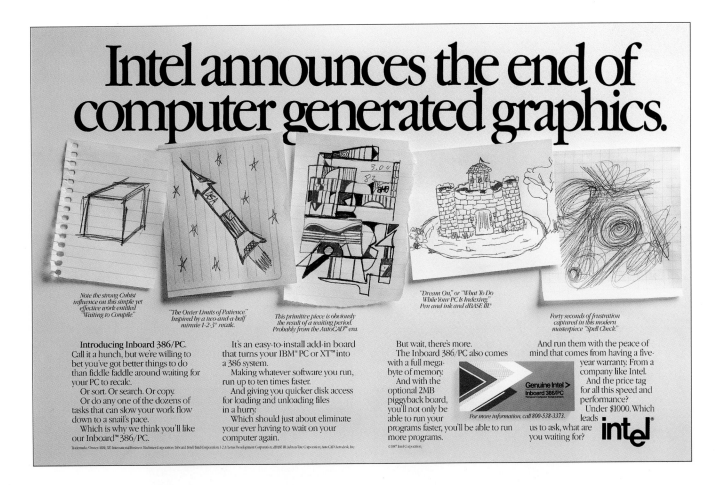

Note the strong Cubist influence on this simple yet effective work entitled "Waiting to Compile."

"The Outer Limits of Patience." Inspired by a two-and-a-half minute 1-2-3® recalc.

This primitive piece is obviously the result of a waiting period. Probably from the AutoCAD® era.

"Dream On," or "What To Do While Your PC Is Indexing." Pen and ink and dBASE III®

Forty seconds of frustration captured in this modern masterpiece "Spell Check."

Introducing Inboard 386/PC.
Call it a hunch, but we're willing to bet you've got better things to do than fiddle faddle around waiting for your PC to recalc.
Or sort. Or search. Or copy.
Or do any one of the dozens of tasks that can slow your work flow down to a snail's pace.
Which is why we think you'll like our Inboard™ 386/PC.

It's an easy-to-install add-in board that turns your IBM® PC or XT™ into a 386 system.
Making whatever software you run, run up to ten times faster.
And giving you quicker disk access for loading and unloading files in a hurry.
Which should just about eliminate your ever having to wait on your computer again.

But wait, there's more.
The Inboard 386/PC also comes with a full megabyte of memory.
And with the optional 2MB piggyback board, you'll not only be able to run your programs faster, you'll be able to run more programs.

For more information, call 800-538-3373.

And run them with the peace of mind that comes from having a five-year warranty. From a company like Intel.
And the price tag for all this speed and performance?
Under $1000. Which leads us to ask, what are you waiting for?

intel®

The memory is always the first to go.

–192K. For all its pluses, networking has a minus.

–66K, –128K, –128K. A word of warning: Too many pop-ups can have a negative effect on your memory.

–128K. Everyone will tell you downloading is where it's at. Which is why expanded memory is where you should be.

–320K. Windowing can give you a whole new outlook. It can also gobble up a whole lot of memory.

It can happen just like that.
One minute you've got a walloping 640K, the next minute, you've got zip.
That's because each new application you add devours precious RAM.
Fortunately, you can avoid playing memory roulette. With an Above™ Board from Intel.
Above Board is more than just another slam bam memory board. It's a long-term memory solution.
It not only takes you up to 640K of conventional memory, it gives you up to 4 megabytes of expanded memory. Based on the EMS standard developed by Lotus,® Microsoft® and the folks paying for this ad.
So now you can take advantage of applications like the ones over there on the left, knowing you've got memory to spare.
Plus (and it's going to be a big plus in the future), Above Board provides extended memory, which will support protected mode DOS. So you won't have to eighty-six your Above Board, no matter what happens in '87. And beyond.
What's more, every board comes with a five-year warranty, toll-free hotline support and a free copy of Microsoft Windows. (–320K. But then, with Above Board, that's no big loss.)
For details, see your favorite computer dealer. Or call us at (800) 538-3373.
And find out why the first thing to go is the last thing to worry about.

intel®

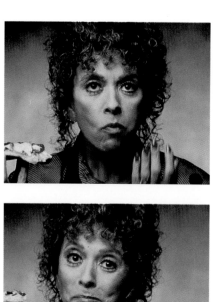

MUSIC: Throughout.

RITA MORENO EATING PIZZA.

MORENO: If I'm feeling mellow. I just want cheese and tomatoes.

TAKES ANOTHER BITE.

MORENO: If I'm feeling attractive, I say "Put on some pepperoni." You know?

CONTINUES TO LOOK BACK AND FORTH BETWEEN CAMERA AND HER SLICE OF PIZZA AS SHE SPEAKS.

MORENO: If I'm feeling wild and crazy, I just tell the guy behind the counter "Throw it all on."

SUPER: Rita Moreno.

MORENO VO: I'm fair game tonight.

SUPER: Pan Pizza with everything . . . when she's in the mood.

MUSIC: Throughout.

MULL: Hello, I'm here to tell you a little bit about pizza etiquette. Can you do this? Yes. It's acceptable. It's good cold in the morning for breakfast. I've done that. I mean how many of you. . . how many have done that? Can you take it and go from the other end? Crust first? No. I'm sorry. You have to start at the point.

MUSIC: Throughout.

CLOSE-UP OF HERBIE HANCOCK AS HE TAKES A BITE OF PIZZA. ALMOST TAKES A BITE SEVERAL TIMES AS HE SPEAKS.

HANCOCK: When people buy pizza, they're very generous with it. It's "Yeah, sure, go ahead and have a slice for yourself. Until there's only one slice left. And when there's only one slice left, the person that wants that slice is the person that bought the pizza.

FINALLY TAKES A BITE.

SUPER: Pan Pizza with mushrooms, green peppers and onions.

MUSIC: Throughout.

MORITA: I like kids. Probably mostly because I used to be one.

DISSOLVE TO MORITA TAKING A BITE OF PIZZA.

MORITA: When my kids get really cookin' and they're, they burn up a lot of energy and stuff...

TAKES ANOTHER BITE OF PIZZA.

MORITA: This is their favorite eating form. They'd take this over anything...french fries, hamburgers, ketchup...uh, rice.

209

"We had to retouch the film frame by frame because you could see the food in her mouth while she talked."

MUSIC: Throughout.

OPEN ON ROSEANNE BARR EATING A SLICE OF PIZZA.

BARR: So my husband says to me, "Roseanne you've been workin' real hard. How 'bout if we take the kids out for pan pizza and you can eat at the salad bar?" So I said, "Well, what a great idea, Honey. While you and the kids are eatin' a hot, steamy, cheesy pizza, I can be off in the corner grazing on a delightful array of sprouts and garbanzo beans. Get real."

MUSIC: Throughout.

OPEN ON HOYT AXTON TAKING A BITE OF PIZZA.

HOYT: I wouldn't marry a woman who didn't like pizza.

HE TAKES ANOTHER BITE.

HOYT: I might play golf with her but I wouldn't marry her.

SUPER: Hoyt Axton.

SUPER: Pan Pizza with extra Italian sausage and extra cheese.

"The truth is, we didn't even know Hagler was going to fight Hearns until the morning of the shoot. We read it in the sports section of the L.A. Times when we got to the set, and then wrote the script."

MUSIC: Throughout.

MARVIN HAGLER TAKES A BITE OF PIZZA. LOOKS AT SLICE AS HE CHEWS PIECE IN HIS MOUTH. TAKES ANOTHER BITE.

MARVIN: Just thinking...wonder what "Whats-his-name" is eating tonight...probably soup.

LAUGHS AS HE TAKES ANOTHER BITE.

SUPER: Marvin Hagler.

SUPER: Pan Pizza with anything he wants.

MUSIC: Throughout.

OPEN ON DOUG AND BOB MACKENZIE HOLDING SLICES OF PIZZA.

DOUG: Oh excuse me, where did you grow up in the woods?

BOB: Okay. Some things fall off of my pizza. eh. But that's only cause it's got so much stuff on it and I...losing my balance.

DOUG: I stole his cheese while he wasn't looking.

DISSOLVE TO DOUG STEALING TOPPINGS FROM BOB

DOUG: Pizza raid! Ah, ah, ah, ah! Use noise to disorient your opponent. That way you can get more of his stuff on your pizza.

SUPER: Supreme Pan Pizza with extra stuff.

MATT SITS DOWN AT A BAR. HE IS IN A COMPLAINING MOOD AND HE GRABS A CALIFORNIA COOLER THAT THE GUY NEXT TO HIM IS DRINKING. MATT BEGINS TO COMPLAIN ABOUT CALIFORNIA . . . OTHER GUY LOOKS AMUSED.

MATT: I hate California, you know what I'm sayin? It's like (sarcastic mimicry) "Have a nice day" . . . "Surf's up—AHuh AHuh." I mean, their idea of culture is yogurt. . . A formal dinner party—means you wear socks. Blonds everywhere . . . Pink Tofu—excuse me? Soy burgers. . . I really hate it.

MATT IS LOOKING AT CALIFORNIA COOLER BOTTLE . . .

MATT: I even hate what they drink.

BARTENDER: What'll ya have buddy?

POINTS TO CALIFORNIA COOLER

MATT: (As if he had not said the above)
One of those.

ANNCR: California Cooler. One more reason to hate California.

OPEN ON STEVE SITTING AT BAR. BARTENDER IS CLEANING GLASSES. STEVE PICKS UP A BOTTLE OF CALIFORNIA COOLER THAT HE'S BEEN DRINKING. HE FROWNS AT THE BOTTLE AND BEGINS TO COMPLAIN ABOUT CALIFORNIA . . .

STEVE: I hate California.

STEVE STARTS TO GET SARCASTIC ABOUT THE CALIFORNIA WAY OF LIFE . . . BARTENDER IS AMUSED.

STEVE: Hollywood!! You know the people out there actually name their kids Moon Puppy?? It's true. . . they have business meetings in swimming pools. . . acres of tanned skin. . . even their junk food is good for ya! (still ranting) 12-car garages, pet cemeteries, 29-grain bread!

STEVE GLANCES AT CALIFORNIA COOLER BOTTLE.

STEVE: I even hate what they drink.

BARTENDER: You want another?

STEVE: Yeah sure.

STEVE DOESN'T SKIP A BEAT WHEN HE ORDERS ANOTHER COOLER—HE THEN CONTINUES HIS COMPLAINING . . .

STEVE: Oh—and vegetarians. . .

ANNCR: California Cooler. One more reason to hate California.

"California Cooler thought what they were was a derivative of the wine category. They thought they should position themselves as a younger wine or a sportier wine or a more useful wine. But we found that the real way the coolers were being drunk, and in fact inherently they were being sold, in single bottles, positioned the cooler category much closer to beer, and that their source of business would not be wine drinkers, but beer drinkers."

||||| ||||| ||||| |||

"Oo mau mau, pa pa oo mau mau.
Glug glug glug glug glug."

In San Francisco, they have gone in eight thousand different directions for the new California Cooler campaign, and the client hates them all. The client wants heritage.

You don't have any heritage, the copywriter says. You've only been in business two years.

The client doesn't care. He wants people to like his drink, and feels he is making a very modest request. After the "One more reason to hate California" campaign, he doesn't want to have anymore west coast weirdness associated with his product. He wants it to be Miller Time, except everybody is drinking coolers.

The creative director in San Francisco calls up the creative director in Los Angeles and says, "I don't know what to tell you, the guy wants heritage."

The creative director in L.A., having grown up at the beach, says "Rent some surf movies, maybe it'll put you in the mood."

So a few of the creative teams in San Francisco are watching surf movies, throwing back some coolers, and a copywriter says, "Y'know, we used to make a drink like this at the beach I lived near." And three other people in the room have the same story about growing up at the beach and mixing this stuff up. They start talking about partying at the beach, the old surf music, "Louie, Louie," "Surfin' Bird," and they start thinking, well, maybe we can do something with this.

Two weeks later the creative guys from San Francisco find themselves working with the creative director in L.A., because, as it turns out, this man did not just live at the beach. This man is the beach. He talks about the big tubs they mixed this stuff up in. He talks about wooden surfboards. He talks about buying ice by the block. He talks about what bikinis used to look like. He talks about friends with names like The Chairman and No Pants Lance. He talks about recreating The California Beach, circa 1965.

Every top executive of California Cooler and its parent company comes to the presentation. The creative director presents the new work. The room is quiet. The number two man from California Cooler rises. He's got to say it, but he is really disappointed with Chiat/Day. First of all, he doesn't like "Louie, Louie," he's never liked "Louie, Louie," and then the thing with making this drink on the beach, it's so unsanitary, and maybe if it was done in a cleaner tub, or maybe if you put the tub on a clean towel, and on and on, he basically dumps on the campaign for what seems like an eternity.

"Is there anything more you'd like to add?" his boss asks him.

The man shakes his head from side to side.

"Well then, I've got to tell y'all, this is the greatest thing I've ever seen. Go make it."

Around the time the California Cooler commercials are being finished, Apple Computer calls and says that they have decided to put their account into review, and that Chiat/Day is invited to try and keep the business. Apple's new chief executive is no longer happy with the work of Chiat/Day. Three months later, Apple is gone. The press will have its opinions why, and the man from Apple will have enough explanations to fill a small book, but to the creative people who worked so long and hard to make Apple the most watched, most read, most talked about advertising in America, it will be a simple case of one man who did not like another man.

The day after Apple announces its decision, the creative director of Chiat/Day's L.A. office will call everyone into the conference room.

"I was here when we lost Honda. And everybody thought that was the end of the world," he says. "And I was here when we lost Fotomat, and Olympia and a lot of other accounts. And each time, it was terrible.

"Chiat/Day is not defined by any one account. Chiat/Day is defined by the work we do. And if Apple doesn't want us, we will find someone else who does, and we'll do great work for them. And if they fire us, we'll do great work for somebody else.

"That's all I have to say."

Towards the end of the year, Guy will decide that it's time to leave Chiat/Day one more time. He feels he's helped to do what he set out to do when he came back three years ago—the agency's success is no longer tied to one large client. There are no big goodbye parties, no speeches, no tears, no testimonial dinners. On his last day, he finishes his work, gets in his car, and drives home to see his wife.

That's Guy.

MAU MAU

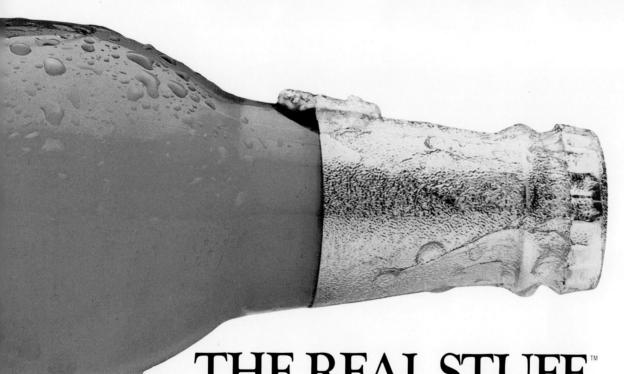

THE REAL STUFF™

THE PRECEDING PAGES ARE A MONTAGE OF IMAGES FROM THE CALIFORNIA COOLER "REAL STUFF" TELEVISION CAMPAIGN. THESE ARE THE SCRIPTS OF THE COMMERCIALS.

OPEN ON GUY READING SURFER MAGAZINE ON THE BEACH

MUSIC: "Gimme Some Lovin'" throughout.

CUT TO SCENES OF PEOPLE CARRYING INGREDIENTS.

ANNCR VO: For years it was made by guys with names like Rabbit . . .

CUT TO BIG BEEFY GUY CARRYING ICE BLOCKS.

ANNCR VO: Quasimodo . . .

CUT TO MAN READING SURFER MAGAZINE.

ANNCR VO: . . . The Chairman.

CUT TO VARIOUS SCENES OF DANCING, FRUIT AND BEACH ANTICS.

SINGERS VO: "Hey!"

ANNCR VO: Real fruit and California white wine. Blended under ideal conditions.

MUSIC: Up "Well I feel so good . . ."

CUT TO BEACH SCENE WITH CHAIRMAN IN FOREGROUND STILL READING SURFER MAGAZINE. CUT TO FRUIT AND PRODUCT SHOT.

ANNCR VO: California Cooler. The real stuff, now in bottles.

SINGERS VO: "Hey!"

BEACH PARTY AT NIGHT WITH BONFIRE.

MUSIC: "Louie Louie."

ANNCR VO: Thousands of people worked late nights . . .

SHOT OF SIX PEOPLE ON TOP OF BUS.

ANNCR VO: . . . weekends . . .

PARTY SHOT OF HOUSE WITH NEAL WILLIAMS IN FRONT.

ANNCR VO: . . . and holidays perfecting the original wine coolers.

ANNCR VO: California Cooler.

SHOT WITH NEAL IN FRONT IN CHAIR.

ANNCR VO: The real stuff.

CLOSE-UP OF COOLER BOTTLE TURNING SLOWLY.

ANNCR VO: The FDA requires that we inform you of the ingredients in every California Cooler.

ANNCR VO: Okay.

MUSIC: "Tutti Frutti."

QUICK CUTS. MAN WITH LIME IN HIS MOUTH. FRUIT ROLLING. PEOPLE PLAYING WITH FRUIT. GUY WITH PINEAPPLE ON HIS HEAD. JUGGLING LEMONS AND LIMES. GUY SQUEEZING GRAPEFRUIT ON GIRL'S BACK. WINE POUR SHOT. COOLER BEING LADLED INTO GLASS. MORE PLAYING WITH FRUIT.

ANNCR VO: California Cooler. The real stuff.

MUSIC: "Green Onions" throughout.

OPEN ON MAN WAKING UP IN VW VAN PARKED ON BEACH AND GETTING OUT OF SLEEPING BAG. CUT TO GUYS RUNNING ALONGSIDE OLD BLACK CAR, PACKED WITH SURFBOARDS.

ANNCR VO: Up and down the coast of California . . .

CUT TO CAR DRIVING BY SANTA CRUZ HIGHWAY SIGN.

ANNCR: . . . the locals made a drink they called "cooler."

CUT TO VARIOUS SHOTS OF SURFING.

ANNCR VO: Using white wine and real fruit . . .

CUT TO SHOTS OF WINE AND FRUIT.

ANNCR VO: . . . on beaches like Rincon, Swami's . . .

CUT TO MORE SURF SHOTS.

ANNCR VO: . . . San Onofre, The Ranch.

CUT TO SHOT OF FRUIT AND WINE BEING POURED INTO A LARGE TUMBLER.

ANNCR VO: And now that original blend comes in a bottle, and you'll find it in places like . . .

CUT TO FRUIT AND PRODUCT SHOT.

ANNCR VO: Shreveport, Newark, Des Moines, Boise . . .

OPEN ON VARIOUS SHOTS OF SURFING.

ANNCR VO: Meet the people who made the original wine coolers.

SFX: Music "Surfin' Bird" throughout.

CUT TO SURFER WIPING OUT AND THE REACTION OF PEOPLE ON THE BEACH.

ANNCR: Years ago they blended white wine and real fruit . . .

CUT TO BEACH SCENES INTERCUT WITH FRUIT AND WINE SHOTS. CUT TO GIRL DROPPING AN ARMFUL OF FRUIT. CUT TO A TUB SETTLING ONTO A TOWEL.

ANNCR VO: . . . in a tub . . .

CUT TO GUY RIDING A COW.

ANNCR VO: . . . at a party . . .

CUT TO GUY DANCING ON BEACH.

ANNCR VO: . . . on the beach.

CUT TO SURFER SHOT.

ANNCR VO: And now that original blend comes in a bottle.

CUT TO BOTTLE POURING.

SFX: Gurgling part of song.

CUT TO FRUIT AND PRODUCT SHOT.

ANNCR VO: California Cooler. The real stuff.

Rock & Roll & Roll & Roll & Roll & Roll & Roll

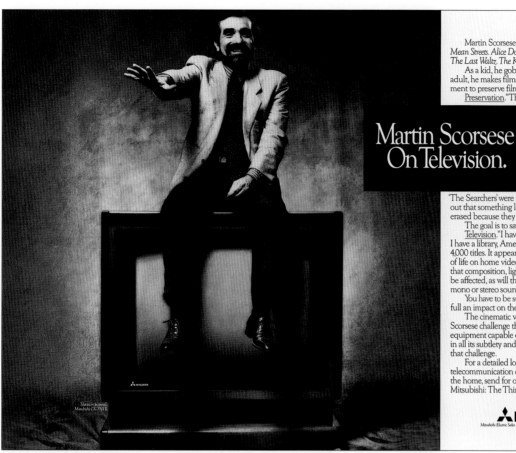

Martin Scorsese is challenging. Like his pictures. *Mean Streets. Alice Doesn't Live Here Anymore. Raging Bull. The Last Waltz. The King of Comedy.*

As a kid, he gobbled up films like popcorn. As an adult, he makes films, collects films, and leads the movement to preserve films.

Preservation. "The idea is to raise the consciousness of the studios, to make them realize that with the advent of cable, they had to start preserving their stuff. Even the stuff they think is no good. You can't make a value judgement. The old pictures that you think are no good, very often are 10 years later the most influential.

Classics like 'Psycho' and 'The Searchers' were panned in their own time. I found out that something like 20 years of Johnny Carson were erased because they needed the space.

The goal is to save everything."

Television. "I have TV on all the time, in every room. I have a library, American directors, obscure films, maybe 4,000 titles. It appears that my own films may have more of life on home video than in the theater. This means that composition, lighting, size of people in the frame will be affected, as will the choice of black and white or color, mono or stereo sound.

You have to be sure what you want to say will have as full an impact on the small screen as on the big screen."

The cinematic visions of filmmakers like Martin Scorsese challenge the manufacturer to offer video equipment capable of capturing the totality of their art in all its subtlety and nuance. Mitsubishi accepts that challenge.

For a detailed look at Mitsubishi telecommunication equipment for the home, send for our brochure, Mitsubishi: The Thinking Inside.

Martin Scorsese On Television.

MITSUBISHI

Jim Henson has achieved extraordinary audience and critical approval from every medium he's had his hand in. Educational TV, *Sesame Street.* Network TV, *The Muppet Show.* Film; a trio of Muppet movies, *Dark Crystal,* and *Labyrinth.* His insightful imagination, expressed through an enduring cast of creatures, artfully exposes the very best in people and media alike.

"I spent a summer traveling through Europe meeting other puppeteers. That was when I first realized it was an art form... the sort of thing a grown man could do for a living."

"Sesame Street surprised everybody, the impact it had on the culture and all. It wasn't like you had to do anything dramatic to do a very good job."

"I think it's important that movies be about something, so that there is that substance to be discovered."

"Frank Oz, who does Miss Piggy, builds layers and levels of character. He knows her background, what kind of painful childhood she's had. Her humor comes from the pain."

"If our 'message' is anything, it's a positive approach to life. That life is basically good. People are basically good."

The vision of people like Jim Henson challenges the manufacturer to develop componentry capable of capturing their art in all its subtlety and nuance. Equipment like the Mitsubishi 2053 Monitor/Receiver with full-square Diamond Vision picture tube shown here.

For a detailed look at Mitsubishi audio/video equipment for the home, from projection to history's first 35-inch direct-view TV, send for our brochure—Mitsubishi Television: The Thinking Inside.

Jim Henson Gives Television A Hand.

MITSUBISHI

Building history's first 35-inch conve
Finding a newspaper big eno

al   tube TV was hard enough.
to see it was impossible.

Its picture area is 86% larger than a 25-inch. Its picture is as rich, as sharp, as bright as a 25-inch. But you can see all that. Only at an authorized Mitsubishi dealer.

 **MITSUBISHI**

Mitsubishi Electric Sales America, Inc., 5757 Plaza Drive, Cypress, CA 90630-0007.

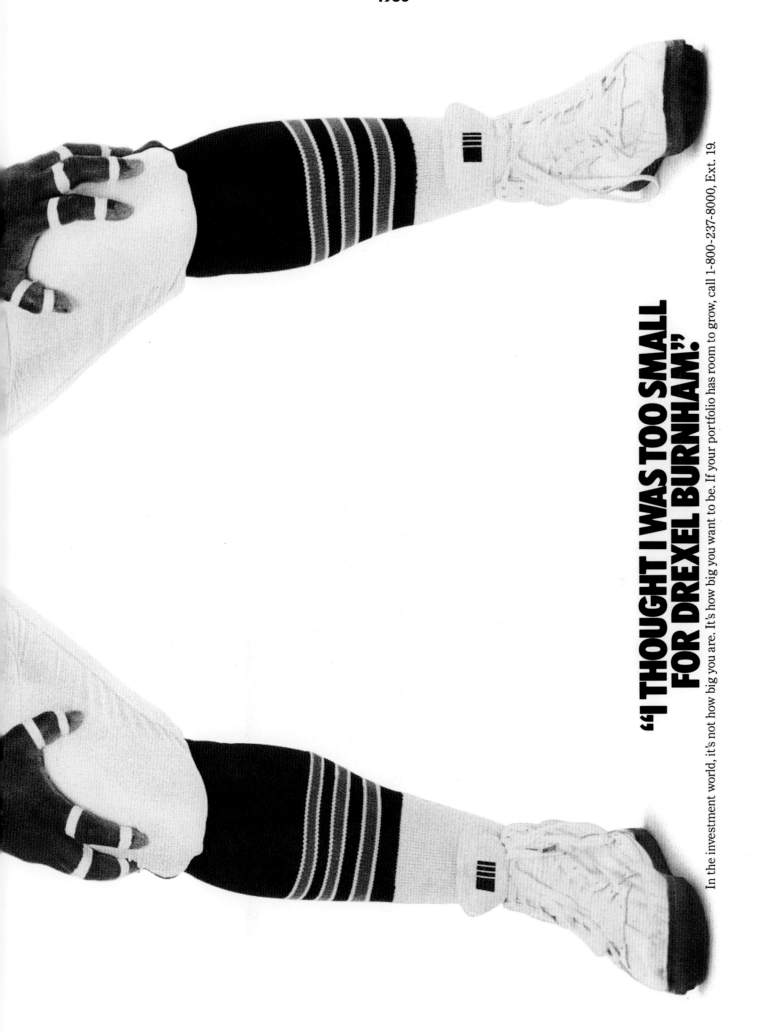

"I THOUGHT I WAS TOO SMALL FOR DREXEL BURNHAM."

In the investment world, it's not how big you are. It's how big you want to be. If your portfolio has room to grow, call 1-800-237-8000, Ext. 19.

"I THOUGHT I WAS TOO SMALL FOR DREXEL BURNHAM."

Most people who know of Drexel Burnham think of us as operating in the rarified "board of directors room" atmosphere of megabuck corporate financing.

But, the fact is, Drexel Burnham offers a full range of financial services to large and small investors as well.

And the investment opportunity could be a substantial one.

When hundreds of millions of dollars are being invested by institutions, it follows naturally that the quality of the research and the investment advice is going to be of the highest order.

When you get your personal financial advice from a firm whose major business is guiding the fortunes of large corporations, you can avail yourself of that wealth of knowledge and insight.

Of course, if you're not a professional investor, you may never have heard of us.

But then, in the investment community it's not how much you're known that counts... it's how much you know.

Find out how much we know.

Call 800-237-8000, Ext. 11 and ask for our *Current Purchase List*.

Drexel Burnham
Drexel Burnham Lambert Incorporated

"I THOUGHT I WAS TOO SMALL FOR DREXEL BURNHAM."

Most people who know of Drexel Burnham think of us as operating in the rarified "board of directors room" atmosphere of megabuck corporate financing.

But, the fact is, Drexel Burnham offers a full range of financial services to large and small investors as well.

And the investment opportunity could be a substantial one.

When hundreds of millions of dollars are being invested by institutions, it follows naturally that the quality of the research and the investment advice is going to be of the highest order.

When you get your personal financial advice from a firm whose major business is guiding the fortunes of large corporations, you can avail yourself of that wealth of knowledge and insight.

Of course, if you're not a professional investor, you may never have heard of us.

But then, in the investment community it's not how much you're known that counts... it's how much you know.

Find out how much we know.

Call 800-237-8000, ext. 16 and ask for our *Current Purchase List*.

Drexel Burnham
Drexel Burnham Lambert Incorporated

"I guess they put me on Drexel because I
couldn't balance my own checkbook."

When we invented high-speed facsimile technology, we knew there was a need to transmit a document quickly and accurately.

We just didn't know how great the need.

Each year, too many children don't return home from their piano lesson. A weekend fishing trip. The mini-market around the corner.

Whether abducted by an estranged parent, or even a total stranger, that's when the nightmare begins.

Parents say the hardest part isn't the hysterical phone call to the police. Or passing the empty bedroom at the end of the hallway. Or looking at the bicycle leaned against the wall in the garage.

The hardest part, is the waiting.

That's why we're proud to assist an organization like Child Find of America in transmitting information on missing children via facsimile machine.

If we can shorten that wait for even one parent, by even one second, we will have put our technology to the best use there is.

If you have any information concerning the whereabouts of this child, please call Child Find of America toll free at 1-800-I-AM-LOST.   Ricoh Corporation, 5 Dedrick Place, West Caldwell, New Jersey, 07006

RICOH

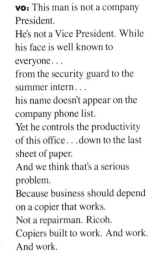

vo: This man is not a company President.
He's not a Vice President. While his face is well known to everyone. . .
from the security guard to the summer intern. . .
his name doesn't appear on the company phone list.
Yet he controls the productivity of this office. . .down to the last sheet of paper.
And we think that's a serious problem.
Because business should depend on a copier that works.
Not a repairman. Ricoh.
Copiers built to work. And work. And work.

It's always there when you need it.

"Nynex came to talk about a one million dollar corporate identity account for Nynex Information Resources, at a time, right after deregulation when no one knew who Nynex was. A woman from Nynex said, 'We want a corporate identity program to tell people what we do within the Nynex family.' And we said, 'What is it that you do?' And she said, 'Well, we publish the Yellow Pages.' 'Well that's great. Why don't we just do some great Yellow Pages advertising for you?' 'Well we want to tell people what else we do,' she says. 'What else do you do?' 'Well, nothing. But someday, we're gonna do electronics and we're gonna do this and we're gonna do that.' And we said, 'We think it's really important, since Nynex is a new name and the Yellow Pages is an old product and someday there's gonna be competition, that you have to tell people that Nynex is the Yellow Pages. That old familiar thing that they know in their home all of a sudden has this crazy new name, but somehow it's the same thing.' So we were in a pitch against two other agencies, and they were pitching for a one million dollar corporate identity program, and we were pitching for the entire Yellow Pages account, which we won. And that led us to our first famous commercial in New York, which was the little kid on the book."

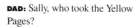

DAD: Sally, who took the Yellow Pages?

SALLY: I dunno.

DAD: Honey, have you seen the Yellow Pages?

MOM: No.

DAD: Susie, where are the Yellow Pages?

SUE: Sally had it last.

SALLY: I did not.

DAD: C'mon, I need the Yellow Pages...

VO: Over the years, one book has been in more homes...

VO: ...helping people throughout New York (New England) find more goods and services.

VO: The Nynex Yellow Pages...

SUE: Mom!

VO: It's always there when you need it.

In 1455, Gutenberg brought the miracle of printing to the civilized world.

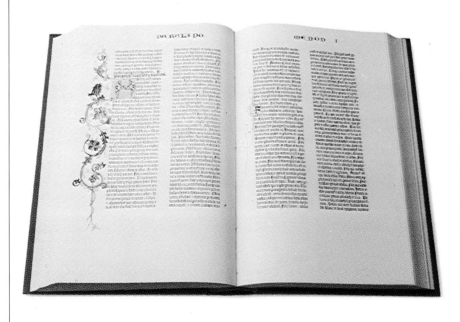

531 years la

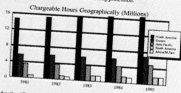

Writing business letters with powerful software programs like Microsoft's Word and Excel can mean the difference between getting read and getting ignored.

Each and every one of the 2,564 pages that compose the Gutenberg Bible represents a technological breakthrough in printing that revolutionized the sharing of information.

Each was painstakingly typeset. Elegantly illustrated. Laboriously printed—over a five year period. Using what was then a state-of-the-art process known as movable type.

Of course, each and every one of the four pages you see above also represents a

technological breakthrough in printing that has revolutionize the sharing of information.

Each was painlessly types Instantly illustrated. And electrically printed—over a cup of coffee. Using a state-of-the-art process we've pioneered, known as the Desktop Publishing Plus™ system. As its name implies, the Desktop Publishing Pl system is practically a des

Thanks, Apple.

Late Monday night, May 19, 1986, we learned that Apple Computer was moving its advertising account from Chiat/Day to BBDO.

This marks the end of the roller coaster adventure our two companies have shared for nearly seven years. Together, we introduced a new technology to the world, founded a new industry in America and changed forever the way business talks to business.

Now we'd like to take this moment to say thanks, Apple.

Thanks for letting us make a little history.

Thanks for demanding our best, and then more than our best.

Thanks most of all for actually running our best, year after challenging year.

You've done for us what VW did for Doyle Dane Bernbach, what Hathaway did for Ogilvy & Mather, what McDonald's did for Needham, Harper & Steers.

So thanks, Apple.

It's been a great ride.

Chiat/Day

Congratulations, Chiat/Day.

Seriously.

Congratulations on seven years of consistently outstanding work.

You helped build Apple and were an integral part of the marketing team.

You took risks, sometimes failed, never compromised.

The personal computer industry is now being handed over from the "builders" to the "caretakers"; that is, from the individuals who created and grew a multi-billion dollar American industry to those who will maintain the industry as it is and work to achieve marginal future growth.

It is inevitable that in this turbulent transition many faces will change.

You created some truly great work—the kind that gives advertising a good name.

The kind people will remember for years. The kind people remain proud to have been associated with.

I'm expecting some new, "insanely great" advertising from you soon.

Because I can guarantee you: there is life after Apple.

Thanks for the memories.

Steven P. Jobs

"Happy birthday to you, happy birthday to you."

Six months ago, he still lived in L.A., his home of the past ten years. He was happy there, loved his house, ran a couple of good accounts in the L.A. office. Then, Jay asked him if he'd like to move to New York to be the creative director there, just for a little while; he could always go home. A month later, he and his family got off the plane to the greeting of a typical New York summer, all humidity and heat. He found himself in an air-conditioned midtown hi-rise with a dog and a kid and a wife, all of whom would rather have been in California.

Everyone knew he was coming, although there was no official notice. There was a meeting where Jay said, "This is the new creative director," and that was about it. He hired some, fired some, promoted some, and for awhile wondered if he was really doing anything at all.

Now, he is getting his chance to find out. Arrow, one of the oldest shirtmakers in America, has awarded Chiat/Day their account. They aren't really sure advertising can help them; they feel the Arrow name doesn't have too much life in it, and they are preparing to sub-brand. He and an art director develop a print campaign which is very clean, very plain, and very simple. The print campaign is successful enough to get Arrow feeling like maybe they should be doing some television. The television does so well that Arrow feels like maybe there's some life left in the Arrow name yet.

Then, there's Nynex, a company formed as a result of the deregulation of the telephone company. They have always printed the New York Yellow Pages, but now they have competition. The New York market is profitable, and other companies are trying to get in; it is Chiat/Day's job to stop them.

The creative director sits with a copywriter and art director for months, trying to come up with a campaign that will prove that Nynex Yellow Pages have more listings with more information than anyone else. They feel they have to prove that Nynex is the phone book you've always had and the only one you'll ever need. They want to make New Yorkers feel the competitive urgency of the problem.

Then, one day, in a moment of absolute clarity, they realize this: Hey, people don't care about the Yellow Pages. People care about crime waves and garbage strikes and air pollution and rent hikes, not which phone book they open up when they need a plumber.

The burden of a Yellow Pages war lifted, they think about a radio campaign they've been doing for Nynex, which centers around some of the stranger headings in the Yellow Pages. The creative director and the creative team talk about doing a television campaign which revolves around some of the interesting headings and types of businesses that are in the Nynex directory. The team goes away, looks through the phone book, and comes back with about thirty scripts which all revolve around some visual or verbal pun and the end line "If it's out there, it's in here."

The creative director believes the campaign will work for these reasons: Logically, it makes

**People Training For Dogs
310 W 87** — — — — — — —

the New York Yellow Pages seem like they have a much wider range of listings than you would ever believe. Emotionally, the commercials don't ask you to fall in love with the Yellow Pages. They are just entertaining enough to make you think about them for a couple of seconds.

The Nynex spots, when completed, are a commercial and critical success, winning in every major awards show. The campaign makes the advertising community focus on the creative work of Chiat/Day New York in a way it never has before, and when it does, it finds that Chiat/Day's New York office has become one of the major creative forces in the city.

He's been creative director for about a year now. His job, he feels, is kind of like waxing a car. You start out with a dirty car, and you wash it, and you start waxing it, and pretty soon, the car is looking great, and then you have the satisfaction of standing back and seeing what you've done. All the creative people ever really needed was someone to be a good sounding board, helping a little here and there, and that is what he has become.

It's a nice night. He walks home to his loft down in Soho. His wife went to a museum, his kid is at a friend's house. Maybe there's a Met game on.

In the L.A. office, they have spent two months preparing to pitch the account of the Nissan Motor Corporation. At one hundred and fifty million dollars, it will be the

biggest single account move in the history of advertising. It is also unusual because Chiat/Day has been cast in the unlikely role of favorite, which makes the L.A. creative director feel this is one he must, must win.

Two nights before the pitch, the creative director is up all night, checking every slide of every ad to be presented. The night before the pitch, he watches as the rehearsal for the three-hour presentation runs seven hours long.

The day of the pitch. The presentation, he believes, has gone great. That weekend, the agency throws a huge party on the beach. And while the creative director is smiling, there is still that little doubt; it is the creative experience that if something can go wrong, it will.

Monday and Tuesday pass. Wednesday is his birthday. He's at work for a couple of hours when Jay comes into his office.

"Nissan wants to talk to us on a speakerphone," Jay says. "The whole place."

They cram into a tiny room with a speakerphone, twenty, forty, a hundred people, till they are spilling out of the room and down the hall. The advertising committee of Nissan is on the speakerbox.

The Nissan guy asks if everybody is there.

Jay says yes.

He asks if the creative director is there.

Jay says yes.

He asks if the creative director can hear him okay.

The creative director says yes.

"In that case," the man from Nissan says, "There is something I'd like to tell you." And then, the man from Nissan does something amazing and wonderful.

He starts to sing.

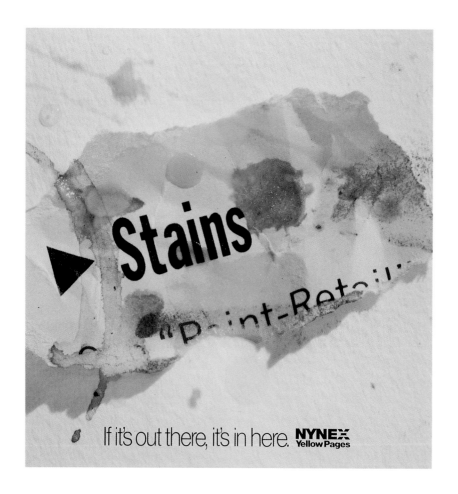

SFX: Opening chime; cocktail chatter, piano.
WOMAN 1: Isn't my hair marvelous? Peter did it, you know.
MAN 1: Didn't we meet in Cannes last year? Or was it Bora Bora?
WOMAN 2: So let's talk about you darling. What do you think of my dress?
WOMAN 3: . . . Then Rod said, let's go to Mick's house.
MAN 2: Both of my Ferrari's are in the shop . . . I hate that!
WOMAN 4: I see modeling as a stepping stone. But what I really want to do is direct!
MAN 3: Uh huh, sure! Oh, you're right. Hi!
VO: If it's out there, it's in here . . . the Nynex Yellow Pages.
SFX: Book slams shut.
VO: Why would anyone need another?

SFX: Opening chime, sound of people talking.
MAN 1: Hey! Herbert Fisher! Have you met Herb Grant?
MAN 2: Herb Grant, Tacoma.
MAN 1: Herb's in the plumbing business!
MAN 2: Yeah, I'm all backed up!
SFX: LAUGHTER.
MAN 3: Herb! You know these bums? Herb Riddick, Herb Kaplan.
MAN 4: Hi!
MAN 1: So, the wife and kids are good?
MAN 5: Herb Junior's almost twelve.
MAN 1: Woo, next thing you know, there'll be a Herbert Junior Junior!
SFX: Laughter.
VO: If it's out there, it's in here . . . the Nynex Yellow Pages.
SFX: Book slams shut.
VO: Why would anyone need another?

SFX: Opening chime. Restaurant sounds.
MAN VO: Excuse me . . .
WAITER: Sir!
MAN VO: What are your specials today?
WAITER: I don't know.
WOMAN VO: Do your entrees come with salad?
WAITER: I don't know.
MAN VO: Do you have escargot?
WAITER: Escargot? (pause) I don't know.
WOMAN VO: May we see a menu?
WAITER (CONFUSED): Yes! No! I don't know.
VO: If it's out there, it's in here . . .
SFX: Plates breaking.
VO: If it's out there it's in here . . . the Nynex Yellow Pages.
SFX: Book slams shut.
VO: Why would anyone need another?

 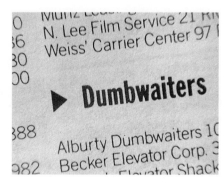 

"It was a real rock and roll shoot because we were shooting three spots a day, we had two stages, and one stage was being prelit while we were shooting the other one, then we'd yank the camera, shoot this one, this one's being prelit, yank the camera back and do another one. And there was no letting up. Sixteen-hour days for four straight days. And it was great because they couldn't be too precious. They were like cartoons. That to me was definitely the lesson, the value of spontaneity in TV. 'Cause I really believe that the spirit of that spontaneity came across."

OPEN ON NICE LIVING ROOM-TYPE SETTING ON WHITE SEAMLESS. A GROUP OF TRAIN CONDUCTORS ARE SITTING AROUND ON CHINTZ-COVERED SOFAS HAVING TEA AND FINGER SANDWICHES. THEY ARE EXTREMELY CORDIAL TO ONE ANOTHER WHILE THEY CHIT CHAT ABOUT TRAINS AND THINGS.
SFX: Violin music.
MAN 1: You know, there's just no substitute for a well-polished train.
MAN 2: Indeed.
MAN 3: (MAN 4 ENTERS) Roy, how nice to see you. (SHAKES HAND OF MAN 4, WHO HANDS HIM BOX OF CHOCOLATES)
MAN 2: Oh!
MAN 3: You shouldn't have.
MAN 2: Do sit down.
MAN 3: May I offer you a cup of tea?
MAN 4 (SITTING): Why, thank you, Wendell. Listen, I do love what you've done with this place.
MAN 1: Yes, this fabric would look lovely in my caboose.
MAN 2: I must remember to pick some up.
MAN 1: Finger sandwiches, gentlemen?
VO: If it's out there, it's in here ...
the Nynex Yellow Pages.
SFX: Book slams shut.
VO: Why would anyone need another?

SFX: Opening chime. As lights go down, stripper music begins. Clapping, whistling. Music and crowd noise continue. Music and crowd noise continue; sound of springs popping off. Music and crowd noise continue.
VO: If it's out there, it's in here ...
SFX: Cat call whistle.
VO: The Nynex Yellow Pages.
SFX: Book slams shut.
VO: Why would anyone need another?

OPENING CHIME. SOUND OF MARCHING. OFF CAMERA DRILL SERGEANT (YELLING): Attend Hut! Funky Chicken!
SFX: Military snare drum throughout.
SARGE: Duckwalk!...Moonwalk!...Disco!... Windmill!...Air Guitar!...James Brown!
SOLDIERS (YELLING TOGETHER): Huh!
SARGE: Jimi plays Monterey!
VO: If it's out there, it's in here...The Nynex Yellow Pages.
SFX: Book slams shut.
VO: Why would anyone need another?

 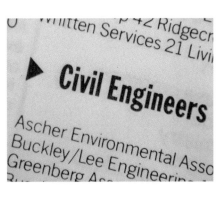 

"For 'Rock Drills' we used the London Ballet guys. The fun of it also is that the references can become a little oblique, like at one point, the drill sergeant yells out, 'Jimmy Plays Monterey!' He could have just yelled 'Heavy Metal,' but we decided, no, this joke is for the .002% that will get it. But if they get it, they're gonna feel really cool about it."

Porsche finishes Daytona ten years ahead of the competition.

1977. Porsche wins the 24 hours of Daytona.
1978. Porsche wins the 24 hours of Daytona.
1979. Porsche wins the 24 hours of Daytona.
1980. Porsche wins the 24 hours of Daytona.
1981. Porsche wins the 24 hours of Daytona.
1982. Porsche wins the 24 hours of Daytona.
1983. Porsche wins the 24 hours of Daytona.
1984. Porsche* wins the 24 hours of Daytona.
1985. Porsche wins the 24 hours of Daytona.
1986. Porsche wins the 24 hours of Daytona.

This year, we not only won our tenth Daytona Endurance Race, but we did it by finishing 1st, 2nd and 3rd. Our congratulations to the winning team of Al Holbert, Derek Bell and Al Unser Jr. To the 2nd place team of A.J. Foyt, Danny Sullivan and Arie Luyendyk. To the 3rd place team of Jim Busby, Darin Brassfield, Derek Warwick and Jochen Mass. And to all the other teams who, over the years, have helped us stay so far ahead of the competition. PORSCHE

*Porsche March car. ©1986 Porsche Cars North America, Inc.

On Feb. 1, 1987, the sun rose in the east, day followed night and Porsche won Daytona.

After winning the 24 Hours of Daytona for the last 10 years in a row, it didn't come as a total surprise this year when we made it 11 in a row.

It was, however, a bit of an eye-opener when we also came in second, third, fourth, fifth and sixth.

The winning team of Al Unser Jr., Derek Bell, Chip Robinson and Al Holbert took the flag in a Porsche 962 endurance racer (seen here with its turbo afterburn giving the dawn a little competition).

That car's performance was virtually flawless, averaging 111.6 mph for 2,681 miles and a record-setting 753 laps. The sort of performance that would tempt most engineers to sit back and take a few bows.

But at Porsche we've never been comfortable resting on our laurels. Even when our laurels include an 11-year winning streak.

That's why our engineers are, as usual, back at their drawing boards, using what they learn from racing to make our cars perform even better. On the track and on the road.

So, while we wouldn't want to predict what will happen next year, there are some things we're pretty certain of.

The swallows will return to Capistrano.
Thanksgiving will fall on a Thursday.
And each new Porsche will be better than the last. PORSCHE

©1987 Porsche Cars North America, Inc., 200 S. Virginia St., Reno, Nevada 89501. For the location of your nearest dealer call (800) 252-4444.

If you were driving a Porsche, you wouldn't have time to read this.

(Dealer Name)

Take it out and open it up.

Porsche 911 Cabriolet

In Germany there are no getaway cars.

POLIZEI

OPEN ON LOCKED SHOT OF A PORSCHE PIT AND CREW. A 962 PULLS INTO THE PIT AND THE CREW SWARMS OVER IT CHANGING TIRES, CLEANING WINDSHIELD, AND REFUELING THE CAR.

SFX: Natural throughout.

ANNCR VO: At Porsche, key personnel meet on a regular basis to discuss alterations and refinements.

THE DRIVER AND SEVERAL TECHNICIANS (SPEAKING GERMAN) ENGAGE IN A HEATED DEBATE ABOUT SOME DETAIL OF THE CAR'S PERFORMANCE.

ANNCR VO: At these times, many important contributions are made in the perfecting of our cars.

THEIR WORK COMPLETE, THE CREW STANDS BACK AND THE CAR ACCELERATES OUT OF CAMERA.

ANNCR VO: We try to keep the meetings short.

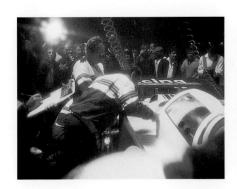  

*"I had one great ad
with a picture of a
shovel that said
'Now that Sara Lee is
making cheesecake
for under 200
calories a serving,
you can afford to
take bigger portions.'
For some reason,
they liked this one
better."*

We think our incredible tasting cheesecake for 200 calories a slice is going to be very popular.
People are already showing some interest. *Sara Lee*

Light Classics: French Cheesecake, Strawberry French Cheesecake, Chocolate Mousse, Strawberry Mousse.

Ditto for our pound cake at 130 calories a slice. *Sara Lee*

DEBRA HARRY: Hi, here comes my commercial.
First of all did I tell you this was bread, from
Sara Lee. Thirteen minutes in the oven. Smells
great. . .fresh, hot. Now it can't get any hotter
than this. I love french bread, ya. . .it's good.
Can I cook.

This Is Our

A dog's first meal comes from a highly developed nutritional source.

Which leaves man with a pretty tough act to follow.

Ideally, a dog food should continue to provide such perfectly tailored nutrition. That's why 10 years ago, Cycle Dry Dog Food was born. It was specifically developed by Gaines

to suit every stage of a dog's life.

But when nature is the standard by which you judge yourself, there's always room for improvement. So in addition to containing

Competition.

...no added sugar, today Cycle has ...no artificial color. And even lower ...odium.

Together, we think these changes ...ring Cycle even closer to our goal

of providing a lifetime of the best possible nutrition.

And that much closer to our competition.

Gaines' CYCLE. A friend for life.

© Gaines Foods, Inc. 1986 Subsidiary of Anderson, Clayton & Co.

MUSIC: Under throughout.

CARMEN VO: Well, I've been saving my money because at our age, my husband and I, you know he's still working and one of these days he's gonna retire, and we would like to travel a little bit.

ANNCR VO: Carmen Cortez. Home Savings customer.

CARMEN VO: I was a widow the first time. With two children.

CARMEN IN KITCHEN.

CARMEN VO: It wasn't easy, I never went anyplace. Because I didn't have the money to do anything or because everything was for the kids you know and pay my bills and make my house payment. And then when I met Mr. Cortez things were a little easier for me. And he wants to take me to

Mexico City and he wants to take me to Cancun . . . and he wants to take me here and there. But, I want to go to New York.

ANNCR VO: Home Savings takes very good care of Carmen's money and about a million other people's as well.

CARMEN VO: Most of all I would like to see Miss Liberty. And up way up on her crown and, uh, get way up to the top and look from there. This is my country.

  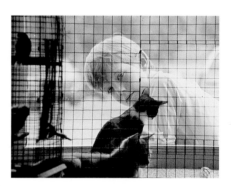

MUSIC: Throughout.

DUSTIN VO: Well, usually sometimes if I keep my room clean I will get an allowance.

PAN OF DUSTIN'S ROOM.

DUSTIN VO: Which I probably will get an allowance this week.

ANNCR VO: Dustin Jensen, Home Savings customer.

DUSTIN VO: Sometimes I'll get money from maybe a birthday or like maybe my Mom, instead of giving me a present, put a hundred dollars in the bank. I'm looking for a paper job that's just the only ways I get money.

DUSTIN MAKING A CAGE.

DUSTIN VO: I'm saving for mainly college and I was kinda hoping to get a scholarship. But my grades aren't that hot.

DUSTIN WITH BIRD.

DUSTIN VO: I think I want to be a veterinarian when I grow 'cuz I really like animals. I have a hamster and a bird . . .

ANNCR VO: Dustin is one of Home Savings' smartest customers. He's in the fifth grade.

DUSTIN VO: I think it's a smart thing to do is to save money because if nobody saved money then it'd be kinda hard to get around in the world.

"These started out as radio commercials that were only going to run in Kansas City. I don't know if it's coincidence or not, but all the people we ended up using had had some sort of tragedy in their lives. I think they were all very brave, strong people, and I think that strength of character comes across on the film."

MILTON: We've always made it and I don't worry because she's a good manager. If we have little or a lot. We make it.

ANNCR VO: Milton and Emma Unger, Home Savings customers.

EMMA VO: We were raised during the depression. It makes a difference. If you have a little money you start saving it.

CUT TO MILTON.

MILTON: One week we were so poor, I bought a bushel of carrots and we lived on carrots all week. Now when we go out to dinner and we see carrots we look at each other and we smile. It didn't hurt us. It was fun.

CUT TO PICTURE OF EMMA IN HER WEDDING DRESS.

MILTON VO: She was very thrifty. She made all her own clothes and she looked like a million bucks. She still does.

CUT TO MILTON PLAYING PIANO.

MILTON VO: My hobby is playing piano at the senior citizens home. It's the only thing I'm good at.

ANNCR VO: The Ungers worked very hard for their retirement. So did Home Savings.

CUT TO MILTON PUTTING ON HAT.

MILTON VO: You know, I'm a character and the little old ladies love that.

MILTON IN OLD FOLKS HOME.

EMMA VO: It really doesn't bother me 'cause I know what he thinks and I know that he cares for me.

CLOSE UP OF MILTON.

MILTON: Best deal I ever made. I couldn't live without her.

MUSIC: Under throughout.

HAROLD VO: My philosophy of life...huh! Well, money's not going to grow out of a tree in the backyard, back there, you gotta earn it.

CLOSE-UP HAROLD.

HAROLD VO: I've made myself pretty secure, definitely have done that.

ANNCR VO: Harold Arlund, Home Savings customer.

HAROLD VO: But like I told you, if I spend a buck I don't have to worry about making it back tomorrow. I'm not cheap, I mean I'll spend a dollar, two dollars. But I want my money's worth. I hate to spend five dollars and get a dollar and a half's worth of work.

HAROLD IN GARAGE.

HAROLD VO: I want to take another trip down to that Caribbean, it's nice sitting on that ol' ship and let her float down the line, can't beat it.

ANNCR VO: Harold Arlund doesn't take chances with his money, neither does Home Savings.

HAROLD VO: The kids won't have to fight over anything, I told 'em that when I go ahead and take a trip, I said, I'm spending your inheritance. (Laugh) They say go ahead and spend it.

If you want how come yo

An Ahmanson Company

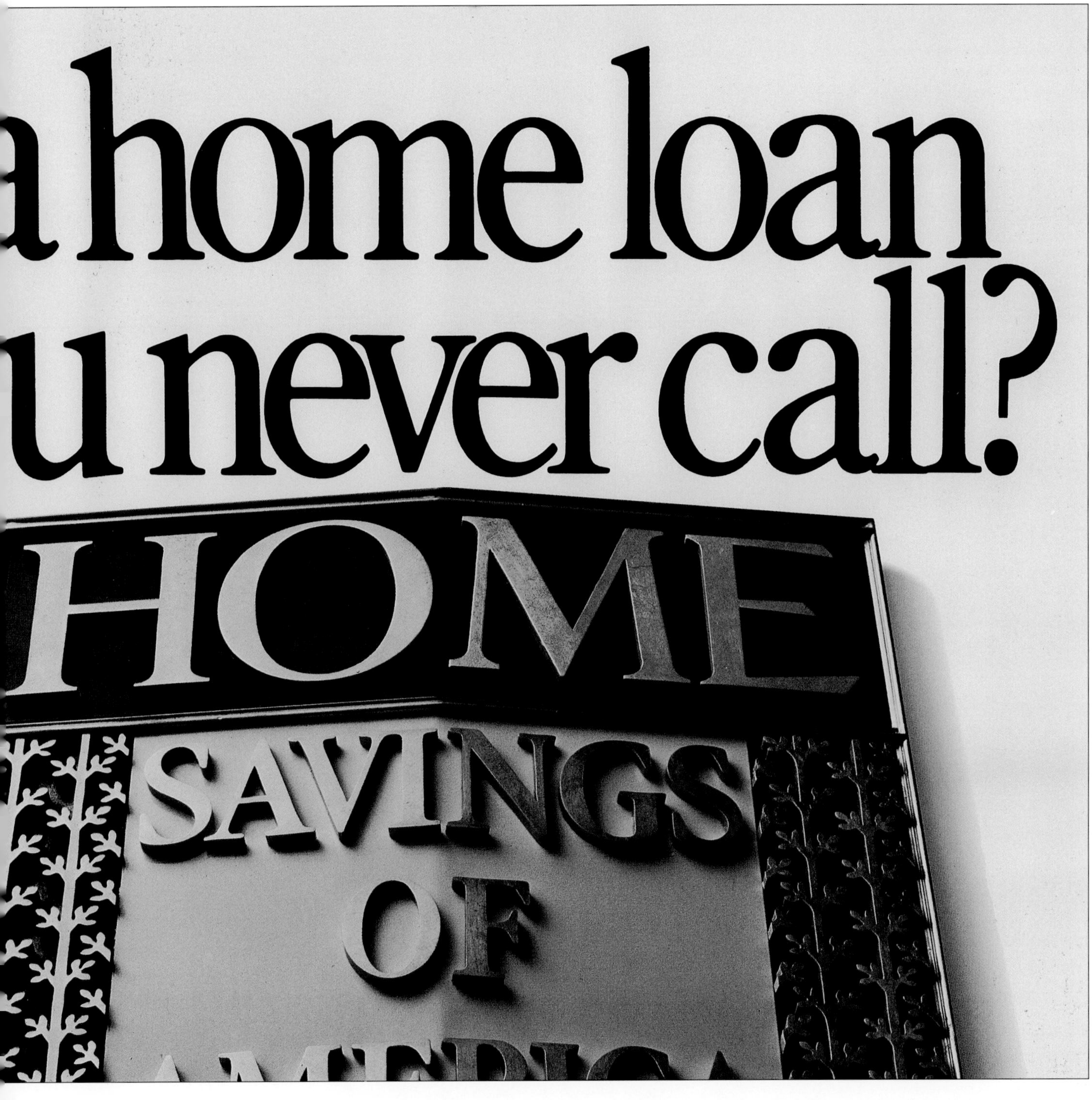
a home loan
u never call?
HOME
SAVINGS
OF

110th and 3rd Avenue, New York City.

Reebok 🏴󠁧󠁢󠁥󠁮󠁧󠁿
Basketball

Stick   Midtown   Money   Johnny B.   Willie   King Neil

Finish line. Pike's Peak Marathon. Manitou Springs, Colorado.

It starts at 6,000 feet above sea level. And ends at 14,000 feet, above the clouds.

Welcome to the Pike's Peak Marathon. Nobody knows exactly how far it is from beginning to end. But from the Colorado sunshine at Manitou Springs to the sub-zero snowstorms at 16 Golden Stairs, the general consensus is about 14 miles. (Give or take another 14 going down.)

Still, there are two points that everyone agrees upon. It's not a run you try on a whim. Or a surface you take lightly on your feet. Which is why a lot of anxious runners prepare for it by lacing up our GL6100 training shoes.

Their lightweight design won't drag you down on your way up Barr Trail's 23° incline.

Their Indy 500 outsoles can withstand any type of punishment. Including a plunge down French Creek's jagged embankments.

And their nylon mesh and nappa pigskin uppers allow your feet to breathe comfortably under the scorching sun that gave Dismal Forest its name.

Of course, taking a mountain in two and a half hours might still cause nausea, dizziness, and shortness of breath. In which case, you might want to try a less mountainous terrain. Like mile 21 of the Boston Marathon.

But we're saving Heartbreak Hill for another story.

Reebok

268

SFX: Breathing and exaggerated
sound effects throughout.
SFX: Silence.

What do you get after spending 75 year

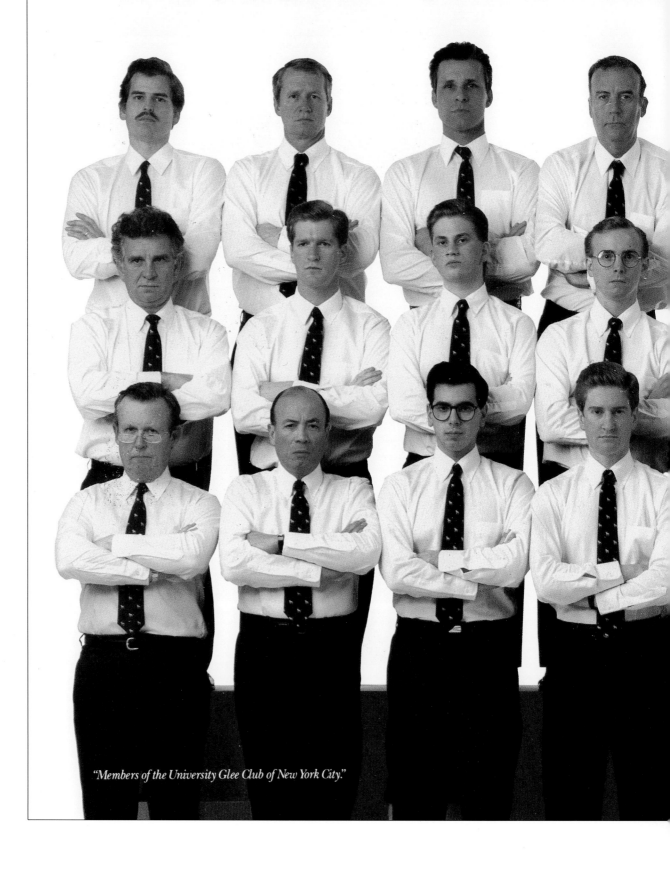

"Members of the University Glee Club of New York City."

making America's favorite dress shirt?

Bored.

Arrow

"They were known for white shirts, and they were this boring, staid brand and they'd lost their edge amongst the 18-34 year olds. That was really the issue: Can we use advertising to get those people in that age group thinking Arrow again? We went out, and we had all these wonderful concepts that the planner was just as excited about as the creative team—things about America's dress shirt with incredibly sexy advertising, like Obsession or something, really experimental, really high fashion. The planner and copywriter took the work out to this 18-34 age group and it just didn't work. And they came back and said, Arrow has an equity and it has a value. It may be my father's dress shirt, but it also is seen as a good value shirt, and it's got a lot of heritage and equity going. So we should bounce off that, that should be our starting point. And then they came up with a print ad that evolved into the TV spot. Literally, we ran one spot right before Christmas, six weeks, and across the next year sales were up thirty percent."

CHORUS (BEGINS SINGING "HIGHER AND HIGHER" IN
SLOW FOUR-PART HARMONY): "YOUR LOVE HAS LIFTED
ME HIGHER . . . THAN I'VE EVER BEEN LIFTED BEFORE.
SO KEEP IT UP."
SOLOIST # 1: (PICKS UP TEMPO): "So keep it up."
CHORUS: "Quench my desire."
SOLOIST #2: "Quench my desire."
CHORUS: "And I'll be at your side for ever more."
CHORUS: (BEGINS TO INCREASE TEMPO AND ENERGY):
"You know your love keeps on liftin.'"
SOLOIST #2: "Keeps on liftin.'"
SOLOIST #3: "Higher."
CHORUS: "Higher and higher."
CHORUS: (INCREASES TEMPO AND SINGS FULL VOICE):
"I said your love, your love keeps on, keeps on
liftin', liftin' me higher and higher."
VO: "Arrow shirts, we've loosened our collar."

"It was a one-night shoot. The amazing thing is that we wrapped at sunrise, at the Pasadena City Hall, and after the last shot was done, when the crew was getting ready to tear apart the set, the big L.A. earthquake happened, and that was the epicenter of the earthquake."

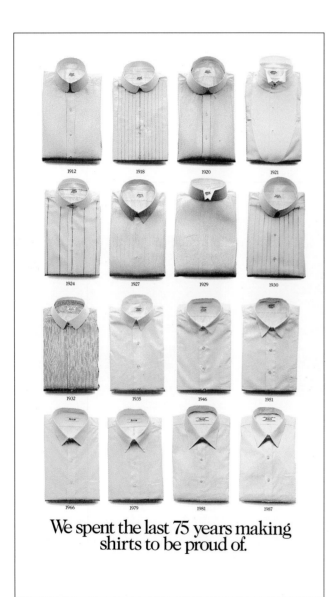

We spent the last 75 years making
shirts to be proud of.

We spent the last six months making
something to cover them up.

To help make the holiday season a little warmer, we designed a bright new collection of sweaters.
In 100% cotton and cotton/ramie blend. With strong, clean lines. Bold, vibrant colors. And the quality you'd
expect from Arrow. We'd never cover our shirts with anything less.

Arrow

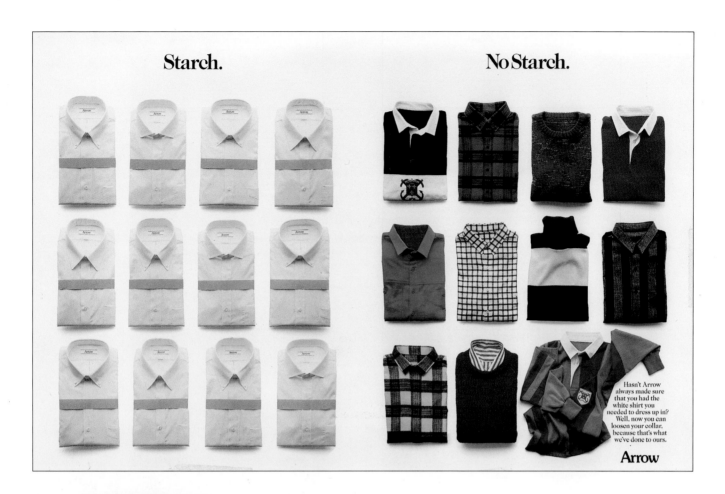

Starch.

No Starch.

Hasn't Arrow always made sure that you had the white shirt you needed to dress up in? Well, now you can loosen your collar, because that's what we've done to ours.

Arrow

Sold.

This Fall, selling dress shirts will be easier than ever.
Introducing Criterion, Original Dover and Kent Classic from Arrow.
Criterion. Full cut and relaxed silhouettes in wide-awake patterns.
Original Dover. The traditional oxford button-down pre-washed for casual comfort.
Kent Classic. The crisp, gentleman's shirt that's always in demand.

Arrow

After 75 years, we've loosened our collar.

That's why this fall you'll be able to wear our colorful new rugbys, sport shirts, and sweaters.
And since you've always expected quality from an Arrow dress shirt, that's what you'll find in Arrow sportswear.
We may have loosened our collar, but we'll never relax our standards.

Arrow

The Canvas.

The Palette.

FOSTER FARMS.
Select Servings

Specially Selected
Hand Trimmed • Low in Fat

BONELESS & SKINLESS
THIGH/DRUMSTICK MEAT

CALIFORNIA GROWN FRYING CHICKEN

The Masterpiece.

Feast your eyes on this work of art: Peking Stir-Fry Chicken.
Thanks to new Foster Farms Select Servings, you can put your
energies into creating masterpieces like these. Not into boning chicken.
Select Servings come from fresh, plump Foster Farms chickens.
Gourmet cuts, already boned, skinned and trimmed by hand.
What's more, our butchers have an eye for æsthetics. So every Select
Servings cut is chosen for size, and of course, presentation.
The next time you feel inspired, pick up Select Servings. Thighs, breasts
or thighs and drumsticks.
Believe us, they'll bring out the artist in you. FOSTER FARMS

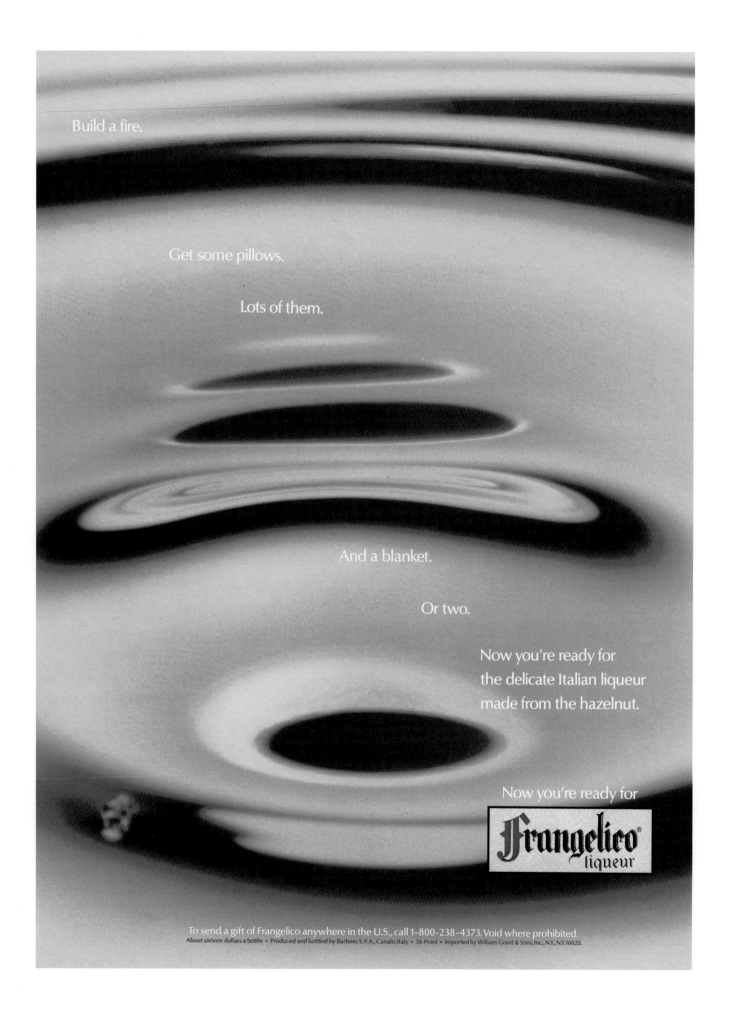

Build a fire.

Get some pillows.

Lots of them.

And a blanket.

Or two.

Now you're ready for the delicate Italian liqueur made from the hazelnut.

Now you're ready for

Frangelico liqueur

To send a gift of Frangelico anywhere in the U.S., call 1-800-238-4373. Void where prohibited.
About sixteen dollars a bottle • Produced and bottled by Barbero S.P.A., Canale, Italy • 56 Proof • Imported by William Grant & Sons, Inc., N.Y., N.Y. 10020.

Whether your kids are 14 years old or 40 years old, we know a sure-fire way of getting them to follow your example.

Jump on a snowmobile.

The only question is, which snowmobile to jump on. A choice made all the more difficult by the fact that Yamaha makes 14 different sleds, each the best in its class.

Such as the Yamaha Phazer—the number-one selling snowmobile in the world.

The Phazer earned that title by combining unique styling, versatility and high performance. And that's something you'll need plenty of, if you hope to stay ahead of your kids.

Because even the Yamaha Bravo and Bravo Long Track, our most economical full-size sleds, offer enough performance to keep young riders* entertained for years.

Then there's the incredibly comfortable, easy-to-learn Inviter. And the powerful Enticer line of sleds, including the luxurious Excel III and the new Enticer Long Track with reverse, designed to haul you and enough gear for your whole family.

You can see the entire Yamaha line at your nearest Yamaha dealer. Then head for the hills with your kids close behind.

Or vice versa.

*The Snowmobile Safety and Certification Committee is committed to your safety and enjoyment, so when you buy a snowmobile look for the SSCC label. Always wear a helmet and eye protection. Observe all state and local laws. Respect the rights of others. *Snowmobiles are not recommended for riders under 14 years old or riders who have not received qualified instruction.

YAMAHA
We make the difference.

How to get your kids to follow in your tracks.

Of the 16 best sleds in the world, 15 are Yamahas.

That's because we make a total of 15 different models, including a whole new concept for having fun in the snow—the SnoScoot. And every Yamaha is famous for innovation, craftsmanship and reliability.

Starting with the economical yet full-size Bravo. The easy-to-learn Inviter for beginners. The Enticer line, including the new Enticer Long Track with reverse and the luxurious Excel III. And our rugged new utility sled, the VK540.

On the other end of the scale, we also make the incredible Exciter and Exciter Deluxe, the epitome of high performance. And the revolutionary Phazer, the most popular sport sled ever made.

So, if you want the best sled for any purpose, there are really only two places to look.

Inside your friendly Yamaha dealer.

Or behind your friendly Husky.

The Snowmobile Safety and Certification Committee is committed to your safety and enjoyment, so when you buy a snowmobile look for the SSCC label. Always wear a helmet and eye protection. Observe all state and local laws. Respect the rights of others. Snowmobiles are not recommended for riders under 14 years old or riders who have not received qualified instruction.

YAMAHA
We make the difference.

No, you don't have to join the Air Force to get one.

It's the 1988 Exciter. With a liquid-cooled 569cc two-stroke engine armed with new slide-valve carburetion this year. Yamaha Telescopic Strut Suspension and rear suspension that's better than ever. And a power-to-weight ratio that gives you the kind of acceleration you'd expect from something like a F-15, not a snowmobile. To get one, see your local Yamaha dealer. Then file your flight plan.

The Snowmobile Safety and Certification Committee is committed to your safety and enjoyment, so when you buy a snowmobile look for the SSCC label. Always wear a helmet and eye protection.

YAMAHA
We make the difference.

Observe all state and local laws. Respect the rights of others. Snowmobiles are not recommended for riders under 14 years old or riders who have not received qualified instruction.

CHIAT/DAY WANTS TO DRIVE YOUR CARS.

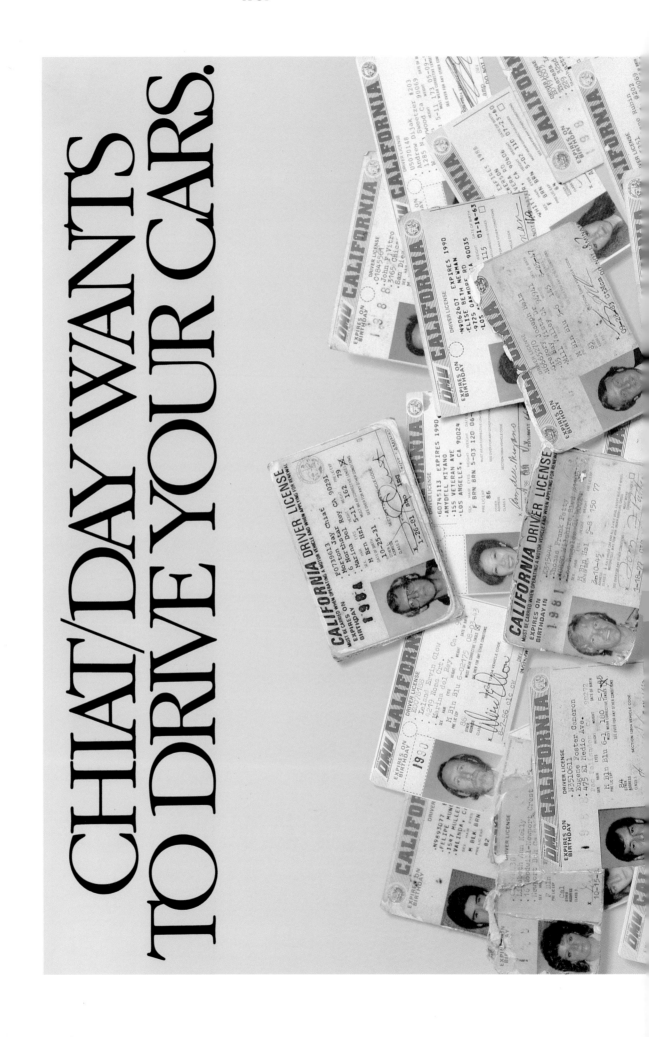

Built for the

Avoid the Human Race. NISSAN

Remember what happened to the last guy who didn't use original body parts?

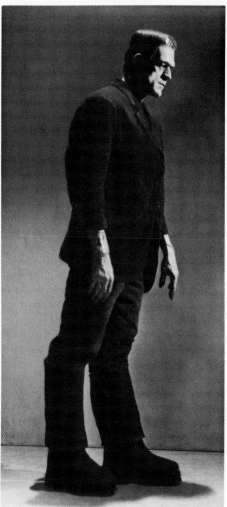

Things didn't work out the way he intended.

Which is exactly why you should always insist on Genuine Nissan® Auto Body Replacement Parts to repair your customer's Nissan car or truck.

Not imported imitation auto body parts.

Only Genuine Nissan Auto Body Parts meet Nissan's exacting original equipment specifications for fit, finish, corrosion resistance and workmanship.

Protect your customer's investment.

Nissans have long been famous for reliability, durability and maintaining a healthy portion of their value for resale.

All these qualities can be compromised by using imitation, imported auto body parts.

That's because only Genuine Nissan Auto Body Replacement Parts are designed and built to be as durable as a Nissan.

Furthermore, every Nissan car and truck is designed and tested as a system. And, if any part of that system is changed, the dynamics of the whole system may change.

All of which adds up to one thing: you may not be returning your customer's vehicle with the same original equipment quality.

And this could diminish the value of your customer's Nissan car or truck.

Yet, many insurance companies insist that imported imitation auto body parts be used to reduce costs.

Your customer has a right to know.

At Nissan, we think your customers deserve to have their car or truck repaired with only the finest body parts.

In short, they have a right to protect their investment.

It's a point of view a lot of people share, too. Currently, many states are investigating the repair policies of insurance companies. In fact, several have recently approved legislation that addresses this matter.

If you'd like to know more about this important issue, we'll be glad to send you an informative brochure on the subject. Write to us at: Nissan Motor Corporation USA, PO Box 191-PD, Gardena, CA 90247.

When you use Genuine Nissan Parts, your customers will be more satisfied in the long run. You'll have a lot better chance at repeat business. And, because they fit right, Genuine Nissan Replacement Parts will be easier and quicker to install.

So why fool around with anything less than the real thing?

Insist on using Genuine Nissan Parts. And don't create a monster.

Built for the Human Race.

Nissan cited for squashing bugs.

Let's face it. Life has enough problems already.

That's why at Nissan, we make sure your new car has the bugs out. Before you get in.

And apparently, we're doing a smashing job of it.

Because the brand-new 1988 J.D. Power and Associates Initial Quality Survey finds that fewer

Nissan owners experienced problems during their first three to four months of ownership than any other manufacturer.

And that includes the high-priced boys. Like Mercedes-Benz, Porsche and BMW.

This extensive study covered 89 critical categories. From engines and transmissions. To steering and

handling. Right down to the leaks, squeaks and rattles.

Which all makes any Nissan a car that's a pleasure to own and drive.

Instead of one that's crawling with problems.

Built for the Human Race.

1987

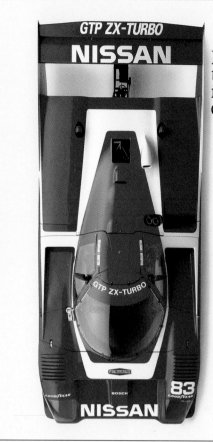

Basically, we took the same idea and added carpeting.

Racing an 800-horsepower, 215-mph projectile like the Nissan® GTP ZX Turbo for hours on-end will teach you a thing or two about performance.

Things we've applied to the latest street-legal version.

The Nissan 300ZX Turbo.

For example, in the car on the right, you'll find the most powerful Z engine ever, a 3.0-liter, turbocharged, fuel-injected overhead cam V6. The same basic engine that's in the car on the left.

You'll also find in the 300ZX a new, high-flow, low-inertia turbocharger that actually reduces lag—a common turbo complaint—by a spirited 40%.

Power rack-and-pinion steering, limited slip differential, and power four-wheel vented disc brakes are all standard.

Of course, we had to make a few concessions to driving in the real world. Like cut-pile carpeting instead of a bare aluminum floor pan.

Beyond that, we've added a six-way adjustable driver's seat; remote controls on the steering wheel; power windows, mirrors and door locks. And other Human Engineering™ touches that help keep you in total control of your environment.

Because, the way we see it, anything that takes away from your performance takes away from the car's performance.

And anything that does that just isn't as much fun.

NISSAN

Built for the Human Race.

Most people who buy economy cars are missing a few screws.

290

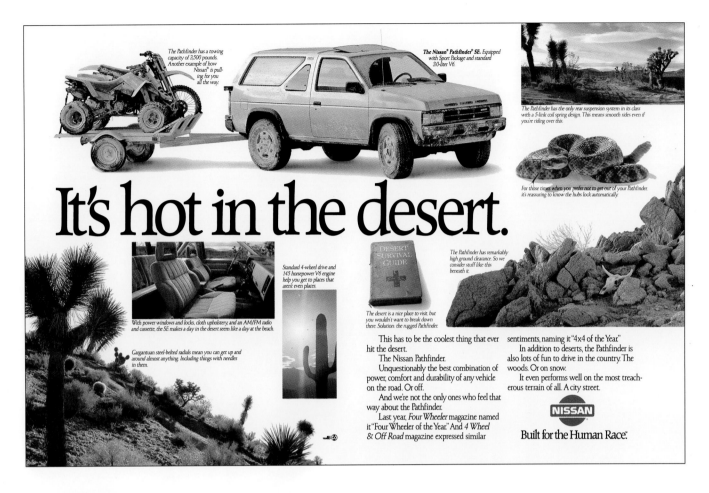

The Pathfinder has a towing capacity of 3,500 pounds. Another example of how Nissan® is pulling for you all the way.

The Nissan® Pathfinder® SE. Equipped with Sport Package and standard 3.0-liter V6.

The Pathfinder has the only rear suspension system in its class with a 3-link coil spring design. This means smooth rides even if you're riding over this.

For those times when you prefer not to get out of your Pathfinder, it's reassuring to know the hubs lock automatically.

It's hot in the desert.

With power windows and locks, cloth upholstery, and an AM/FM radio and cassette, the SE makes a day in the desert seem like a day at the beach.

Gargantuan steel-belted radials mean you can get up and around almost anything. Including things with needles in them.

Standard 4-wheel drive and 145 horsepower V6 engine help you get to places that aren't even places.

The desert is a nice place to visit, but you wouldn't want to break down there. Solution: the rugged Pathfinder.

The Pathfinder has remarkably high ground clearance. So we consider stuff like this beneath it.

This has to be the coolest thing that ever hit the desert.

The Nissan Pathfinder.

Unquestionably the best combination of power, comfort and durability of any vehicle on the road. Or off.

And we're not the only ones who feel that way about the Pathfinder.

Last year, *Four Wheeler* magazine named it "Four Wheeler of the Year." And *4 Wheel & Off Road* magazine expressed similar sentiments, naming it "4x4 of the Year."

In addition to deserts, the Pathfinder is also lots of fun to drive in the country. The woods. Or on snow.

It even performs well on the most treacherous terrain of all. A city street.

NISSAN

Built for the Human Race.

"I'm hot."
Who says Mom and Dad should be the only ones who get a sunroof? Not us. Our van has an optional double sunroof.

"I'm thirsty."
Someone should have thought of this when we were their age. It's a refrigerator with a built-in ice maker (and it can keep drinks warm, too).

"I wanna bring my bike."
Go ahead and bring it. There's plenty of room for bikes, camping gear, whatever. Even Stacey's teddy bear. The big one.

"I'm cold."
The rear has its own air conditioner/heater, too. And since kids will be kids, there's a master control in the front.

"Stacey's on my side."
Not in the Nissan® You can get swivelling, reclining captain's chairs in the second row as well.

RR HEATER

The Nissan van reduces road noise.

When you start shopping for a new car, make sure to bring your kids.

Because if you don't listen to what they have to say before you buy, you probably will afterward.

NISSAN

Built for the Human Race.

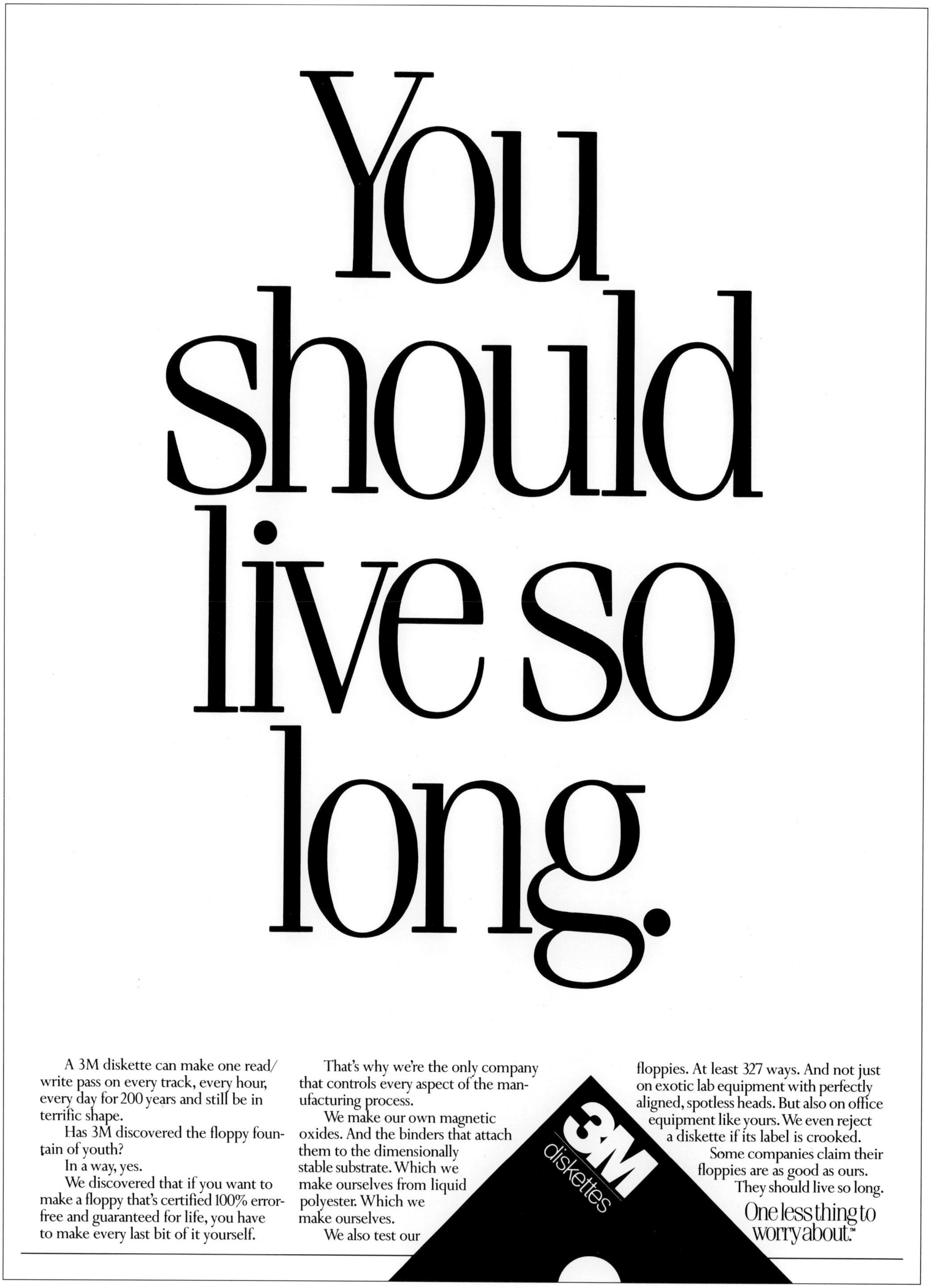

You should live so long.

A 3M diskette can make one read/write pass on every track, every hour, every day for 200 years and still be in terrific shape.

Has 3M discovered the floppy fountain of youth?

In a way, yes.

We discovered that if you want to make a floppy that's certified 100% error-free and guaranteed for life, you have to make every last bit of it yourself.

That's why we're the only company that controls every aspect of the manufacturing process.

We make our own magnetic oxides. And the binders that attach them to the dimensionally stable substrate. Which we make ourselves from liquid polyester. Which we make ourselves.

We also test our

floppies. At least 327 ways. And not just on exotic lab equipment with perfectly aligned, spotless heads. But also on office equipment like yours. We even reject a diskette if its label is crooked.

Some companies claim their floppies are as good as ours.

They should live so long.

3M diskettes

One less thing to worry about.™

The cure for worry warts.

It's not a pill or a potion, and it's cheaper than psychotherapy. It's a 3M diskette, certified 100% error-free and guaranteed for the life of the diskette.

Which we conservatively estimate to be 200 years, at the rate of one read/write pass on every track, every hour of every day.

We can make this guarantee because every 3M diskette must live up to 327 of the most demanding standards ever devised.

Standards that even reject a floppy if the label's a little off.

Of course, some people might think we're a little off.

Who else spends so much time and

energy worrying about diskettes?

Well, better us than you.

One less thing to worry about.

3M introduces one less thing to worry about.

We can't do anything about your taxes. Or the rush-hour traffic. Or the person who keeps stealing lunches out of the office refrigerator.

But we can take a big load off your mind when it comes to diskettes.

3M diskettes are certified 100% error-free. And guaranteed for life.

No floppy is more reliable.

There's no way one could be. Because only 3M controls every aspect of the manufacturing process.

We make our own magnetic oxides. And

the binders that attach them to the dimensionally stable substrate. Which we make ourselves from liquid polyester. Which we make ourselves.

We also test our floppies. At least 327 ways. And not just on exotic lab equipment with perfectly aligned, spotless heads. But also on office equipment like yours.

We even reject a floppy if its label is crooked.

Some people think we're a little crazy to go to all that trouble. After all, do you really need a diskette that can make one read/write

pass on every track, every hour, every day for the next 200 years?

Not really.

But now that you know a 3M floppy can do it, you can relax.

And worry about other things.

Like who stole your lunch from the office refrigerator.

One less thing to worry about.

DR 3179

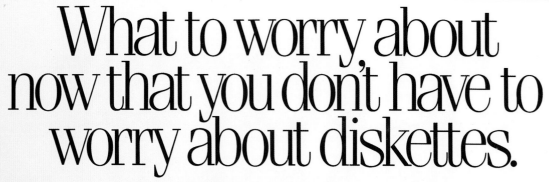

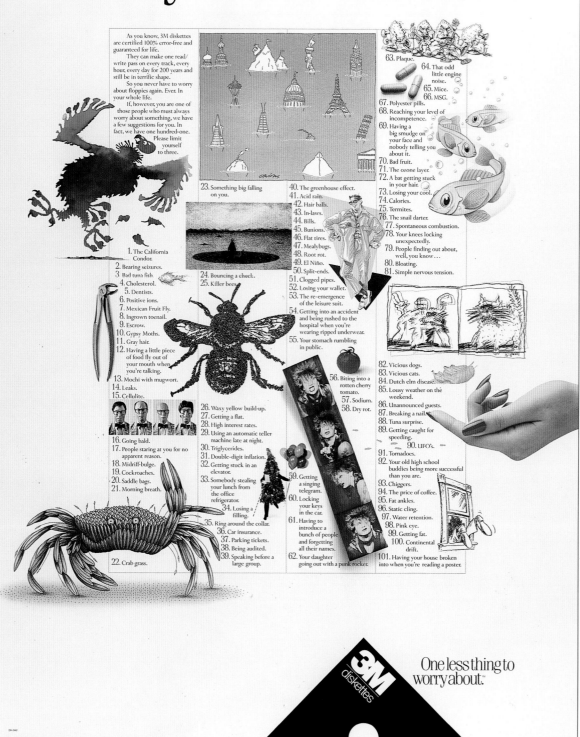

OPEN ON WOMAN SITTING BEHIND DESK LOOKING OVER CALENDAR NOTES.

ANNCR: Are you worried about being audited next Thursday?

WOMAN: (casually) Not at all.

ANNCR: Are you worried that a woman has never made it to Senior Vice President?

WOMAN: No.

ANNCR: Worried about your daughter going out with a punk rocker?

WOMAN: (laughs) Not really.

WOMAN GETS VERY NERVOUS . . .

ANNCR: Are you worried about a floppy disk losing all your payroll records?

SHE PICKS UP COFFEE CUP AND IT SHAKES IN HER HAND, SPILLING ON HER DESK. SHE PULLS A TISSUE FROM BOX AND ONLY GETS A TINY PIECE BUT STILL NERVOUSLY TRIES TO MOP UP SPILL. SHE STARTS PLAYING WITH PEARL NECKLACE, IT BREAKS AND BEADS FLY ALL OVER DESK. SHE IS VERY NERVOUS.

WOMAN: (Visibly shaken) No. . . No (trying to sound convincing).

ANNCR: If you had 3M diskettes, you wouldn't have to worry. 3M floppies are certified 100% error free. No floppy is more reliable.

3M Diskettes. . .One less thing to worry about.

ANNCR: Two years ago, Sallye Blake went back to work. As part of her job, Sallye would often work long hours at a stretch. A job she couldn't afford to give up. But, like millions of other working parents across America, Sallye had an even tougher job than this. She had to find a place where she'd feel secure leaving her children.

CRAWL: Kinder-Care was among the first to see the need for high-quality, affordable child care. Over the years, Drexel Burnham has arranged more than $300 million in financing. Today there are over 1100 Kinder-Care Learning Centers throughout the country. Proof that innovative thinking is not just good business. But for everyone.

ANNCR: Drexel Burnham

VO: This plant could have employed a lot of people. It could have helped us compete in foreign markets. But like 95% of the mid-sized companies in America, the company that wanted to build this plant couldn't get an investment grade rating. So it couldn't afford to raise the capital it needed to grow. Or, for that matter, survive.

CRAWL: Since 1977, more than 300 companies have been able to fund their growth with the help of high yield bonds financed by Drexel Burnham. Today, those companies employ over 1.7 million people. Proof that innovative thinking is not just good for business. But for everyone.

ANNCR: Drexel Burnham

VO: In 1983, over 16% of the population of Vidalia, Louisiana were unemployed. So when plans were announced for a new hydro-electric plant there was a lot of new hope. Then something happened. Shortly after the project began, more money was needed. Unfortunately at the time, most investment bankers never heard of the town of Vidalia, let alone want to invest in it. So the plans for the hydroelectric plant were left unresolved. And the unemployed of Vidalia, Louisiana were left unemployed.

CRAWL: In December 1986, the Catalyst Energy Corporation began construction on the Vidalia hydroelectric plant, financed with the help of high yield bonds managed by Drexel Burnham. Today, with the help of this project, unemployment has been reduced by 30%. Proof that high yield bonds are not just good for business. But for everyone.

ANNCR: Drexel Burnham

VO: Chances are, the rising cost of liability insurance doesn't affect you a great deal. Unless, of course, you're a 5-year-old living in California. A place where increased claims and other factors had made liability insurance so costly, a number of community parks and playgrounds were threatened to be closed. Ultimately, making it very hard for a 5-year-old to be a 5-year-old.

CRAWL: In 1987, money was raised to pay the liability insurance. Today the parks and playgrounds in California remain open. Financing was secured with municipal bonds provided by Drexel Burnham. Proof that innovative thinking is a very powerful tool. Not just for business. But for everyone.

ANNCR: Drexel Burnham

The Official Oakley Eye Chart

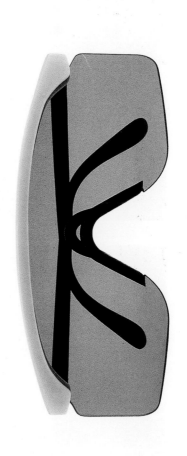

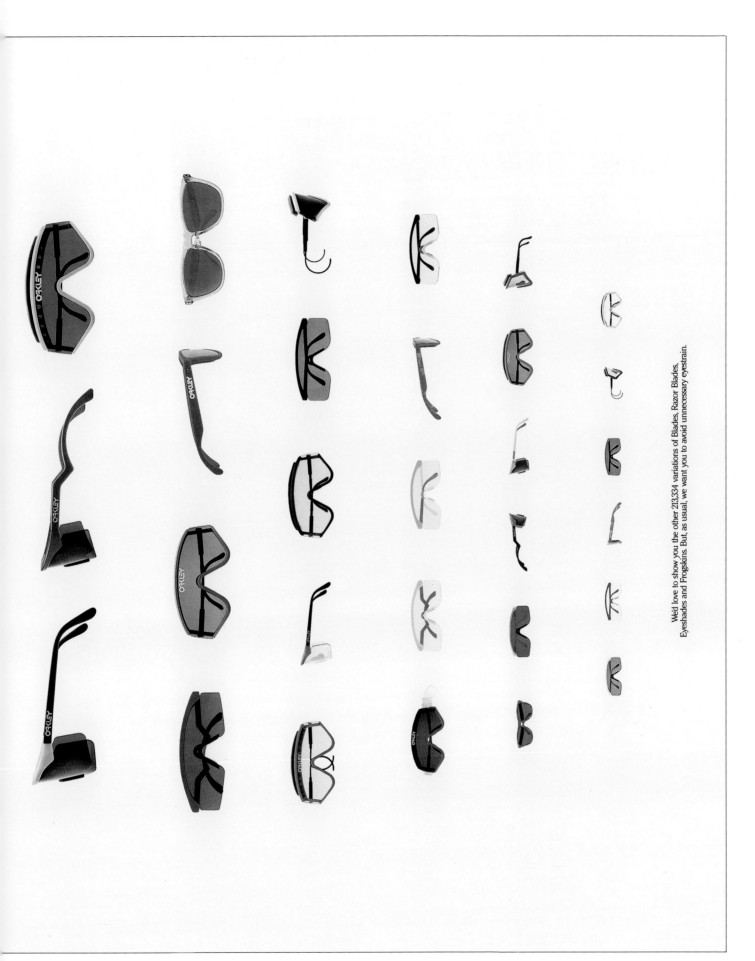

We'd love to show you the other 213,334 variations of Blades, Razor Blades, Eyeshades and Frogskins. But, as usual, we want you to avoid unnecessary eyestrain.

"This was the best Oakley ad we did in the daytime."

_____ **bells,**
_____ **bells.**

We don't do jingles.
Season's Greetings from Chiat/Day.

Chiat/Day turns over a new leaf.

After 20 years in the States, we've just opened our first international office. Our thanks to the people of Toronto
for making us feel welcome. And, of course, to Nissan® of Canada for making it all possible.

Chiat/Day Toronto

卌 卌 卌 卌

"How big can we get without getting bad?"

At a hotel restaurant in Los Angeles, Guy Day is having breakfast. He is talking about the future of the agency that has his name.

"You take Jay's well-known line—'I want to see how big we can get without getting bad.' It's just that, I don't want to know. That's pretty much the basic philosophical difference."

He smiles when he says it, and you wonder if he really means it.

"When you've been around long enough to have witnessed what Bill Bernbach means when he talks about good advertising, and what David Ogilvy means, and Mary Wells—and you know they really mean it. It's not some veneer or some pitch. And then you see what happens—Bernbach lives to see everything he stood for erode...I think at some point in time, to protect your sanity, you have to detach yourself.

"The only hope is, and whether it can be done is still yet to be determined, there has to be the ability for the culture to replicate itself in the next generation. Because you can't expect the same core of people to hold it together forever. And, you take Chiat/Day, when you have four offices and five-hundred people, to hope that all the right people will step forward at the right point in time and assume the reins with the same passion and enthusiasm as two or three guys had when there were thirty people on Olympic Boulevard, you know, the odds aren't with you. You still try and do it, but you need that next generation to stand up and say, "Okay, I want to work as hard as the first generation."

In a conference room in the New York office, Jay Chiat is leaning back in a chair, talking. He is talking about the agency that used to determine its president with a yearly coin toss.

"I think the question has become, how many clients can you do great work for? It isn't a case of size. Size is measured in dollars. It's really a case of, can you do great work for a hundred clients? The jury's out on that. We now have 47 that we're doing great work for. And that work's all being done by the second generation. My influence may still be there, because I'm still around, but the reality is, we're doing better work now.

"If you dissect the agency business, it's almost more like a guild than it is a corporation. It's not a typical corporation, because you can't send creative work to Taiwan, to Korea, to get it done cheaper. You can't copy a campaign and have it built off-shore. You don't have the ability to computerize your manufacturing line or increase the productivity of your production capabilities. It's really a little guild, a handful of people, almost like during the Renaissance, making armor for knights.

"If you took a look at advertising horizontally that way, then look at all the things we've done to accommodate that kind of growth, like de-departmentalizing—getting rid of geographic departments so that a group of people can work together for a client instead of a department head—you can see that what we've done is say, hey, you can grow, because what you do is, you break the agency down into forty or fifty small businesses, each dedicated to one client. And then, size is no longer an issue.

"I never thought of us as big. Even now I still look around and say, it's not really big because you could do 500 million, a billion dollars in one year. And I don't think it really matters how big your clients are or just how many people are working at the agency, as long as they're good people, and the environment is right to do good work, and you insist on doing good work.

"To me, the key is environment. I think there was always an intellectual commitment to the kind of environment we wanted to create. I wanted to be working at a place where you wouldn't be embarrassed to say you worked in advertising."

He pauses for a second.

"Listen, I have to go pick up a suit. You wanna come?"

"With any account, it's not so much doing good work. It's selling it. It's sitting on it till it's out the door."

REEBOKS LET U.B.U.

Reebok

REEBOKS LET U.B.U.

Reebok 🇬🇧

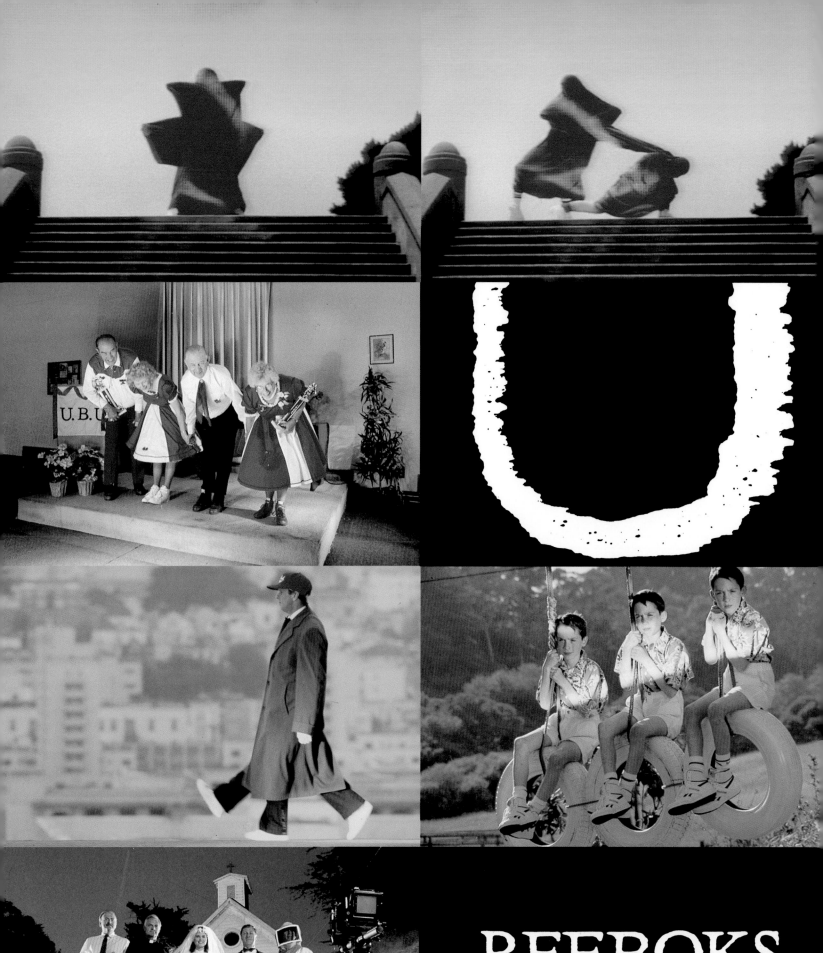

REEBOKS
LET U.B.U.

REEBOKS
LET U.B.U.

U.B.U.

MAN CHANGING WARDROBE THROUGHOUT.
ANNCR VO: The latest news in fashion is this:
Now there's an iron that actually lets you adjust
the steam from a light setting for silks...to an
extra-heavy setting for denims...so you can
steam iron everything. No matter how extensive
your wardrobe. The new Select Steam Iron
from Sunbeam.

We feature GM cars like this 1956 Chevrolet Belair

You Don't Have To Rent The Same Old Car Anymore.

They wore fender skirts. Acres of chrome. Two-tone paint. Three-deuce carbs. And they turned heads from Seattle to Savannah.

Now, you can relive the days of ducktails and hanging dice. At National's Los Angeles International Airport location. Just ask about the "California Classics". Pick out your favorite. And you'll be cruising the streets faster than you can say "Beach Blanket Bingo".

The "California Classics" are just another way National is bringing a new level of fun and excitement to renting a car. Another way we're working to make choosing National more rewarding than ever.

So grab your bobby sox. Brush up on your twist. And take a cruise down memory lane. For details, call **800-CAR-RENT**. **National** Car Rental

We feature GM cars like this 1957 Chevrolet Corvette.

You Don't Have To Rent The Same Old Car Anymore.

They wore fender skirts. Acres of chrome. Two-tone paint. Three-deuce carbs. And they turned heads from Seattle to Savannah.

Now, you can relive the days of ducktails and hanging dice. At National's Los Angeles International Airport location. Just ask about the "California Classics". Pick out your favorite. And you'll be cruising the streets faster than you can say "Beach Blanket Bingo".

The "California Classics" are just another way National is bringing a new level of fun and excitement to renting a car. Another way we're working to make choosing National more rewarding than ever.

So grab your bobby sox. Brush up on your twist. And take a cruise down memory lane. For details, call 800-CAR-RENT. **National** Car Rental

MUSIC: Throughout.
CAR SFX: Wheez, sputter.
DRIVER: Uh oh!
CAR SFX: Screech!
ATTENDANT: Out of juice?
MUSIC: Continues to end.
CAR SPEEDS AWAY.
VO: Veryfine. Juice it up!

Top sellers in their glass.

Our rice and noodles are feeling their oats.

It's no longer news that The Quaker Oats Company bought Golden Grain. What is news, is all the things Quaker® has done since.

And what it all means to you.

Take a look at these two pages. You'll see a lot of reasons why you're going to have your best year ever with Golden Grain.

All of which should make you feel just a twinge of excitement yourself.

Our traditional brands aren't so traditional-looking anymore.

We've always been the market leader for what goes inside our boxes. But there was some room for improvement on the outside.

Now with more contemporary-looking Rice-A-Roni® and Noodle Roni® packages, your new sales figures should far exceed your traditional ones.

On May 7, the cable cars will stop running.

After 25 years of dedicated service, the old Rice-A-Roni advertising campaign will come to an end.

Stay tuned for the new campaign. One that promises to be impossible to miss. That's because the advertising is so strong.

And so are the media dollars. Overall we're spending twice as much on advertising and promotions this year.

Trademark/owner: Golden Grain, Quaker/The Quaker Oats Company; Rice-A-Roni, Noodle Roni, Savory Classics/Golden Grain Macaroni Company; Uncle Ben's, Country Inn/ Uncle Ben's, Inc.; Gatorade/Stokely-Van Camp, Inc.

A lot of people will be leaving Uncle Ben's® Country Inn.™

Introducing Savory Classics™ Rice Dishes. Broccoli Au Gratin, Zesty Cheddar, Garden Pilaf and Chicken Florentine.

We've combined delicious flavors with easier one-step recipes to make Savory Classics the easiest flavored rice to sell.

We're making our move into the growing premium rice category.

It'll be worth it to make room.

Quaker put the country on a steady diet of rice cakes and Gatorade® Thirst Quencher.

Since Quaker took over Gatorade four years ago, sales have tripled. Since they bought Arden Rice Cakes two years ago, sales have quadrupled.

If they're any indication of what's to come with Rice-A-Roni, Noodle Roni and Savory Classics, you're about to go on a much steadier diet of the very thing you thrive on.

Profit.

DOGS: Woof. Woof. Woof. Woof.
A SERIES OF WOOFS SOUNDING LIKE
A TRAIN
SFX: Train bells.
SUPER: New beef basted nuggets.
DOGS: Woofs continue.
SUPER: New beefier gravy.
DOGS: Woofs continue.
SFX: Train bells, hissing.
VO: New Gravy Train has crunchy
beef basted nuggets and even
beefier gravy. New Gravy Train.
It's the beefiest Gravy Train ever.

Why Our Piña Coladas Are Better Than Their Piña Coladas.

Even if both drinks were made in exactly the same way with exactly the same ingredients, the one you sipped on a Royal Caribbean ship would taste better. Because you'd be sipping it in our famous Viking Crown Lounge. A beautifully designed club 12 stories above the water that gives you a perfect view of the sea and the sunset. And only Royal Caribbean ships have one.

And there's something else only Royal Caribbean ships have. The kind of personal service that leaves you free to enjoy every aspect of your vacation. To leave you feeling happier and more relaxed than you've ever been. So that even if there was no such thing as a Viking Crown Lounge, our Piña Coladas would still taste better.

⚓ROYAL CARIBBEAN

When you're ready for something better.

Most 7 day cruises from $1210–$3550 per person, including airfare. Song of Norway, Sun Viking, Nordic Prince, Song of America, Sovereign of the Seas. Ships of Norwegian and Liberian Registry. See your travel agent.

CARIBBEAN MUSIC THROUGHOUT

ANNCR VO: The officers and staff of Royal Caribbean Cruise Line invite you to join them for seven days of absolute perfection.

R.S.V.P. your local travel agent. Don't just cruise the Caribbean. Cruise the Royal Caribbean.

In The Best Theaters, The Sound Is As Big As The Picture.

From the people who brought you big screen television comes the sound to go with it. Introducing Mitsubishi Home Theater Systems. For the Mitsubishi dealer nearest you, call (800) 556-1234, ext. 145. In California, (800) 441-2345, ext. 145. © 1988 Mitsubishi Electric Sales America, Inc.

△ MITSUBISHI

The Best Way To Watch A Movie Has Always Been On The Big Screen.

With a screen that's 86% larger than conventional 26-inch sets, our 35-inch direct-view TV will even make bad movies look good. For the dealer nearest you, call (800) 556-1234, ext. 245. In California, (800) 441-2345, ext. 245. © 1988 Mitsubishi Electric Sales America, Inc.

△ MITSUBISHI

One Measure Of A Great Theater Is The Size Of Its Screen.

With our 60-inch big screen TV, you can literally turn your living room into a screening room. For the Mitsubishi dealer nearest you, call (800) 556-1234, ext. 245. In California, (800) 441-2345, ext. 245. © 1988 Mitsubishi Electric Sales America, Inc.

▲ MITSUBISHI®

THE FOLLOWING PAGES ARE A MONTAGE OF
IMAGES FROM THE MITSUBISHI "HOME THEATER"
TELEVISION COMMERCIAL. THIS IS THE SCRIPT
OF THE COMMERCIAL.

SERIES OF CLASSIC MOVIE AND CARTOON CLIPS
THROUGHOUT.
GROUCHO: And now, on with the opera...
SFX: Scream...Scream...Aaaaaaaaaa...
CLOSE-UP SHOT OF THE MITSUBISHI HOME THEATER. CUT
TO CLOSE-UP SHOT OF THE MITSUBISHI LOGO ON A HOME
THEATER SYSTEM.
SFX: Aaaaaaaaaa...
ANNCR VO: From the people who brought you big
screen television...
CUT TO CLOSE-UP SHOT OF THE MITSUBISHI HOME THEATER.
ANNCR VO: ...comes the sound to go with it.
CUT TO CLOSE-UP SHOT OF THE MITSUBISHI LOGO ON A
HOME THEATER SYSTEM. CUT TO SHOT OF A MITSUBISHI
HOME THEATER SYSTEM TV SCREEN SHOWING MOVIE CLIPS.
CLARK: Frankly my dear, I don't give a...
ANNCR VO: Introducing Mitsubishi Home
Theater Systems...
CUT TO A WIDE SHOT OF THE MITSUBISHI HOME
THEATER SYSTEM.
ANNCR VO: ...now playing at a dealer near you.
CUT BACK TO A CLOSE-UP SHOT OF THE TV SCREEN.
ORSON: Rosebud.

INPUT VCR 1

SURROUND DOLBY

AUDIO FUNCTION

RECORD SELECTOR

CD—V ◄AUDIO FROM► VCR 2
VIDEO FROM

VOLUME

SCAN

INPUT

PUSH OPEN

UNIFIED REMOTE CONTROL/C

UBISHI

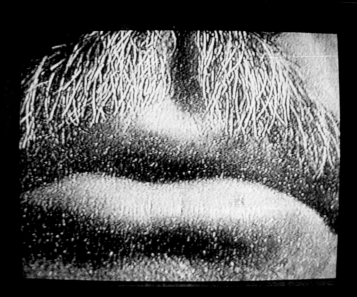

Give J&B Some R&R.

Walk through our homes naked.

We've got nothing to hide. Cultured stone, Owens Corning insulation, dual-glazed windows, and engineered trusses are just a fraction of the features found inside the inside of a Kaufman and Broad home.

And we're not afraid to show you any of them. In fact, we're rather proud.

That's why many of our home sites have two homes for you to see. The finished one. And, the unfinished one.

Where you can actually see floors before they're carpeted. Examine walls before they're painted. Study plumbing before it's covered in cabinetry.

We welcome it. And so do our contractors.

For unlike most other builders, we contract out almost every part of our homes to specialists. From architects to landscapers, to even soil engineers. Each an expert in their field. And each very happy to show off their work.

So when you look at a Kaufman and Broad home, we make sure nothing is left up to your imagination.

Except, of course, deciding how to decorate it.

But that's a whole other story.

Kaufman △ Broad

9 out of 10 people in California have a drinking problem.

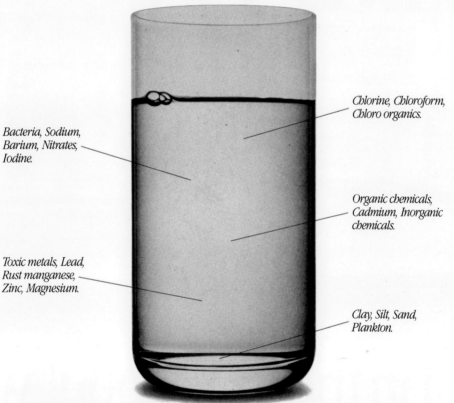

Bacteria, Sodium, Barium, Nitrates, Iodine.

Chlorine, Chloroform, Chloro organics.

Organic chemicals, Cadmium, Inorganic chemicals.

Toxic metals, Lead, Rust manganese, Zinc, Magnesium.

Clay, Silt, Sand, Plankton.

The facts are clear. Unfortunately, the water isn't. That's why there's a Watermark™ Water Center. A place where you can get the clearest, healthiest, premium pure water available.

The world's first complete water center.

You can buy our pure water by the bottle. Or you can bring in your own container. Or we can even hook up one of our Ultrapurification Systems to your sink at home.

At Watermark, we can handle just about any water problem you have. Whether it's hard water. Dirty water. Or just plain bad tasting water. Bring in a sample from home and we'll test it for free.

If you're one of the 9 out of 10 people in California with a water problem, see the expert. Visit the Watermark Water Center. There you'll find the perfect solution.

Watermark™
Water Centers™
We make one thing perfectly clear.

We're located at Snell and Blossom Hill in San Jose (408) 629-6000. Steven's Creek and De Anza in Cupertino (408) 257-0900. Opening soon on Calaveras in Milpitas. El Camino in Mountain View.

Still in the dark about what to give for Christmas?

If you're looking for a great Christmas present, here are a few shining examples.

Eveready® flashlights.

They come in all sizes and shapes, for every imaginable use. Like warning flashers to keep in the car. Extra-bright halogen lanterns for camping trips. Powerful little Squeeze Lights for a key ring or purse. And dozens more.

Remember Eveready when you make out your Christmas list this year. And you'll get your shopping done in a flash.

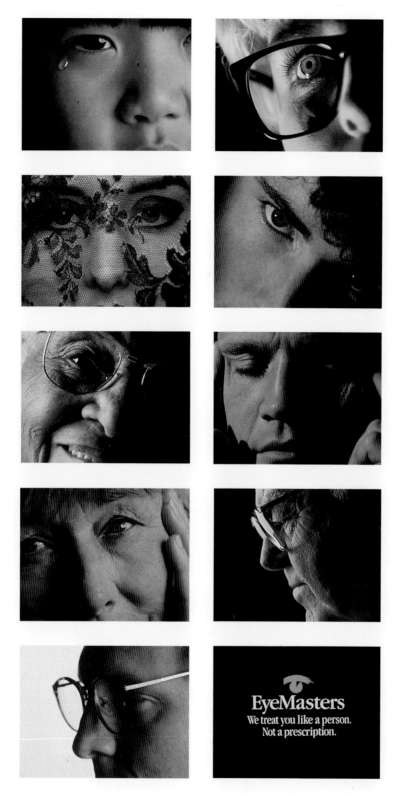

ANNCR VO: Look into someone's eyes and you can discover a lot about them. At Eyemasters the more we can discover about you the better. So we ask a few more questions and spend a little more time to get your glasses right. Because we know, you can always get another pair of glasses, but you never get another pair of eyes.

EyeMasters
We treat you like a person.
Not a prescription.

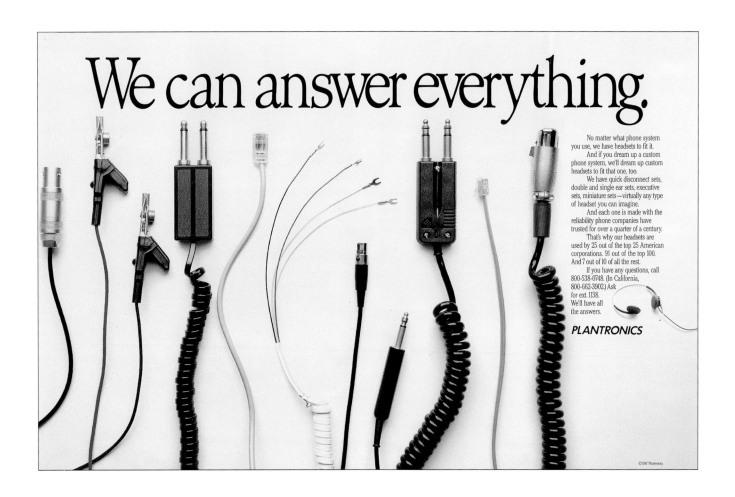

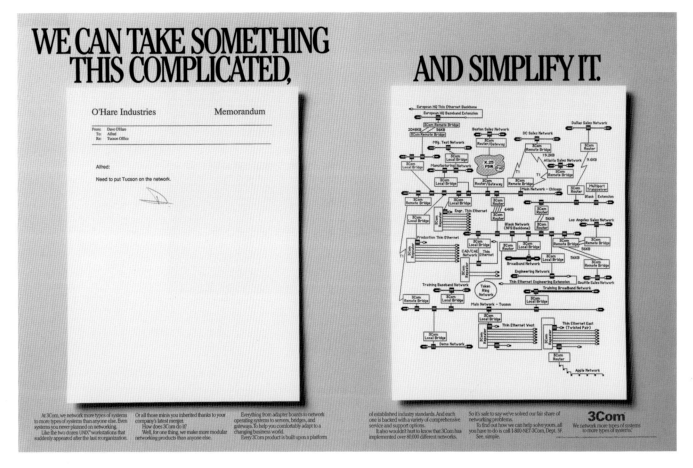

A BUSINESSMAN IS IN A CHAIR WITH WHEELS ON IT. HE'S TALKING ON HIS OMNISET WHILE HE'S WORKING ON HIS COMPUTER KEYBOARD.

MAN: Sure, I can talk (pause) I'm all yours . . .

HE SPINS CHAIR SO ONE HAND IS WORKING WITH FILES, AND THE OTHER IS PECKING AT HIS KEYBOARD. HE SWIVELS BACK AND FORTH WITH HIS HANDS STILL STRETCHED BETWEEN THE TWO DESKS. FILM STARTS TO SPEED UP.

ANNCR: Introducing OmniSet— The phone designed for the normal modern workload: two jobs at once.

MAN: Let's do it now before I get busy.

BUSINESSMAN LEANING BACK IN HIS CHAIR READING FILES. HE SPEAKS INTO HIS OMNISET PHONE.

MAN: Yes sir.

VO: Introducing the OmniSet business phone . . .

MAN: You want to give us your account.

HE SLAPS FILES DOWN ON DESK.

VO: . . . Because you never know when you'll need your hands free.

HE LEAPS OUT OF HIS CHAIR, CLENCHES FISTS AND THROWS HANDS INTO THE AIR.

MAN: Thank you very much.

HE PRETENDS HE'S HIGH-FIVING FRIENDS, BEATS HIS CHEST, CARRIES ON.

MUSIC: Up-tempo, classical throughout.

A SERIES OF VIGNETTES, SHOWING JUST HOW MUCH NISSAN OWNERS THINK OF THEIR CARS. THE VISUAL TONE IS FUN AND UPBEAT. IN THE FIRST SCENE, A MAN WASHES HIS CAR IN A VACANT ALLEYWAY. A WOMAN PULLS HER PULSAR NX INTO A PARKING SPACE. CAMERA PULLS BACK TO REVEAL SHE'S PARKED IN A FAR CORNER OF THE LOT, AWAY FROM ALL THE OTHER CARS. A FATHER VERY RELUCTANTLY HANDS THE KEYS TO HIS MAXIMA TO HIS SON. A YOUNG WOMAN KEEPS A WATCHFUL EYE ON CAR WASH ATTENDANT, THEN USES HER SKIRT TO CLEAN A FRONT HEADLIGHT. HEAD SHOT OF PROUD PULSAR NX OWNER.

ANNCR VO: Have you ever noticed how cars mean a little more...

CUT TO PULSAR NX.

ANNCR VO: ...to some people than they do to others?

CUT TO PROUD OWNER WITH A BIG SMILE ON HIS FACE.

ANNCR VO: Nissan has.

PROUD OWNER OF THE HARDBODY "BIG FOOT" SHOOS AWAY A DOG WHO HAS JUST URINATED ON ONE OF THE FRONT TIRES.

ANNCR VO: That's why we build ours the way we do. We understand that a car fulfills a number of human needs.

CUT BACK TO MAN WASHING HIS NISSAN IN A VACANT ALLEYWAY. AS HE WALKS AWAY FROM HIS NISSAN HE LOOKS BACK AT IT TWICE, TO ASSURE HIMSELF THAT IT LOOKS GREAT.

ANNCR VO: And transportation...is only one of them. Nissan. Built for the Human Race.

OPEN ON PAIR OF FEET WALKING ON A CONCRETE SURFACE.

MUSIC: Suggestive of something to come.

ANNCR VO: Nissan builds cars for people who have a certain...enthusiasm for the cars they drive.

MAN'S HAND REACHES FOR HANDLE ON CORRUGATED METAL GARAGE DOOR. DOOR OPENS DRAMATICALLY TO REVEAL THE NISSAN GTP CAR IN A RACETRACK GARAGE.

MUSIC VO: Exciting, SFX start.

HAND REACHES FOR SECOND GARAGE DOOR.

ANNCR VO: Of course...

DOOR OPENS DRAMATICALLY TO REVEAL GTO RACER SUCH AS THE NEWMAN/SHARP CAR.

ANNCR VO: ...some drivers...

HAND REACHES FOR THIRD GARAGE DOOR.

ANNCR VO: ...are a little more enthusiastic...

DOOR OPENS DRAMATICALLY TO REVEAL ROGER MEARS' RACING TRUCK.

ANNCR VO: ...than others.

AN EXCITING, HIGH-ACTION SERIES OF RACING SCENES BEGINS HERE AND CONTINUES FOR THE REMAINDER OF THE SPOT, UNTIL IT CRESCENDOS AND ENDS ABRUPTLY AND DRAMATICALLY WITH THE NISSAN LOGO.

ANNCR VO: Nissan. Built for the most demanding race of all...the Human Race.

 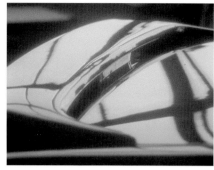 

OPEN IN NISSAN MOTORSPORT GARAGE. WE SEE GTP CAR, OTHER HIGH-PERFORMANCE CARS. A GROUP OF MECHANICS HOISTS A BLACK SPORTS CAR, WE JUST SEE PARTS OF IT. BEAUTY SHOTS FOCUS ON DETAILS OF THIS SPORTS CAR. WHEELS, SPOILER, BLACK/WHITE GAUGES, TACH, DUAL EXHAUST, DEEP PAINT, TAIL LIGHTS, ETC.

ANNCR VO: Nissan has developed a new high-performance sports car. With a modified Z-Car engine. Anti-sway bars front and rear, and anti-lock brakes. The cockpit was designed for one 6-foot 2-inch driver...

REVEAL ENTIRE CAR WITH FOUR DOORS OPEN.

ANNCR VO: ...and four 6-foot 2-inch passengers. Introducing the new Nissan Maxima.

SFX: Clunk, clunk, clunk, clunk.

ANNCR VO: The four-door sports car.

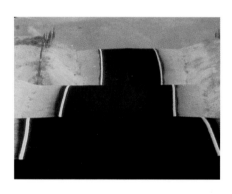  

OPEN ON SHOT OF ROAD. CUT TO QUICK CLOSE-UP DRIVE BY. CUT TO EMPTY ROAD. CAR ENTERS. CUT TO CLOSE-UP OF CAR.

ANNCR VO: When the engineers at Nissan designed the 240SX they wanted it to have certain acceleration.

CUT TO ADJUST MIRROR. BEAUTY SHOT. TACHOMETER. BEAUTY SHOT. STICK SHIFT. FOOT. TACK.

ANNCR VO: characteristics.

CAR LEAVES FRAME. POINT OF VIEW OVER HILL. POINT OF VIEW ROLLER COASTER. CUT TO BEAUTY SHOT OF FRONT OF CAR.

ANNCR VO: The Nissan 240SX. It's a lot of sports car, but you can handle it.

"The guy who held the camera
threw up while getting this shot."

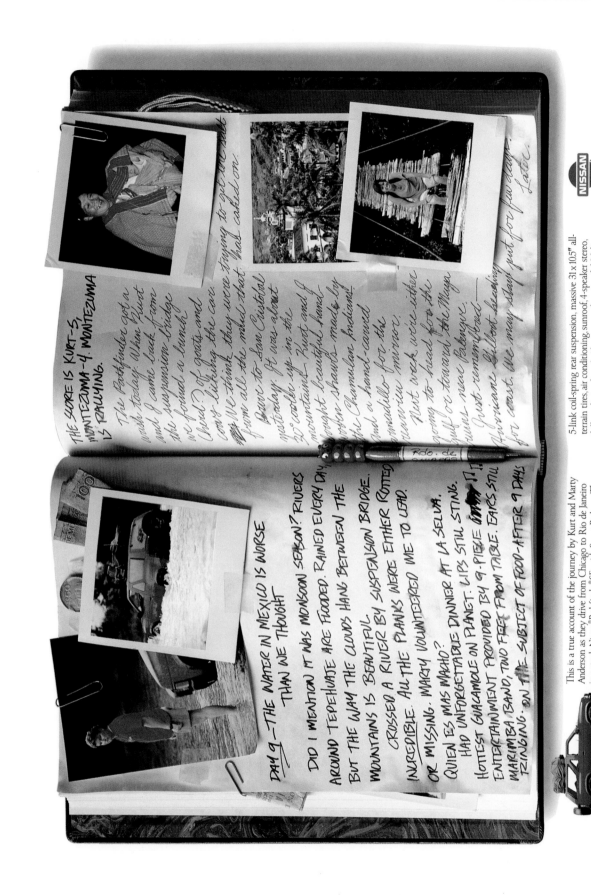

Pathfinder on the road to Rio : Day 29, The Amazo

*"I think you get permission
to be large. You get your
first million dollar
account, then you're given
permission by clients to
be able to handle it. Then
you get a five million
dollar account, and you
can handle it, and you
work your way up."*

Built for the Human Race.

Day 1 On the Road to Rio.

MEXICO

Botatulan

Day 9 On the Road to Rio.

PELIGRO A 200

BOTATULAN

AMAZON

Macapá

Rio de Janeiro

Day 35 On the Road to Rio.

THE PRECEDING PAGES ARE A MONTAGE OF IMAGES FROM THE NISSAN "ROAD TO RIO" TELEVISION CAMPAIGN. THESE ARE THE SCRIPTS OF THE COMMERCIALS.

SFX: Packing, conversation in living room.
SPONTANEOUS CHATTER
MARTY: Those are my special jungle tights.
KURT: Jungle tights? Jungle tights.
CUT TO KURT AND MARTY LEAVING HOUSE WITH LUGGAGE.
KURT VO: That's us, Kurt and Marty Anderson.
CUT TO KURT AND MARTY ANDERSON LOADING UP THE PATHFINDER IN THE DRIVEWAY OF THEIR SUBURBAN HOME. CUT TO SEVERAL QUICK CUTS OF KURT AND MARTY PACKING AND LOADING THE PATHFINDER WITH GEAR.
KURT VO: We had always talked about getting away, on a trip. A real trip. You know, wild jungles, mountains, an adventure.
THE PATHFINDER HEADS THROUGH TOWN TOWARDS THE FREEWAY.
KURT VO: So we're going to drive a Nissan Pathfinder 7,000 miles. From Chicago to Rio. We figure the trip to Brazil will take about 6 weeks...
IT'S IMMEDIATELY ENGULFED IN RUSH HOUR.
KURT VO: ...depending on traffic.
SFX: Freeway noise.

MUSIC: Under throughout.
SFX: Under. Outdoors, insects, birds, wind.
OPEN ON WIDE SHOT OF MEXICO WITH PATHFINDER DRIVING.
SERIES OF SHOTS OF THE PATHFINDER TAKING ON THE DIFFERENT TYPES OF ROADS AND TERRAIN IN MEXICO.
KURT VO: You wouldn't believe what the Pathfinder went through on the road to Botatulan. I guess when they ran out of asphalt, they used cobblestones. When they ran out of cobblestones, they used rocks. When they ran out of rocks, they used gravel. When they ran out of gravel they used dirt.... They never ran out of dirt.

OPEN ON BELIZE AIRPORT, VARIOUS SCENES OF TRAVELERS, AIRPORT PERSONNEL, ETC. CAPTURING THE LOCAL COLOR. WE SEE KURT AND MARTY TRYING TO MAKE ARRANGEMENTS TO PUT THEIR PATHFINDER ON A CARGO PLANE TO BELEM. THEY TALK TO VARIOUS OFFICIALS OF THE AIR CHARTER, THEY'RE ON THE PHONE EXASPERATED, AT EVERY TURN IS A CONFRONTATION. SUCCESS DOES NOT COME EASILY.
MARTY: In Belize, we ran into Hurricane Gilbert...
KURT: ...and an even bigger problem.
TICKET AGENT: No way.
KURT: That's what we gotta do, that's what we gotta do.
CUT TO KURT AND MARTY ON THE TARMAC, THE PATHFINDER BEING LOADED, THE ROAR OF THE PROPS.
KURT: The State Department strongly advised us not to drive through Central America, so we're hopping this plane to Belem, Brazil. Let's not kid ourselves, the Pathfinder is tough...but it ain't bulletproof.

SFX: Under. Primitive village, natives, Pathfinder engine.
MARTY VO: This is the first time Waeimpie Indians have ever been filmed. They have never seen red hair...or anything like a Pathfinder. Here on the equator, the air conditioner was a big hit. And they seemed to like our music. But we discovered, we like their music...ever more.
MUSIC: Native instruments and singing.

SFX: Under. Outdoor Walla, Pathfinder driving.
SUNSET, THE PATHFINDER IS ON THE OUTSKIRTS OF RIO, HEADING TOWARDS DOWNTOWN.
MARTY VO: Rio. We made it.
KURT VO: It's been 35 days in the Pathfinder. Marty and I have gone through jungles, rain forests, primitive villages, and eleven deodorant sticks.
IN LIGHT OF DUSK, OUR HEROES PULL THE MASSIVE PATHFINDER UP TO A MODEST HOTEL.
KURT VO: We really needed a good night's sleep.
KURT AND MARTY OPEN THE PATHFINDER'S MUD-ENCRUSTED TAILGATE. A BATTERED AND MUD-SPLATTERED STEAMER TRUNK IS OPENED TO REVEAL A SEQUINED, BRIGHT BLUE EVENING GOWN.
MARTY VO: But that could always wait 'til tomorrow.
CUT TO KURT AND MARTY IN ELEGANT EVENING WEAR, DANCING TO A LATIN BEAT, CELEBRATING WITH LOCALS AT AN OPEN-AIR NIGHTCLUB DOWNTOWN.
MUSIC: Under throughout.

Everyone who we can remember that ever worked at Chiat/Day.

Michael Aarons · Rick Abel · Dan Abramson · David Acosta · Dorothy Adams · Robert Adelman · George Adels · Michele Afshar

Mary Agresta · Vicki Ahrens · Crispin Alapag · Rick Albert · Kristy Albrecht · Steve Alburty · Scott Alee · Eileen Alexander · Susan Alexander

Pam Alexander · Andrea Alfano · Sara Allbright · Gary Alpern · Linda Altus · Steve Amato · Ruth Amir · Catherine Anderson

Judy Anderson · Jeffrey Andrews · Hank Antosz · Lorraine Arado · Jamee Ard · Pam Armstrong · Susan Armstrong · Lisa Arnett

Ronald Arnold · Bruce Ascher · Karen Aseltine · Susan Ashmore · Steve Astorino · Silvia Athans · John Attebery · Bob Austin · Susan Avant

Loren Averick · Melanie Axtman · Eric Ayzenberg · Cheryl Bailey · Brooke Baker · Darcy Baker · Daryl Baker · Tom Baker · Gayle Baldauff

Licia Baldwin · Laura Ball · Patricia Baltrusaitis · Morton Baran · Jennifer Barber · David Barberis · Mary Bardes · Jerry Barnhart

David Barr · Jane Bartesch · Gail Bartley · Jay Barton · Judith Barton · Diana Barton · Roxanne Bartush · Annette Barzilai · Steve Bassett

Kenneth Battiest · Daniel Baxter · Steven Bayer · Suzanne Bazoian · Steve Beaumont · Caroline Beck · Valentine Beck · Kristine Becker

John Beckett · Susan Beebe · Theresa Beindorf · Brian Belefant · Gillian Bell · Maggie Bell · Jon Belzer · Brian Bennett · Jamie Benson

David Berger · Beth Berlin · Barbara Bernau · Deni Bernhardt · Melissa Bernhardt · Doris Berry · June Berry · Robert Berry · Mattie Betts

Scott Bicking · Charlie Bidwell · David Bigman · Jeff Billig · Ingrid Blaauw · Reggie Blackshear · Jeffrey Blish · Betsy Bloodgood

Dawn Blume · Patricia Boardman · Stephanie Boardman · Jeff Bockman · Matt Bogen · Steven Bond · Brent Bouchez · Susan Bowers

Linda Bowles · Chic Bowling · Shannon Boyd · Rick Boyko · Bob Bradley · Elizabeth Bradley · Sharron Brady · Kenneth Brandt

Penny Branstetter · Amanda Brauman · Anne Brazil · Jill Brean · Timothy Breen · Susie Breen · Kim Bresser · Diana Bridges · E. Kim Briggs

Walter Brindak · Frederich Briski · Marina Brock · Corinne Brohme · Sally Brommage · Jack Brotherton · Alison Brown · Bob Brown

Mindy Brown · Robert Brown · Tracey Brown · Michael Brownstein · Judy Brumelle · William Brussow · Pamela Bucher · Bryan Buckley

Nancy Budd · Judith Buehler · Chris Buell · Lori Burgess · Patrice Burling · Nelsens Burt · Devon Burton · Ann Burton · Brian Butler

Dave Butler · John Butler · John Buttress · Claudia Byrum · Orlando Cabalo · Marrissa Cagnolatti · David Cairns · Victor Caldwell

Rosann Calisi · Wanda Calvello · Alan Campbell · Joyce Campbell · Mari Campbell · Irene Cange · G. Sharron Cannarsa · Mary-Regina Cano

Frank Carlile · Patricia Carlisle · Charles Carlson · Carolyn Carlson · Karen Carlson · Maria Carmazzi · Bicente Caro · Jane Carpenter

Nigel Carr · Thomas Carroll · Pat Carson · Theodora Carter · Barbara Casado · Maureen Casey · Robyn Cass · Joan Cassin · Lorraine Castillo

Robin Castillo · Joe Castro · Veronica Caudillo · Joseph Caulfield · Tom Cavanagh · Annette Cerbone · Dyanne Chae · Alma Chaidez

Maria Chakarian · Janet Chambers · Keith Chambers · Judith Chandellor · Robert Chandler · Diane Charbonic · Sherry Charles

Glenda Charrette · Barbara Cheatham · See-Fown Cheng · Mark Chernansky · Beverly Chesler · Tulip Chestman · Carolyn Cheung

Elyse Chiat · Jay Chiat · Marc Chiat · Andrew Chinich · Carolyn Christensen · Nicole Christensen · Shari Christensen · Heidi Christenson

Carol Chua · Shelly Chung · Dan Ciccone · Alex Cichy · Mike Ciranni · Greg Clancy · Michael Clancy · Charles Clark · Julie Clark

Leslie Clark · Linda Claussen · Lisa Claymen · Anne Cleary · Lee Clow · Anita Coakley · Bess Cocke · Robert Cockrell · Cathy Coe

Ted Cofsky · Alisa Cohen · Lory Cohen · Suzee Cohen · Nick Cohen · Francesca Cohn · Lisa Cohn · Michael Cohn · Paul Cohune

Edward Cole · James Coleman · Courtney Compton · Richard Condon · Kathleen Connelly · Carolyn Connelly · Kelly Connelly · Ed Connor

Elaine Cook · Lisa Cook · Marilyn Cook · Martin Cooke · Michaela Cooney · Eugene Cooper · Kathryn Cooper · Geoff Coopland

Laurie Coots · Karen Corcela · Thomas Cordner · Robert Cosinuke · Barbara Costaperaria · Jim Cox · Carol-Anne Craft · Jennifer Cripe

Mathew Crisci · Richard Crispo · Eugene Crocker · Caroline Crosby · Margo Cruz · Bart Culberson · Lyn Cummings · Roger Cummings

Daniel Cunha · Pamela Cunningham · Dina · Niola Cusati · Peter Cusick · Lori Cutick · P. Meredith Cutler · Dennis D'Amico

Gisele D'Amour · Suzette Dacuag · John Dailey · Robin Daily · Valerie Dainer · Marilyn Dalisay · Dede Dalton · Mary Dalton

Karen Danehe · Sally Danto · Kieran Darby · Susan Dasaro · Susan Daugherty · Nancy Daves · David Davis · Steven Davison · Guy Day

Adilson De Almeida · Kathy Deavila · John De Bonis · Thomas De Cerchio · Betty Deepe · Robert De Florio · Robin Deidler · Jeff De Joseph

Jose De La Cuadra · June Delaney · William Delaney · Maria Delano · Richard Delap · Francisco De La Plata · Lidia De La Rosa

Cynthia Delgado · Michelle Deli Santi · Laura Della Sala · Thomas Delmore · Marie De Marco · Pam Den Hartog · Roxanne Dent

Emily Denton · Remy Deperalta · Janice De Ryss · John De Salvo · Marc Deschenes · Peter Devaux · Denise Devine · Cynthia De Vito

Salvatore De Vito · Felice Diamond · Steve Diamond · Cynthia Dickerson · Douglas Dickinson · Andrew Dijak · Mary Dmyterku

Steve Doctrow · Ellie Dodge-Seddon · Margaret Dods · John Doepp · Jane Dolin · Paula Dombrow · Neil Donavan · Deidre Donnelly

Christine Donohoe · Rose Dorn · Derek Dowden · Mark Doyle · Madeline Drake · Nancy Drew · Milton Dubane · Josh Dudley · Teresa Dumphy

Edith Dunker · Tom Dunker · Frances Dunn · Richard Durante · Norman Durkee · Holly Dysart · David Easter · Bryan Easton

Patricia Eaton · Shirley Ede · Peggy Edwards · Josh Einhron · Glennis Eisele · Alison Elizabeth · Estreilla Elkaim · Sandra Elliot

Kevin Ellis · Marci Ellis · Donald James Elms · Marilyn Elpern · Ellen Elshelby · Carolanne Ely · Minton Emerson · Jacqueline End

Carole Engle · Heidi Epling · Judy Epstein · Richard Esterbrook · Rosalinde Estes · Patricia Eure · Dana Eurich · Hilary Evans · Linda Evans

Patricia Evans · Donald Everett · Carole Fanning · William Fanning · Lori Farber · Annamarie Faro · Lisa Farwell · John Fautz · Patrick Faw

Ann Fay · Rob Feakins · Judy Fehrlage · Anne Marie Feldman · Bob Feldman · Joseph Feldman · Julie Feldman · Beverly Felix

Tammy Ferrey · Gina Ferrigno · Paula Ferrigno · Linda Filby · Victoria Filice · Susan Fingerett · Len Fink · Joseph Fiore · Shelley Firth

Ardsley Fischer · Stacy Fischer · Patricia Flaherty · Mary Jean Flamer · Cynthia Fleig · Neil Fleischer · Jennifer Fleming · Scott Flood

William Flora · Francine Foerster · Ann Fogelhut · Doris Fogg · Clyde Folley · John Follis · Steven Fong · William Foote · Paul Forbath

William Ford · Charlene Foreman · Wendy Foreman · Winfield Foreman · Barbara Fox · Evelyn Fox · Theresa Foye · Karen Frank · Patrick Frank

Libby Frankcom · Peter Franke · Bonita Freehill · Renee Freifeld · Diane Frerichs · Amelie Friedlander · Martin Friedman · Steve Friedman

Linda Frohman · Anthony Froio · Lisa Frole · Dennis Frusciano · Kim Fujikawa · Wayne Fulcher · Paul Fuller · Linda Furlong · Kim Furniss

Paula Fuszard · Florence Gaa · Lori Gaffney · Yvette Gaines · Ann Galbraith · Claire Gallo · Michael Gamache · Therese Gamba

Michelle Gannon · Pam Garcia · Scott Garell · Steve Garey · Georgia Garrett · Joseph Garrett · Joan Gelfand · Suzanne Gelinas

Catherine Gerber · Rick Gershon · Lauren Gertz · Rose Gervais · Sheri Gettleman · Hugh Gibney · Susan Gimple · Oksana Glass

Sheriann Glass · Andrew Glickman · Fred Goldberg · Paul Goldberg · Rachael Golden · Gail Goldman · Maurice Goldman · Steve Goldman

Jeanette Goldner · Gary Goldsmith · Sharon Goldwasser · Neal Gomberg · Susan Gomes · Consuelo Gomez · Esther Gonzales

Teresa Gonzalez · Jamie Goodman · Linda Gordon · Susan Gordon · Jeff Gorman · Douglas Gotthoffer · Karen Gottschalk · Jack Gowdy

Art Gramer · Gayle Grant · Pauline Grant · Lisa Gray · Stephen Gray · Judith Green · Kathy Green · Patti Green · Paul Greenburg

Frederick Greene · Pamela Greene · Randi Greenwald · John Greer · James Gregovich · Leslie Grenier · Fritz Greve · Michelle Griswold

Richard Groff · Marsha Grossman · Neal Grossman · Frank Grubich · Mario Guia · Christopher Guillet · Jean Guillot · Terry Guimond

Gary Gusick · Lisa Haake · Laurie Habiby · Catherine Habiger · Bernie Hafeli · Colin Hagen · Harry Hahn · Yvonne Hailer · Natalie Hale

Theresa Hale · Matt Haligman · Janice Hall · Mary Hall · Jack Hallahan · John Hallahan · Jennifer Hamburg · Elaine Hamill

Betsy Hamilton · Bill Hamilton · Pamela Hamilton · Jennifer Hammond · Julie Hampel · Jane Hampson · Geraldine Hanan · Steven Hancock

Tim Hannell · Roula Hanson · Mia Hanusek · Thomas Harbeck · Anne Harding · Stuart Hardman · Karen Hargrove · Debra Harper

Ty Harper · Heather Harris · Mindi Harrison · George Hartley · Diana Hartman · Sharon Harvey · Tracy Hastings · Glenn Hatfield

Christie Havens · Stephen Hayden · Elizabeth Hayes · Harold Hayes · George Haynes · Patt Healy · Paul Heath · Steve Hecht

David Heldman · Hendrika Hellendoorn · Greg Helm · Marrianne Heltai · Terry Hemerson · James Hendry · Paul Henman · Eric Henry

Joseph Heppt · Tomas Hermogeno · Charlot Hernandez · Emma Herrador · Susanne Higgens · Kerry Higgins · Mary Hildebrandt

James Hill · Mark Hill · Pat Hilton · Helen Hinkle · Perez Hinton · Elaine Hinton · Jeffrey Hirsch · Roberta Hoechster · John Hoefer

Monica Hoentsch · Bill Hoffman · Bill Hogan · Alan Hogenauer · Jonathan Holburt · Cindy Holden · Liz Holden · Shelley Holden

Charlotte Holden · Kurt Holg · Gregory Holladay · Michael Hollander · Elaine Hollifield · Virginia Hollinger · Steve Hollingsworth

Fern Homan · Irene Hook · James Hoover · William Hopkins · Sara Hopley · Lisa Horowitz · Vickie Horowitz · Adelaide Horton

Sara Hopley · Lisa Horowitz · Vickie Horowitz · Adelaide Horton · Leslie Horvath · Brianne Howard · Doris Howard · Douglas Howatt

Jill Howell · Cynthia Hoyes · Fanny Huang · Juanito Huang · Deidre Huberty · Celine Hubler · Lori Huerta · Alexandra Hughes

Laurie Hughes · Susan Huhndorf · Bob Hulme · Steve Hunt · Terri Hunt · Blake Hunter · Edna Hunter · Nora Hutton · Kaikay Hwang

Carol Hyde · Gene Icardi · Jon Inazaki · Elizabeth Irion · Darren Isabelle · Claudia Ishino · Gayle Jacot · Arlene Jaffe · Michael Jaglois

Kathryn Jaibur · Carolyn James · Lisa James · Robert Janoff · Mimi Janopaul · Marie Janssen-Rioux · Michael Janz · Lauren Jeffers

Robert Jeffrey · Lenlee Jenckes · Steve Jett · Gary Johns · Ann Johnson · Camille Johnson · Cass Johnson · Colleen Johnson · Terrie Johnson

Angela Johnson · Ann Johnston · Diana Johnston · Gary Johnston · Greg Johnston · Susan Johnston · Teresa Johnston · Michael Jolivette

Claylene Jones · Jean Jones · Louellen Jones · Lynn Jones · William Jones · Amy Joseph · Ellen Judson · Mindy Kaehler · Rita Kalimian

Patricia Kanan · Hildy Kane · Julie Kaneshiro · Steve Kaplan · Penny Kapousouz · Arnold Karol · Shari Kasch · Rebecca Kason

Harold Katkov · Lilyane Katz · Helen Katz · Carolyn Kaufman · Tracey Kaufman · Sandra Kaumeyer · Patricia Kavanagh · Christine Kay

David Kaye · John Kazan · Mary Keaveney · Patt Keefe · Pam Keehn · Laura Keelan · Nancy Kelber · Holly Keller · Gerri Kelley

Richard Kelley · William Kelley · Carol Kelliher · Debby Kelly · Lizabeth Kelly · Nancy Kennedy · Wendy Keough · Alan Kerr · John Kerr

Stephen Kessler · Theresa Kibe · Jean Kieling · Caroline Kim · Jim King · Lynne King · Phyllis King · Dorrit Kingsbury · Laura Kinney

Jean Marie Kirkpatrick · Lianne Klapper · Lorraine Klarl · Corey Klein · Kelli Sue Klein · Iona Kligman · Joan Klitzke · Steven Klosterman

Philip Koenen · Catherine Kolberg · Virginia Kollewe · Rikki Komachi · Gary Korpi · Leslie Koyama · David Koza · Christina Kracke

John Krass · Amy Krentzman · Gretchen Kribs · Daniel Krippahne · Nanette Kroupa · Fern Krupnick · Bob Kuperman · Eileen Kuramoto

Jennifer Kurtz · Monica Kuth · Larry L'Hommedieu · Joline La Mond · Elaine La Monda · Lisa La Prath · Charles Labiner · George Lafleur

June Lagmay · Frank Lagoria · Joan Laiche · Deborah Lalla · Kevin Lally · Susan Lamski · Steve Landsberg · Douglas Lang · Julia Langford

Lisa Langhoff · Phillip Lanier · Ann Lapham · Larissa Lapin · Irina Lapin · Judith Larkin · Debra Larsen · Cindy Larson

Torri Latimer · Helene Lavine · Kirsten Lawson · Ray Leal · Cliff Lee · Cynthia Lee · James Lee · Jonathon Lee · Nan Lee · Susan Lee

Jeff Leedy · Linda Leggiere · Jean Lehman · Sara Leiman · Richard Leiter · Joan Lennartz · Zachary Leonard · Lora Levenson

Nancy Levine · Gary Levitan · Harvey Levy · Arleen Lew · Helen Liao · Martha Lightcap · Sharon Lillis · Heather Lim · Lorie Lim

Keith Linde · Betsy Lindsay · Alfred Link · Gwen Lipsky · Gale Litt · Abigail Littman · Michael Liuzine · Dalila Lizcano · Richard Lobel

Joann Lobono · Margaret Lochmann · Laurie Locke · Sharon Lockette · Heather Lockwood · Nina Lockwood · Gina Locurcio

Mary Loeffler · Randall Lofgren · Hans Logie · Gina Long · Deborah Longley · Sarajane Looney · Carol Lopez · Felipe Lopez

Lydia Lopez · Toy Louie · Ray Lovasz · Sandra Lovejoy · Diane Lozito · David Lu · David Lubars · David Luhr · Karen Lutkin

Steven MacDonald · Douglas MacGibbon · Charlotte MacLeod · Sheryl MacPhee · Garrison Macri · Karen Madajczyk · Ramon Madrid

Cari Mager · Laurie Mahler · Debra Mahoney · Valentin Maiquez · Virginia Maiquez · Adam Mandel · Mitchell Mandell · Renee Mangini

Merike Manley · Rebecca Manning · Donna Margeotes · Mary Marhula · Carol Markman · Robin Markowitz · Linda Marks

Mary Maroun · Robert Marscovetra · Thomas Marshall · Carolyn Martin · Craig Martin · Diane Martin · Jeff Martin · Roland Martinez

John Martini · Susan Marvin · Vishwa Marwah · Tracy Masco · Charles Mascola · Michael Massaro · Barbara Massey · Sally Masters

Ira Matathia · Darlene Mathews · Henry Mathews · Diane Matiska · William Matlack · William May · Mike Mazza · Rene Mazziotti

Kathleen McBride · Marion McBride · Lauren McCloskey · Beth McConnell · Douglas McCoy · John McCrea · Paula McCune

James McDonald · Pamela McDonald · Denise McDonnell · Charlotte McGee · Greg McGee · Jean McGoldrick · Daniel McGrath

Nora McGuiness · Kim McGuinness · Louise McInerney · Betty McIntyre · Todd McIver · Michael McKay · Thomas McKay

Montgomery McKinney · Susan McLaughlin · Ronnie McMillan · Peggy McMullen · Dennis McVey · Douglas McVikar · Linda McWhinnie

Linda Meily · Hugh Mendelsohn · Shelly Menning · Jay Mercado · Anne Merriam · Maile Meyer · Dennis Mickaelian · John Milke · Dana Miller

Floyd Miller · George Miller · Janis Miller · Monika Miller · Robert Miller · Robin Miller · Sarah Miller · Thomas Wain Miller, III

April Milliken · Duncan Milner · Mary Mirisola · Leonard Miropol · Steve Mitsch · Amy Miyano · Shinya Miyata · Alan Moffatt

Denise Mohr · Mark Monteiro · Denise Moon · Casey Mooney · Keith Moore · Sara Mora · Judy Moran · Bill Moreland · Steven Morenberg

Kathleen Morency · Sharon Morgan · John Morrison · Julie Morrison · Robert Morrison · Roger Morrison · Belinda Morton

Francesca Moscatelli · Michael Moser · Dorothy Mosheim · Larry Mosley · Bruce Mowery · Dawn Moxley · Mark Mullin · Laure Mumford

Scott Munz · Beth Murphy · Carol Murphy · David Murphy · Michael Murphy · Joyer Muse · C. Dodds Musser · Dan Muttart · Amy Nachman

Anne Nagamoto · Julie Nakagama · Joseph Naporano · David Nathanson · Charlotte Neal · Jan Neely · Kim Nelson · Lisa Nelson · Ralph Nelson

Georgia Nelson · Lyssa Newhall · Burke Newman · Jane Newman · Elise Newman · William Kelly Nice · David Nichols · Timothy Nichols

Beth Nicklen · Grace Niimi · Michael Niles · Simone Nittel · James Noble · Stephen Nobles · Michael Noonan · Richard O'Connell

David O'Hare · Tim O'Kennedy · Dori O'Leary · Patrick O'Malley · Brian O'Neill · Kathleen O'Neill · Regina O'Neill · Michelle O'Neill

Richard O'Neill · Colleen O'Reilly · Megan O'Shaughessy · Jeanne Marie Obeji · John Odean · Blake Olson · Patricia Orr · Andrew Orth

Adina Ortiz · Sara Ortiz · Ken Orvidas · Debra Ostrow · Stacy Osugi · Mati Otsmaa · Gina Otteson · Barbara Overlie · Joe Palladino

Cari Palmer · Jeffrey Palmer · Robert Palmer · Robin Palmer · Kristin Pankokin · Mohan Pannu · Denise Papararo · George Pappas

Deborah Parisi · Arthur Park · Corinne Parker · Samantha Parker · Bonni Parsons · David Patrycia · Doug Patterson · Frank Patterson

Tom Patty · Vickie Pearson · Dusty Peterson · Amy Peterson · Lester Pekins · John Pelkan · Rob Pellizi · A. Patterson Pendleton, III

Sharon Penland · Lisa Penney · Robert Pennington · Susan Perches · Lisa Perez · Margaret Perlstein · Joan Perrella · Don Perry · Pamela Peters

William Peterson · Sonja Peterson-Yarger · Lynn Petrulas · Susan Petrulas · David Peusner · Charles Phillips · Ellen Phillips

Kathleen Phillips · Mona Philpott · Margaret Pickford · Michelle Pickholz · Joyce Pierce · Maralee Pierson · Ralph Pina · Robert Pinzler

Houman Pirdavari · David Platt · Julia Platt · Dale Plowden · Joel Poets · Richard Polk · Barbara Poncher · Henry Porper, Jr. · Brian Portzel

Sandra Portzel · Patrick Posey · Andy Powell · Richard Powers · Carol Prater · Deborah Premazon · Julie Prendiville · Tania Presby

Lauren Press · David Prince · Robert Pringle · Rodney Pringle · Frank Priscaro · Colleen Proctor · Gayle Prophet · Danna Prosser

Ronnie Sue Puccinelli · Royce Pullen · Mona Purcell · Sherry Pusateri · Sarah Putnam · Juliana Quan · Jackie Quattrocchi · Steve Rabosky

Donna Rafdal · M.T. Rainey · Robin Raj · Marion Ralls · Mary Ramos · Rachel Ramos · Carol Lee Randal · Penelope Raphaely

Emanuel Rappaport · Valerie Raszka · Harry Ray · Mary Lea Ray · Desiree Rechter · Margaret Reede · Kathleen Reese · Charles Reincke

Larry Reinschmiedt · Patty Reis · Jim Rellas · Barbara Reynolds · Henry Reynolds · Joshua Reynolds · Loren Rhea · Rodney Rhodes

Kim Rice · Tracey Rice · Jody Rich · Marvin Rich · Dale Richards · Toni Richards · M. Lauren Richford · Danette Riddle · Robert Riddle

Kristi Roach · Jean Robaire · Jeanne Robinson · Sharon Robinson · A. Harry Robinson, Jr. · Geoffrey Roche · Saul Rodriguez

Florence Rogers · Jennifer Rogers · Gretchen Rollins · Kathy Romagnoli · Edward Ronk · Deborah Rose · John Rose · Mark Rosenberg

James Rosenfield · Ila Rosengarten · Lisa Rosenstein · Amelia Rosner · Robin Rotenier · Stacey Rotner · Janine Rowitch · Olga Roxas

Janet Rubin · Mary Ruby · Ira Ruderman · Lauren Ruetz · Mignon Ryan · Diana Sacks · Cynthia Salcido · Steve Salinaro · Leslie Salmon

Michele Salmon · Scott Salmon · Melanie Saltzman · John Salvati · Jannette Sanchez · Gary Sanchez · Laura Sanchez · Tracy Sanders

Nancy Sanders · Maralee Sanserino · Gyorgi Sapojinikoff · Fred Sattler · Emma Sayao · Amy Saypol · Michael Scardino · Donna Schaffer

Frank Scherma · Thomas Scherma · Dolores Schiller · Karen Schneider · Linda Schneider · Richard Schoeman · Lori Schrader

Michael Schram · Karrie Schreiner · Janet Schrimmer · Janet Schultz · Charlene Schwabe · Ari Schwartz · Beth Schwartz · Robin Schwartz

Bonnie Schwartz · Pamela Scott · Terry Seago · Lynne Seale · Eleanor Seddon · Melissa Segal · Susan Segall · Ken Segall · John Seid

Edward Seidman · Pearl Sell · Saralee Sells · Jamie Seltzer · Lowdean Session · Joseph Shak · Jan Shambaugh · Kevin Shanahan

Margie Shank · Martha Shaw · Riley Shearer · Boo Maureen Sheehan · Michael Sheldon · Susan Sheldon · Lisa Sheptin · Allison Sher

Linda Sherman · Cynthia Shern · Patrick Sherwood · Mike Shine · Richard Shintaku · Renalee Shnairson · John Shrair · Victor Siegel

Barbara Silbert · Steve Silver · Charles Silverman · Howard Silverman · Christy Simmons · Monica Simon · Suzanne Sinenberg

Kishari Sing · Margaret Singh · Diane Sinnott · Carol Siodmak Madonna · Lucy Sisman · Mark Sitley · Dick Sittig · Brian Skiles

Francine Slow · Pam Smalley · Bernice Smith · Charters Smith · Cheryl Smith · Florina Smith · Jan Smith · Janie Smith · Katherine Smith

Michael Smith · Phil Smith · Russell Smith · Suzanne Smith · Yvonne Smith · J'Nise Smith · Walter Smith · Matthew Smith · Suzanne Smith

Catherine Sobel · Judith Soelzer · Mary Sohnen · Larry Sokolove · Andrea Sommer · Gloria Sorkow · Joe Sosa · Dalina Soto

Brigette Souva · Elizabeth Spain · Deanne Sparkes · David Specland · Susan Spiekerman · Ruth Spitzer · Jon Spurney · Joel Squier

Paul Stabile · Suzanne Stack · Kim Stahlman · Darcy Stamler · Marcie Stander · Sharon Stanley · Katy Stanley · Layne Staral

Michael Staveley · Jean Steadman · Sharon Stein · John Stein · William Stenton · Jane Stephenson · Pamela Stern · Jody Stevens

Marlene Stewart · Abigail Stimpson · Barbara Stolar · Corey Stolberg · Jane Stoner · Gaynor Strachan · Sandy Stratman · Karen Stratman

Judy Streppone · Sandra Stretke-Gaylor · Elizabeth Stuart · Margaret Sturner · Scott Suhr · Leslie Sullivan · Pamela Sullivan

Angela Sumser · Bob Sundland · Mark Supachana · Fran Sussman · Marcia Sutton · Christina Svensson · John Swartzwelder · Leslie Sweet

Kathina Szeto · Nami Takashima · Carol Talbert · Jay Talwar · Sargina Tamini · M.J. Tarr · Thomas Tawa · William Taylor · Michael Tchong

Sharon Teal · Nancy Temes · David Thall · Brent Thomas · Dean Thompson · Hylie Thompson · Jeandra Thompson · Kristopher Thoren

James Tindaro · Ed Tinney · Amy Tompkins · Marten Tonnis · Kee Sang Too · Richard Topkins · Margaret Tortorelli · Jose Totgengco

Timothy Tousant · Woo Sui Trainor · Tally Trentini · Susan Trible · Carol Trick · Debra Trotz · Mike Trujillo · Virginia Trujillo · Bill Tucker

Tamara Tucker · Graham Tumer · Joy Turnage · Darlene Turpin · Miles Turpin · Marcy Unger · John Upton · Elizabeth Urban

Jan Ushijima · John Uusitalo · Mary-Lauren Vagt · Nora Vaivads · Peter Valentine · Megan Van Camp · Ross Van Dusen · Gary Van Fleet

John Vandenburgh · Robert Vander Kamp · Bernard Vangrin · Shirley Vann · Lynn Varsell · John Varty · Richard Vasquez

Jean Marc Vaudreuil · David Verhoef · Lucie Verschueren · John Vertigan · Kyle Verwers · Margherite Vetrano · Juanita Villa · Craig Vinsky

Sandra Vitawski · Mark Vitkun · Jim Vogel · Karen Vogel · Gigi Volk · Amelie Von Fluegge · Andrew Vucinich · Stephen Vye · Mark Wagner

Wendy Wainwright · Susan Walker · Catrina Wallace · Glenda Walsh · Leland Walsh · Leslie Ann Walter · Kelly Waltos · Timothy Ward

Linda Ware · Hal Wasserman · Annette Weber · Jill Weed · Donna Wehr · Beverly Weich · Mitchell Wein · Bella Weinstein · Dina Weinstein

Mimi Weisband · Jocelyn Weisdorf · Jane Weiss · Lee Weiss · Marty Weiss · Holly Welch · Michael Welch · Anne Welisch

Christine Welisch · Karen Weller-Watson · Martin Wenzell · Nicholas West · Barry Wetmore · Jill Wetmore · Bradley Wetmore · Sally Wetzler

Gary Wexler · Clive Whitcher · Alfred White · H. Elliott White · Jan White · Jenny White · Jill White · Larry White · Robbi Jo White

Robert White · Jay Whitehead · Nat Whitten · David Wiener · Karen Wiese · Keen Wilkins, III · Gail Williams · Paul Williams

Trisha Williams · Virginia Williams · Frank Williams · Robert Wills · Scott Wilson · Sheena Wilson · Carol Ann Winkler · Junko Winningham

Darby Winterhalter · Patricia Winters · Cheryl Winthrop · Richard Wittstadt · Roger Wojahn · Janice Wojdula · Dora Wolf · Robert Wolf

Sharon Wong · Karen Wood · Dave Woodside · Beth Woollard · Penny Wright · Lisa Wright · Cynthia Wrobel · Cynthia Wulfsberg

Thomas Wynbrandt · Bonnie Wyper · Hy Yablonka · Mike Yablonka · Michael Yamada · Jill Yamashita · Masao Yamashita · Josephine Ybarra

Judy Ybarra · Kathleen Yip · Dave Yoder · Greg Yost · John Yost · Ed Yost · Patricia Young · Tia Young · Helen Young-Fliegel

Chris Yuengling · Robert Zach · Paula Zahakos · Lucile Zahrt · Kerri Zane · Maria Zasada · Bo Zaunders · John Zeeman · Carey Zeiser

Judy Zell · Barbara Zerhusen · Laurie Ziebell · Tom Ziegler · Karen Zollman · Laura Zubeck · Michael Zucker · Louis Zuckerbraun

"It's harder than I thought to do a book.
Thanks, everybody." Lee.